Eugene McGee

The GAA In My Time

Eugene McGee

The GAA In My Time

Ireland's foremost GAA analyst reflects on 50 years of activity on and off the field

Ballpoint Press

*This book is dedicated to my wife Marian
and children Conor and Linda
for putting up with me while writing this book.*

*Also to my late brother Fr Phil McGee
who inspired me to become involved in
Gaelic football in my formative years.*

Published in 2014 by Ballpoint Press
4 Wyndham Park, Bray, Co Wicklow, Republic of Ireland.
Telephone: 00353 86 821 7631
Email: ballpointpress1@gmail.com
Web: www.ballpointpress.ie

ISBN 978-0-9926732-1-5

Book design and production by Elly Design

Cover photograph: The ball used in the 1982 All-Ireland final
between Offaly and Kerry. Photograph by Eugene McGee

Printed and bound by GraphyCems

Contents

Introduction

GAELIC football and hurling are more than mere games for recreational purposes. Right from the origins of the GAA in 1884 there were important national issues inculcated into the organisation that set it apart from all other sports in Ireland at the time. Amazingly, 130 years later that special fervour attached to these games has now strengthened to its highest level and while the strong nationalistic origins of the GAA have become less central they have provided the structures which leave Gaelic games an integral part of Irish life today to an extent that no other sport in the country can equal.

Gaelic football has been a major part of my life for half a century, a period when the role of the GAA, the stature it has achieved in Irish society and the pivotal contribution it makes to communities all over Ireland has been fascinating to watch. I have been fortunate to be intimately involved with Gaelic football at several different levels from club activity to All-Ireland final level and also with administration in all its aspects. I have watched historic events on and off the field, the exultation of great playing achievements as well as the despair after losing an All-Ireland final, a county final or a colleges' final.

It has been amazing to observe and be involved in all those developments and in this book I aim to give some perspective on how the GAA, and Gaelic football in particular, has unfolded over five decades during which monumental changes took place in all aspects of the GAA and its games in parallel with the changing nature of Irish society.

As the GAA advanced during the second half of the last century massive changes took place in the organisation from both the playing an administrative perspective which attracted national debate at various times, proving the stature that the GAA had obtained in Irish society.

The hugely controversial debates about Rule 27, The Ban as it was known, had raged in the GAA for most of the century until it was eventually done away with in 1971, making everybody eligible to play all sports. On the playing field, we had the historic All-Ireland final of 1960, which saw the Sam Maguire Cup crossing The Border for the first time when Down beat Kerry in the final.

In recent times we saw the opening of Croke Park to rugby and soccer to much acclaim from all sections of Irish life and the abolition of Rule 21 which had debarred RUC members from membership of the GAA. These four events were just a few of many which had nationalistic overtones in the GAA's history and marked the organisation as different from most other sports bodies.

Today, it is mainly the games that influence Irish people most of all. The involvement of football in every corner of the country, rural and urban, as well as in about 50 centres around the world has a never-ending appeal to Irish people. Massive crowds attend the big games at national level and the real strength of the GAA is the involvement of over 2,500 clubs. Heroes are created in the parish when a county championship is won, replicating what happens when a county wins an All-Ireland. Otherwise ordinary young men become legends in their own lifetime and are revered in their local communities.

In my time, I have witnessed and often been part of the amazing eclectic mixture of events that are part and parcel of Gaelic football. Controversial matches, rows about fixtures, controversies regarding referees, objections to opposing players, appeals against suspensions, melees at club matches, debates about rule changes: there is an everlasting supply of talking points in football that keeps the public interested and agitated time and time again. Gaelic football abounds with personalities, be they players, referees, managers, officials or mentors. I have met and known hundreds of them and a better cross-section of Irish life you will never find.

There is always great fun and repartee among football people. We have hob-lawyers who think they know the rulebook inside out, and potential comedians at every GAA meeting, many of them equipped with a supply of Fox's Glacier Mints to keep their vocal chords in order.

So, it is true to say that in the ranks of Gaelic football all human life is there and that life is never boring. Great players and great games are the very life-blood of a sport that constantly uplifts the spirit of Irish people. I am privileged to have encountered so many football people around Ireland and abroad and I hope this book will reflect the marvellous panorama of Irish life that can be found in the world of Gaelic football.

Chapter 1
September 19, 1982

'**R**EMEMBER lads today you are playing for yourselves, for your family and county but also for people you will never see, people you will never meet. You will have people all over the world, in America, Australia, New Zealand who will have their chests out Monday morning if Offaly beat Kerry, but you will never see them or have the feeling they're feeling.

"There's two days people take off in the year: the Grand National and the All-Ireland football final. They are the two events people watch all the time. There are old women living down lonely roads in Donegal, Clare and Fermanagh and they're rooting for you today, but you'll never meet them. You'll never realise the lift you'll give them if you beat Kerry today.

"You are carrying a great and noble tradition, generations of players from Walsh Island, Ferbane, Rhode, Edenderry and other Offaly clubs could never have imagined that an Offaly team could be so close to history. We cannot lose this game."

●　　●　　●

These were the last words spoken in the Offaly dressing-room in the bowels of Croke Park on September 19, 1982 by Sean Lowry as the players prepared to take part in an All-Ireland football final that for the Irish public at large seemed to have only one purpose – to crown Kerry as the greatest football team of all time. To do that, they had to do something never achieved previously by winning five successive All-Ireland finals.

Those last few minutes in the dressing-room before an All-

Ireland final are always very tense and for some players they can be overwhelming if their mental attitude is not right.

This occasion was particularly demanding for the Offaly players because seldom had there been such publicity for a final because of the possibility of that five-in-a-row. That was the impression the public had because they regarded Offaly that day as being in the 'lambs to the slaughter' category. However the players were in a totally different frame of mind as they realised that the real pressure that day was in the Kerry dressing-room. For Offaly the game, while very important, was just another All-Ireland final, and they had already played in the previous year's final, but for Kerry the stakes were infinitely higher because they were attempting what had never been done before.

As team manager, I would normally be the last person to speak in an Offaly dressing-room in those days but on this occasion it was Seán Lowry, a real leader on the team and an All-Ireland winner in 1972, who spoke those words in the hushed dressing-room. In the context of the moment, his intervention was brilliant because at the end of a week of unlimited coverage across all media, there was a danger that the sense of occasion would overwhelm some Offaly players. Lowry dismantled those fears by going back to what is the very essence of Gaelic football, especially in County Offaly, by linking the big stars around him in that room with the people in the highways and byways of their native county and abroad. He brought everyone back to the grassroots.

His words were perfect for the moment and as the door burst open, the players set off on a great adventure into the unknown feeling good about themselves and knowing that their own people, men, women and children, were behind them.

It was inevitable because of the historical context of that 1982 final that the actual game of football would largely pass by a lot of people. All everybody wanted was to find out if the Five-in-a-Row was going to happen and they were not very concerned with the details of how the result was achieved. It was a very different story for Offaly and Kerry players as they went through the pre-match formalities. For them, the usual routines had to be carried out, the advice had to be given, well rehearsed tactics had to be remembered, players who tend to be nervous and tense had to be comforted by colleagues and mentors in the two dugouts had to show confidence and self-belief with every move they made.

I will remember many things about that '82 final but as time has gone by, three decades and more, my abiding memory remains the standard of play served up by both teams. Paddy Downey, the revered Irish Times writer, stated the following day it was the best All-Ireland final he had seen for the previous 25 years and any time the game is replayed on television down the years, people constantly remark to me on the high quality of the game.

As manager that day, this is what gives me the most personal satisfaction and the players from each side deserve great praise for their part in that assessment. Bear in mind that rain started falling in the first-half and was very heavy in the second period as well but the quality of football remained very high.

The first-half was bordering on the spectacular in terms of the quality of the scoring and ended with us a point ahead – Offaly 0-10 Kerry 0-9. The first score of the game did not come until the eighth minute but was spectacular and hugely important from a psychological point of view. Liam Currums was a wing half-back whose chief attribute was speed and certainly not scoring from far out. He suddenly took off on a solo run under the Cusack Stand and ran and ran and ran until he crossed the Kerry 50-yard line. Then he closed his eyes and belted the ball as hard as he could. The huge roar told him he had scored. For everybody in the Offaly camp, this was a moment of incredible significance, scoring was not Liam's forte and if he could score a point like that, then it meant Offaly had absolutely no inhibitions. Lack of inhibition was something very few opponents managed to achieve but now Offaly had done it.

To copper-fasten that belief the other two half-backs, Seán Lowry and Pat Fitzgerald also went upfield to score a point each in the first half – a very rare occurrence in an All-Ireland final.

From the moment the 1981 final was lost by Offaly, the management team and players began preparing to take out Kerry the following year. So lopsided was the All-Ireland championship that time that we were confident we would reach the final again, even though we had a very close shave in the semi-final against Galway, only winning by a point. We gambled as it was all about preparing for Kerry and we felt it was safe to gamble on that basis.

In the 1981 final Tim Kennelly won the Man of the Match award and our first priority was to curb the influence of the Listowel man, who was a powerful physical presence as well as a great player. We decided early on to move our normal centre half-back and the captain, Richie Connor, to mark Kennelly if the teams met in '82. Richie's strength, football brain and ability to distribute the ball intelligently turned out to be a pivotal factor as the '82 final progressed. It is also important to point out that our planning to cope with the Kerry defence from 1981, which only conceded 0-8 to us, was greatly facilitated by the unfortunate injury suffered in training early that spring to Jimmy Deenihan. He was the regular right corner-back and an imposing figure in those times when that position was a specialist job. His absence cost Kerry dearly.

I was slightly disappointed at half-time as I had hoped we would be at least three points ahead. I had a habit of setting scoring targets for the players and I told them I wanted them to be ahead by three points after 15 minutes and the same at half-time. We ended up one ahead, after Kerry got the last two points of the half, which was not too bad a position for us to be in.

In the second half Kerry initially seemed less tense than previously and began to play much better. They got points to go ahead and then came the penalty when John Egan was fouled.

Martin Furlong, the oldest Offaly player, saved Mikey Sheehy's kick and Pat Fitzgerald was there to safely collect the rebound. Kerry were ahead by a point at that juncture but a goal would probably have been too much for us at a time when Kerry were on top. Then in the next Offaly attack Johnny Mooney equalised and the whole psychological structure changed with Offaly players visibly buoyed by that score. Kerry were still dominant and scored four unanswered points, the final one after a typical upfield sortie by Páidí Ó Sé which really lifted the Kerry crowd and seemed to be the clinching score.

Personally, I didn't feel that way at all because we had spent a whole year working on Offaly players individually and as a team to convince them that you usually only manage to beat Kerry in the final 10 minutes of a game. Fortunately, the players believed that. A couple of frees by Matt Connor kept the pressure on Kerry and the fact that they had scored fifteen goals in their previous five All-Irelands and none so far this time around must have worried many Kerry people, not least their dugout.

My selectors and I were worried too. We were unable to get enough ball into our talented full-forward line in the driving rain and wind, so a substitution was called for. Wing forward John Guinan was taken off with about seven minutes to go and Seamus Darby entered the fray.

It was customary in those days that when a sub came on, the player who was marking the man taken off would take up the sub. But when Guinan left the field and Darby came on, it was to the left corner-forward position he went to. Tommy Doyle, who had been marking Guinan, followed him. This move probably changed the course of football history as Doyle had hardly ever played at corner back before with Kerry.

When Matt Connor scored his third successive free to leave the score 0-17 to 0-15 in favour of Kerry, a strange thing happened in the stadium. Suddenly, I heard an amazing burst of sound all around the ground like I have rarely experienced before in Croke

Park. The spectators realised that something big could be about to happen with the margin down to two points.

The Kerry players had by then started to show signs of confusion, maybe even panic, and several forwards moved back to help the defence. Nowadays that is the norm but it certainly wasn't the case in 1982.

As desperation seemed to set in with Kerry, Offaly stayed remarkably composed. It was a poor clearance from in front of the Kerry goal – of all places – that led to the famous goal. Mikey Sheehy's kick was intercepted by Seán Lowry, who gave the ball to Pat Fitzgerald. Eoin Liston made a desperate but illegal tackle on Fitzgerald. He chipped the resultant free to Richie Connor who, in turn, gave it to our full-back Liam O'Connor who had gone into the Kerry half of the field at that stage. Liam sent a long, well presented crossfield kick towards the Kerry goal which was fielded by Seamus Darby.

That famous goal followed as Darby's fabulous left-footed shot arched over the head of Charlie Nelligan and into the roof of the Kerry net. It is a matter of opinion whether Darby would have been able to field that ball had a regular corner-back, like Jimmy Deenihan, been marking him but the die is long cast on that by now.

With total pandemonium engulfing Croke Park as the rain lashed down, I remember glancing across at the Kerry dugout a few yards away. It was a scene of desolation. That image has lingered long in my memory and it is not with any great pleasure that I recall it. There was actually a few minutes still left to play but it was played out in a surreal atmosphere as everybody seemed to accept that Kerry had missed the greatest prize ever placed before them. This was strange because Kerry still got a couple of chances to level the score but over-anxiety, understandable at the time, ruined their attempts to save the game.

The final whistle went in an atmosphere of unreality as many in the attendance found it hard to grasp what they had just witnessed.

The pitch was invaded by Offaly supporters and I found myself surrounded near our dugout while the players and subs gravitated to the area in front of the Hogan Stand.

The first thing I did was to kneel down and thank the Almighty and my late brother Fr Phil for what we had achieved. Having sneaked away from the initial onslaught of delirious fans, I moved to a less populated area. I'd decided beforehand that I wouldn't go over for the presentation because once the game ended I had achieved my own personal ambition. As I saw it, the match aftermath was for the players.

In truth, I have little other recollection about what happened afterwards. I recently spoke with former Kerry chairman, Gerald McKenna, and he told me an amazing story about that day of which I had no recall whatsoever. He said that as he and the Kerry medical man, Dr Dave Geaney, were walking across to the dressing rooms at the corner of the Hogan Stand, they passed by the goals at the Canal End. They saw me with both arms outstretched standing in that goalmouth seemingly oblivious to what was taking place around the stadium. As Dave Geaney said (probably very accurately) at the time: 'McGee is totally spaced out'. I was astonished to hear about this incident after a gap of 32 years but I have no reason to doubt the veracity of those two stalwart Kerrymen.

Generally, the occasion of winning an All-Ireland in any capacity takes hold of the person completely and one gets caught up in the overall celebrations without many specifics registering. In my case, the overwhelming feeling was one of satisfaction that Offaly had won, the players had achieved their ambitions and the people of Offaly were going to stand tall for many months to come. Preventing the Five-In-A-Row was never a target for me – I was merely aiming to win an All-Ireland as a team manager and get satisfaction for a coaching and management programme that started on August 24, 1976 and ended on September 19, 1982.

A very long but fruitful journey.

Below was the note for Scorpio, my star sign, in The Sunday World on the morning of the 1982 All-Ireland final.

'Athletic interests will dominate you activities during the week ahead. Perhaps you participate in some real competitive sport. If your particular interest is football you should get a lot of satisfaction as a result of being on 'the right side' just now. A particular feature of the week's events is the way success comes in the most unlikely situation. Start off the week on a very positive note and you really can't go wrong.

Chapter 2
How I Was Almost Shafted In Offaly

ALTHOUGH Dublin and Offaly have only met six times in Leinster senior football finals, a very strong rivalry has developed between the counties since Offaly won their first Leinster in 1960. The counties have met on numerous occasions in semi-finals games which very often ended up being played in Portlaoise.

Games between these rivals for many years epitomised the traditional attitudes from both counties. Dublin were regarded as the cultured players from the city and Offaly were seen as solid country lads intent on playing the game in a very traditional manner. The individual battles were tough and demanding especially when the games took place in Portlaoise.

In 1962 Dublin stopped Offaly winning a three-in-a-row in Leinster when they beat them in the final by 2-8 to 1-7. A decade later when Dublin were the poor relations in Leinster, Offaly won finals in 1969, 1971, '72 and '73 by overcoming Kildare three times and Meath once with the Dubs totally out of contention.

Offaly won back-to-back All-Irelands in 1971, '72 and were fancied to make it a treble in 1973 but were tripped up by Galway in the All-Ireland semi-final. The following year Dublin came from nowhere to snatch victory with a famous late point by Leslie Deegan and thus began one of the most successful periods in the county's history which led to four All-Irelands in 10 years.

The glorious seventies ushered in no less than six Leinster titles in succession – a feat only achieved once before when Wexford did it from 1913 to 1918. By the late seventies that winning Offaly team was breaking up but new talent emerged following three successive Leinster U-21 final appearances that brought two titles.

I took over as Offaly manager in August, 1976 and on the first day I met the players, I told them that we would have to beat two of the best football teams of all-time if we wanted to achieve Leinster or All-Ireland success. My first target was to get out of Leinster and to do that Dublin would have to be beaten. It was a tall order as Heffomania had by now engulfed Dublin football and only Kerry were reckoned to be able to compete, bearing in mind that Dublin had won three of the previous four All-Irelands.

The first signs of resurgence came in 1978 when Offaly and Dublin met in Portlaoise in the Leinster semi-final before a near full-house. Offaly led for most of the match and Kevin Heffernan had to spring Kevin Moran, then playing for Manchester United and whose presence in Portlaoise was a closely guarded secret. Eventually Dublin won by three points but Offaly followers were happy enough with the result.

All we in Offaly could do was to diligently prepare for the 1979 season and the quality of fitness training was stepped up under Tom Donohue, a graduate of the famous Strawberry College of Physical Training in London who was also a member of the Offaly hurling team. Gym work was undertaken in the winter months at a time when such preparation was rare enough for GAA teams. We decided on this course because we knew that both Dublin and Kerry had built up a big advantage in fitness levels because of the residual effect of several years intensive work under Kevin Heffernan and Mick O'Dwyer.

The Leinster campaign of 1979 led to a Dublin-Offaly final and a game that was a battle in every sense of the word. Westmeath's Paddy Collins, the leading referee of the time, had his hands full in the opening quarter when a series of ferocious tackles by both sides often crossed the border line of legality and even the great commentator Michael O'Hehir was exhorting that the referee would have to do something.

Well, something did take place and it was sensational. Shortly before half-time Offaly defender Ollie Minnock from Clara was coming out with the ball when Jimmy Keaveney flattened him. The crowd went berserk as referee Collins immediately sent off Jimmy. For me it was one of those occasions when I had mixed feelings; for selfish reasons I was not unhappy to see a top player out of the game yet Keaveney was one Dublin player whom I always liked and respected even when we had many battles in Parnell Park against St Vincent's.

I remember after one violent final which Vincents won, Jimmy came into the UCD dressing-room, a rare enough thing by the way in those games, and finished his condolences to the college players with the words: 'Ah Jaysus lads, sure a UCD-Vincent's game wouldn't be the same without a bit of blood being spilt.' You never said a truer word Jimmy!

That sending-off against Offaly was a very costly episode for Jimmy, the man who Kevin Heffernan coaxed out of retirement in early 1974 to become an iconic figure in the entire Dublin football set-up for the next five years. In those days a sending off meant an automatic one-month ban so he missed the All-Ireland semi-final against Roscommon and he also missed the final against Kerry.

The game turned into a real war of attrition in the second half and Offaly decided at half-time to leave the spare man, Liam O'Connor, in the full-back role where he had been playing. The scores were very scarce in the second-half and we certainly did not gain from having an extra man. It took a substitution from Heffernan, Jim Roynane from Clontarf, to break the scoring deadlock when he fisted a couple of points although Offaly people were convinced they were throw balls.

Anyway, with time almost up and Offaly leading by 0-9 to 0-8, a free was awarded to Brian Mullins in front of the tunnel under the Hogan Stand. But Mullins threw the ball at Offaly's Gerry Hickey and Collins cancelled the free and instead threw up the ball.

Mullins made a huge leap into the air to dispatch all and sundry around him, grab the ball and set off towards Martin Furlong's goals accompanied by his midfield partner Bernard Brogan. At the right moment, he slipped the ball to Brogan who side-footed it into the net – and that was that. There was no time left, Dublin had won, Offaly were devastated and the Dublin crowd went wild on The Hill. Final score: Dublin 1-8 Offaly 0-9.

Before the game a crate of champagne had been delivered to the Offaly dressing-room, without my knowledge, from a well meaning Tullamore publican and when I saw it I got uneasy as it was tempting fate in a way that was never part of my team preparations. But at least my friends and I enjoyed the champagne during the long winter months!

After that disaster for Offaly repercussions soon set in the county. There had been, since my arrival in Offaly in late 1976, an element that did not approve of my appointment, and felt I was too inexperienced for the job. There was also an element of trying to retain the aura of the '71/'72 winning team by having players from that time more directly involved. I had been handed four selectors when I was appointed by the county executive and as far as I was concerned they were capable and honourable people but the anti-McGee faction did not see things that way and were pushing for the recent winners to be involved.

At a subsequent county board meeting my four selectors were voted out and, again without any consultation with me, four people were named as selectors who were less than enamored with me as Offaly manager. They were former players Noel McGee, Johnny Cooney and Mick O'Rourke along with current goalkeeper Martin Furlong. To say we had a strained relationship from the start would be a major understatement. They had their own ideas as to how Offaly should play football and how the team should be selected – my ways were different in many aspects.

We went through the national league from October to April where I was, in effect, just the messenger boy as I was constantly overruled on team selection, switches, substitutions etc. The situation was untenable from my point of view but, of course, I always respected their right to behave as they did – that after all is GAA democracy and they were all very genuine Offaly football people.

It was obvious the situation could not continue as we prepared for the 1980 championship and it was equally clear that many of the players could sense the uneasy situation that existed. For a big tournament game between Offaly and Galway played in Ferbane on a Thursday Church holiday in 1980 I selected my own team and handed it to the selectors in the dressing-room.

They took umbrage with that and went out and stood by themselves on the sideline. I stood with the subs on the other sideline. Luckily, Offaly won the game and in a tense atmosphere it was obvious that the situation had been brought to a head.

A couple of hours later the four selectors dropped a resignation note into chairman Fr Seán Heaney's door stating they could no longer work as selectors if I was the manager. Before morning, a letter had been handed into all their homes from Fr Heaney accepting their resignation and thanking them for their services. So a saga that threatened to torpedo everything the players and I had worked for during the previous two years had been avoided. As was the custom in the GAA in that sort of situation the Chairman, Secretary (John Dowling) and Assistant secretary (Bro. Sylvester) were co-opted as selectors pro tem and things got back to normal.

None of the three appointees particularly wanted to be selectors as they had enough to be doing so after much thought and consultation with knowledgeable football people I approached two former Offaly greats, Seán Foran and Paddy Fenelon, to ask them to be selectors and after an interesting meeting in a pub in Kinnegad they agreed. They turned out to be excellent selectors with a wonderful knowledge of the game. Foran had often played for Leinster along with Kevin Heffernan and had he not been injured for the 1961 championship campaign, the result of that year's All-Ireland could well have been different.

Some time after we won the 1980 Leinster Final. We played very poorly in the first-half but no less than 12 half-time switches changed everything and a brilliant goal from Matt Connor against the new Dublin goalkeeper that day, John O'Leary, helped Offaly to victory by 1-10 to 1-8. That was to be the first of three successive Leinster titles. Subsequently, I had a happy relationship with the four previous selectors who had no trouble putting the welfare of the Offaly football team ahead of all else.

Undoubtedly, 1979 was the most difficult year of my managerial career in County Offaly but thankfully it also led us all closer to the Holy Grail that culminated in 1982. The All-Ireland semi-final in 1980 was against Kerry, then at the height of their power and it gave us that amazing high-scoring result: Kerry 4-15; Offaly 4-10, but in reality that scoreline seriously flattered Offaly because Matt Connor scored 2-9 that day and the only other scorer was Gerry Carroll who got 2-1.

By the way, three of the Kerry goals were hand-passed into the Offaly net but such scores were banned the following year. However, the experience of playing Kerry in Croke Park was very important as was the fact that we had run them much closer than most neutrals expected.

Chapter 3

Johnny Wore A Waistcoat In The All-Ireland Final

IT was in August 1981 when I got a phone call from one of my Offaly selectors, Edenderry veterinary surgeon Paddy Fenelon, himself an Offaly and Leinster great in the past that brought very bad news. In his usual cryptic comment he spat it out: "Johnny Mooney is after falling off a trailer load of turf on Fahy Hill and has dislocated his shoulder". Although Offaly had qualified for the All-Ireland final against Kerry I said to myself straight away that our All-Ireland chance was gone for that year.

Offaly is a small county with, in those days, a population of around 60,000 but the county was fairly evenly divided north and south between football and hurling. So high quality players were always scarce on the ground as they always are in counties with populations of that size. And Johnny Mooney was no ordinary footballer. He was a brilliant performer and even at a young age he was one of the best fielders of a high ball in the country at a time when that skill was regarded as the pre-eminent one in Gaelic football. He bore many similarities to the great Mick O'Connell in that regard and in his use of the ball through incisive passing and he was also a prolific scorer who complemented the great Matt Connor when he joined the Offaly team.

But what really caused me to be worried with this news was that his other regular midfield partner, Tomas O'Connor, was also injured for some time and was rated doubtful for the final against Kerry. Bearing in mind that the two players lining out for Kerry were Jack O'Shea and Sean Walsh, easily the best pairing in the country at the time, it was obvious that Offaly were going to be in trouble as we awaited developments over the late August and early September period.

Needless to say the best medical advice was called in and I'm sure the great Ossie Bennett, masseur or 'rubber' to famous Tipperary hurlers and others in the past was trying to help out as well at a different level. We looked at the various possibilities of having Johnny wearing protective devices to save the shoulder but it became clear as the weeks before the All-Ireland drew near and Kerry were heading for four-in-a-row that the Rhode man would not be on the team-sheet for that final.

So great was the desire of the Offaly public to find out if there was anything that could be done to even get a few minutes out of Mooney, who was a huge crowd-pleaser at the time, in the final that there was huge pressure not to rule him out of the game completely. In the event, his name was not on the official match programme but at the last minute he was listed on the official team sheet for the match. All sorts of protective devices were suggested even though medical people and players who had themselves suffered the same injury were very sceptical. Their experience was that time was the only thing that could heal the damaged shoulder.

On one occasion during an American visit I took home several items of sports equipments that were not available in Ireland and which I felt might be useful for future use back home. Even ice-packs were very rare in Ireland in 1981. One of the items I bought was an upper-body harness that American footballers wear as huge padding for shoulders. We looked at this for Johnny but decided it was not suitable – it was too bulky for one thing.

In the end, in desperation and rather than do nothing, we fell back on an old reliable – a plain old tight-fitting waistcoat with some padding underneath for the shoulder. So at least Johnny was able to tog out and sit in the dugout. But the game was only about 10 minutes old when Seán Walsh hit Tomas O'Connor with an almighty, but fair, shoulder close to the Offaly dugout and that really put the tin-hat on our midfield prospects as Tomás struggled for a long time before having to go off in the second half.

And yes Johnny Mooney did come on near the end of the game, a match that was decided by a late and spectacular goal scored by Jack O'Shea. That ended the Offaly challenge for that year but at least Johnny went down in history as probably the only man to play in an All-Ireland final wearing a waistcoat.

P.S. Some years later I lent that American football harness to Eoin 'Bomber' Liston who would have been well fit to wear it. But being a Kerryman he forgot to send it back to me so I gave it to him as a souvenir of his time playing against Offaly.

Chapter 4
When Heffo
Won Over A City

ISPENT nearly 20 years living in Dublin as student and worker from about 1960 onwards. GAA games where I lived around Ranelagh, Leeson Street, Rathmines and Donnybrook for all practical purposes did not really exist in that part of the city.

In fact once you crossed to the south side of the river Liffey you would search very hard to find the existence of any GAA activity. The UCD club was always present on the south side, first in Terenure in the first-half of the last century and later in Belfield to which the university campus moved from its original location in Earlsfort Terrace beside St Stephen's Green. However it did not have the local involvement with the community that other GAA clubs have.

The Clanna Gael club was located around the Ringsend area and in the 1960s an amalgamation between two southside clubs Kilmacud and Crokes hurling club produced Kilmacud Crokes, based in Stillorgan.

Over the years other clubs came and went but in general there was very little GAA impact on the citizens of south Dublin. When the All-Ireland finals were on in Croke Park they would scarcely be noticed in south Dublin except when Wexford were playing as they would pass through the area on their way to the game.

It was very different on the northside of Dublin where there was a selection of long-standing GAA clubs such as O'Tooles and St Vincent's who were founded in 1931 and made a colossal impact on GAA life in the city. There were numerous other successful GAA clubs all over the northside and, of course, north county Dublin.

But then came a sea-change in GAA life in the city and county in 1974 when Kevin Heffernan revolutionised the GAA influence all over Dublin when he inspired them to win the All-Ireland by beating Galway in the final. In the 32 years before 1974 Dublin had won just two All-Irelands, 1958 and 1963, so it was difficult to make an impact in the city.

Where I was living on the southside, Shamrock Rovers were the big sporting attraction and when they were based in Glenmalure Park in Milltown, crowds of 15,000 on a Sunday afternoon were quite commonplace.

But then came 1974 and over the space of a few months in that summer Irish sport went through an amazing change. The image of Gaelic football was transformed by the arrival of this brash new county team with a huge following that grew with every passing game in Croke Park. Modern publicity methods came into play and media coverage exploded almost overnight.

The Dublin team caught the imagination of the Dublin public including many people not previously involved with the GAA. The newspapers took note and suddenly instead of a page or two on All-Ireland finals there was saturation coverage as rival newspapers vied for a share of this new sporting market. And crucially The Ban on soccer and rugby had gone in 1971 which created a totally different sporting environment in the capital.

It all started insignificantly when Kevin Heffernan was appointed trainer, later to be called manager, of the Dublin team in late 1973. This decision emanated from the county board chairman Jimmy Gray who realised that the management of the Dublin football team had become rather chaotic and decided that Heffernan was the only man capable of making the necessary changes to bring back respectability to the county team.

I remember well being a board delegate at the meeting at which the decision was made and there was no opposition to the package of Kevin Heffernan, Donal Colfer and Lorcan Redmond presented by the County Board Executive. It was a triumvirate that worked out very well. The progress Heffernan made in the short term is now the stuff of legend, such as cajoling Jimmy Keaveney out of retirement, changing training methods and generally restoring pride in the Dublin jersey. The breakthrough came in 1974 when Dublin played recent All-Ireland champions Offaly in the Leinster championship semi-final and won by a very late point to cause a sensation around the GAA world, added to when they beat Meath 1-14 to 1-9 in the Leinster final, Cork in the semi-final and Galway in the final.

The media went mad at that stage and four or five pages in the Irish Press and Irish Independent were given to covering Dublin's victory and the aftermath. There were even a couple of the Dublin team from south of the Liffey and suddenly a whole new audience for Gaelic football had been created overnight. 'Deffo Heffo', 'Heffos Army', 'The Jacks are Back' – it went on and on.

I have no hesitation in saying that in my lifetime no man has made as great a personal contribution to winning an All-Ireland than Kevin Heffernan with Dublin in 1974. But he did not just win one All-Ireland, he transformed a whole county and city with an energy that sport had rarely done in Ireland before. Dublin never had massive crowds prior to 1974 for games other than finals until he came along. The GAA nationally were huge beneficiaries of that new-found interest and of course that really took off in 1975 when a young Kerry team beat Dublin in the final and the wonderful Kerry-Dublin battles that lasted until 1985 on and off and included six All-Ireland finals were set in motion.

Most managers of top county teams have a personal motivation apart from the general motivation of the team and in Heffernan's case it was to beat Kerry in an All-Ireland final.

For the first half of the last century Dublin teams in football and hurling were heavily populated with players from the country who were working in the capital and indeed for about 15 years early on in the GAA your residence decided your county affiliation. Many country lads decided to stay playing with Dublin and that was mainly because in those years when you went to work in Dublin you rarely visited your home place, unlike nowadays when travel is easy.

In 1942 when Dublin beat Galway in the final there were half a dozen country players, mostly from Kerry, on the winning team. Clearly this was not an ideal situation for any county particularly Dublin and from a young age it was Kevin Heffernan's target to rectify the situation. When the club he played for, St Vincent's in Marino, was founded back in 1931 by two Christian Brothers the core principle was to field only Dublin-based players on the team. This turned out to be a dramatic move because after a few years teams from that club began to dominate Dublin championship football and from 1949 when they won their first title they would have won a remarkable 14 titles in a row but for the intervention of Erin's Hope, the teacher training college in Drumcondra in 1956. Another possible seven-in-a-row was thwarted by UCD in 1963 and in the 1970s Vincent's won six more titles before several other Dublin clubs began to strengthen their sides, ironically with the help of many country players to this day, and of course Vincent's also won the All-Ireland club championship in 1976, 2008 and 2014 and the club has been using non-Dublin players regularly, including their last two All-Ireland wins.

It could be said that St Vincent's was the vehicle by which Heffernan stamped the brand name of Dublin GAA very clearly as an all-Dublin team. The first time that was exemplified was in the National League final of 1953 when 14 Vincent's players helped Dublin win that title by beating the then All-Ireland champions Cavan. But that was only the start of Heffernan's crusade as he was adamant that and all-Dublin team would not be totally proven until they beat Kerry in an All-Ireland final. The counties did not meet very often, it was 13 years from 1942 when Dublin next reached the final, and it was against Kerry. That was one of the massive All-

Ireland finals because of the build-up beforehand and Dublin were favourites, having demolished All-Ireland champions Meath in the Leinster final by 5-12 to 0-7. On that day Heffernan caused a sensation by becoming a roaming full-forward whereby he abandoned the then traditional full-forward role of standing close to the goals. Instead he roamed far outfield and this caused havoc to the previously dominant Meath defence in which full-back Paddy O'Brien was an iconic figure that time.

But when the 1955 final came along it was a major disappointment for Dublin and Heffernan as Kerry won the game so his lifelong ambition was put on hold. One All-Ireland win in the fifties when Heffernan was captain and another in the sixties kept Dublin ticking over but it was not until that fateful county board decision to appoint the Three Musketeers in 1973 that the whole GAA scene in Dublin and the country changed dramatically.

It was convenient from Kevin Heffernan's point of view that Kerry produced the best team of all time in the seventies and eighties because it meant that there would be many Dublin-Kerry finals and there were six from 1975 to 1985 of which Dublin won only one – but what a victory that was in 1976. That was the achievement of Heffernan's life ambition and when Dublin beat Kerry in the semi-final the following year it copper-fastened the legitimacy of the 1976 victory and banished the Kerry demons from his mind. He had often stated that beating Kerry in a final was worth two All-Irelands.

Chapter 5

Heffo: 'McGee And I Would've Spat At Each Other Up And Down Sidelines'

I HAD many football battles with Kevin Heffernan over five county finals and a few more semi-finals between St Vincent's and UCD. After those club battles, we met in four Leinster finals and two semi-finals between Offaly and Dublin and several league and O'Byrne Cup games with honours more or less even.

I understood Kevin, probably as well as anybody ever did, from a football point of view. I saw close up his ruthlessness, his cunning and his incredible intellect. He never spoke to me before, during or after a game in any of these encounters but I gather that was the norm for him with other managers too.

I hadn't the slightest doubt about Kevin's modus operandi in relation to myself and UCD or indeed later on with Offaly. Long after those events, I was made aware that I was used as some kind of 'hate figure' by Heffernan, in the best sporting context I should add, as he used every device to get his team to win matches. A reference in former Dublin goalkeeper John O'Leary's biography, 'Back to the Hill', sheds further light in the form of a comment during the build-up to the Leinster final of 1983. "The fact that Offaly were All-Ireland champions really whetted our appetite. They were managed by Eugene McGee, who for some reason, we didn't like. Maybe it was his style or his manner, but we took a dislike to him and decided to use it as a motivating force in the run-up to that final."

Many team managers over the years have used the same approach and that is all part of the mix that makes up sporting rivalry. I can honestly say I never fell out seriously or permanently with any opposing player or mentor, and particularly not with Kevin Heffernan, who I regarded as being a cut above myself, especially because of his own playing record and also because he was a bit more ruthless in dealing with players, both opponents and his own players, than I was.

It was inevitable that Heffernan would up the ante when his club was facing UCD for high stakes in Dublin because competing against 'culchies' was always a bait that he could never resist. The same role in earlier years was filled whenever St Vincent's played the Garda who had some marvellous teams, all country fellows. He regarded himself as a genuine home-grown Dub even though, as I only discovered many years later, his father was a native of Clonbullogue in Offaly, of all places. I doubt very much if he actually hated country players per se but rather they represented a suitable vehicle for him to create a war situation every time Dublin or Vincent's faced country opposition – bearing out the saying that all's fair in love and war.

A very respected Dublin GAA man of my acquaintance who was close to Kevin used to point out to me that Heffernan's playing days in the Leinster championship were responsible for colouring his views later on. This man would say that as a player Kevin, who was one of the very best of his generation and very clever too, was often the subject of much physical abuse in games down the country and it left a lasting impression on him. Those were the days of the infamous third-man tackle, often seen as a licence to kill by defenders.

Heffo was determined when he became Dublin manager that never again would a Dublin football team be thrown around the place as sometimes happened at Leinster venues up to then.

The first panel of players he selected in 1973 was made up of big, strong, aggressive players even including some 'country' lads from north county Dublin. The players quickly learned what Heffernan had in mind, that in future there would be no surrender against any opponents and they could play the fine football once that was established. Maybe it was because Offaly, in the sixties and seventies, had a reputation of being the hardest and toughest team in the country that he was going to give special attention to Dublin standing up to Offaly jersies and fighting fire with fire at all times.

As far back as the early sixties there were some ferocious battles when Dublin played Offaly in Portlaoise and indeed the last Leinster final to be played outside of Croke Park was a particularly violent encounter that Offaly won. All the Dublin teams that played under Kevin Heffernan in those glory days were hard men, as well as being outstanding footballers, and that was one of the big factors in the hordes of Dublin followers converging on Croke Park in unprecedented numbers. They came there happy in the knowledge that no country teams would be able to tramp on Dublin anymore – the 'culchies' would be kept at bay and most times they would be devoured, metaphorically of course, by Heffo's Army on Hill 16.

This was not the first time that Kevin Heffernan was in charge of the Dublin football team, something that is often forgotten. He was trainer, the term used then, of Dublin in 1969 and 1970 but only small signs of a new team were surfacing at that time and they achieved nothing of note.

When myself and Kevin Heffernan had long left the inter-county football battlegrounds behind us, I rang him one day when I was preparing a book on famous football games and I wanted to talk to him about that 1955 final.

'Don't you know I never talk to journalists, so what are you ringing me for,' was his opening comment, which did not bode well. Almost immediately though, he relented by declaring: 'Ah look, you are supposed to know something about football so come over to my office in the ESB and we will have a chat'. And a very long and stimulating chat it was. As it transpired, we met several times at social events in the following years. Some years later, in a book written by Tom Humphries, when asked about me this is what Heffernan said: 'In the seventies McGee and I would have spat at each other up and down sidelines, first when he was with UCD and I was with Vincent's, then when he was with Offaly and I was with Dublin. We would have disliked each other intensely. Now we can be civil to each other. Now we can have a chat and I think we are both surprised that we have a lot of views in common about the GAA. Back then, however, he was the enemy.'

I would echo those words. I always had immense regard for Kevin and what he did for the GAA in those years. He was an extremely intelligent man who was never afraid to break barriers, such as when he entered Trinity College at a time when Catholics were banned from that institution. I always believed that he regarded his contests with opposing team managers as contests of intellectual excellence.

He seemed determined to personally outwit the football intelligence of opposing managers as much as the contest between the two sets of football teams involved. As a result he was very hostile in football terms to anybody who he regarded as a threat to his ability as a manager and that was what probably drove him to the high levels of dedication that was his hallmark.

That along with his strong desire to beat 'culchies' whenever he got the chance with St Vincent's or against any other county team. I would never have regarded Kevin Heffernan as anti-rural people and indeed he had many close friends in all parts of the country, such as a wonderful Leitrim player of the sixties Tony Hayden with whom Kevin worked in his younger days in the ESB. Rather he saw Dublin beating country teams and country players as the ultimate challenge and eventually the ultimate satisfaction.

I had a very good example of the sort of thinking that permeated Heffernan's attitude as a team manager in 1983. As the teams were leaving the field in Croke Park after the Leinster final of 1982 when Offaly crushed Dublin by 1-16 to 1-7, an Offaly player said within Heffernan's earshot to a colleague: 'I thought Dublin would have given us a better game of it'. Now, that was the sort of comment that a manager like Heffernan, or indeed myself, would never forget and I have no doubt that from that moment on he was determined to rectify what he must have regarded as a slight on the Dublin team. When the teams met the following year in another Leinster final he had a largely new-look team on duty and they beat Offaly as All-Ireland champions by 2-13 to 1-11. Unfortunately for me, I never heard about that comment until 24 years later when Offaly had a reunion because had I been aware of it I would have known that Heffernan was going to go to any lengths to teach that player a lesson, and also Offaly, and McGee, and I would have been prepared for a Heffernan onslaught.

Instead, for probably the one and only time in my football life, I took an opponent somewhat for granted. Offaly had beaten Kildare in the semi-final by 2-16 to 0-6 and the week before that Leinster final Kerry had for the second year in a row been beaten by a last minute goal by Cork in the Munster final so it was looking like a second All-Ireland for Offaly even at that stage. But Heffernan had been planning for a year to get revenge and boy how he must have revelled in doing so!

I hope when the time is right in a few years time that the next new bridge to be built over the river Liffey will be named 'The Heffo Bridge'.

I would regard Kevin Heffernan as one of the greatest GAA persons I have ever met and when he passed away a couple of years ago, I felt genuinely very sad but privileged to have fought and sometimes won many battles against such a warrior down the years.

Chapter 6
'McGee A Manager –
But Sure That Fella
Never Played Football'

I'VE lost track of the number of times I have been asked by media colleagues of mine, and others, as to how I became a football manager seeing as I could scarcely kick a football when I was growing up. Going back through the years, we have seen that the vast majority of managers at club and county level were former players of distinction.

Right back to the time of legendary figures like Dr Eamon O'Sullivan, who won several Sigerson Cup medals in the 1920s, through to John Dunne and Brendan Nestor of Galway who were on the Galway team of 1938 that were the first to beat Kerry in a replay and then managed the great Galway three-in-a-row team of the sixties. Later, Kevin Heffernan and Mick O'Dwyer won and managed All-Ireland winning teams, so the tendency has been to have ex-players as team managers.

But perhaps we should first refine the use of the words 'team manager' in the GAA because it is actually a relatively new term. From 1884 when the GAA was founded until the mid 1970s there was no such thing as a team manager.

Instead the main man, and it was always a man then, was simply called 'The Trainer' even though most teams in all those years had a person who actually acted as trainer in that he was in charge of physical fitness. Very often in the early years, this position was filled by an Army or ex-Army person who was supposed to have had some training in physical education.

Then like many developments that took place in the GAA in the last 50-odd years, the organisation began to imitate what was happening in British sport and that was caused mainly by the arrival of television in Ireland in the early sixties.

The first development was calling trainers of yore managers and Heffernan and O'Dwyer soon became established with those titles handed to them. Subsequently, we got advertising on jersies, sponsorship of teams and competitions, in fact everything we saw in British sport was copied, and still is, here in Ireland and nobody passed any remarks. Irish people have a wonderful capacity for being modernisers overnight when it suits. Anyway for my time in UCD in the seventies I was still being described as a 'Trainer', among other things by the students. When I first went to UCD, the only person who had responsibility for organising or running the team was the captain, which explains why the captaincy was always a prized possession in that particular university and probably in all of them. But when third-level games began to expand, both because of the arrival of a host of new third-level colleges and the consequent increase in third-level competitions, it was clear that colleges like UCD would have to set up new structures to handle the increased numbers playing football. Suddenly in a college like UCD, things moved from just having one team to five or six.

That was how I gravitated into training the senior team while other people were appointed to look after all the other teams. I was there for over a decade – from the late sixties until 1977 – when I was solely involved with UCD. I had plenty of time to learn the trade of being a trainer. I went to great lengths in a personal capacity to improve, starting with attending the first coaching courses in Gormanston College organised by Joe Lennon, Jim McKeever, Frankie Byrne from Meath, Eamon Young from Cork, Michael Ryan from Dublin and many others along the way.

I later went to a couple of residential courses in the famous Loughborough College in England where so many famous sports people studied, included Joe Lennon himself. I acquired books on a wide range of coaching methods from various countries, particularly the USA and Britain, and at that time sports coaching around the world was being transformed as more universities and colleges everywhere began to apply themselves and set up degree courses in all aspects of sports preparation and application. When I graduated from UCD with a BA and Higher Diploma in Education, the latter course included a module on psychology which I found very useful as it allowed me to acquire further knowledge of that subject after learning the basics.

Sports psychology is now commonplace but back then very few people even bothered about it as an aspect of training GAA teams. All those teachers who have become trainers-cum-managers over the years also had acquired the fundamentals of psychology and one has only to recall the number of teachers involved with All-Ireland winning teams to realise that this link with psychology in third level qualifications has been very beneficial to the GAA.

We need only mention Dr Eamon O'Sullivan, himself a pioneer away back in the medical psychological field but in modern times we have had Brian Cody, John O'Mahony, John Allen, Donal O'Grady, Michael Bond, Dermot Healy, Fr Tommy Maher, Billy Morgan, Jack O'Connor, Mickey Harte, Ger Loughnane, Mickey Moran, who were or still are teachers.

The glib explanation for the success of these teachers is that they have holidays all summer and have plenty of time to look after teams but I feel there is a bit more to it than that.

Among very useful books I read in the 1970s was 'Sports and Psychology' by Frank Ryan who held a PhD from Columbia University and was a former champion athlete. Chapter headings included: Mental Rehearsal, Role Playing, Regression under Stress, Figuring out Personality and Psychological Limits.

One of the items dealt with which often intrigued me was the statement: 'Skill can be trusted, effort can't.' It is a comment I have often had to argue about with Gaelic football people but it is one I have always agreed with.

Another American book I found useful and sensible, and these topics don't always come together in relation to sport, was: 'Sports Psyching – playing your best game all the time'. I wonder how many players could have made use of that over the years? Chapter headings there included: The Social Pressures of Sports, The Personal Pressures of Sport, Failure as a Self-Fulfilling Prophecy and The Mechanics of 'Fight or Flight'.

'Understanding Soccer Tactics' written in 1969 by Conrad Lodziak was a book I found very informative as a means of outlining various tactical options in soccer which could also be applied, with variation, in Gaelic. At the front of that book there was a quotation from the great Hungarian football player Ferenc Puskas who scored 84 international goals in 85 games as follows. 'The history of war proves that tactics are the most important thing in winning battles. The same thing applies in football matches. Here too, one must consider the opportunities of both sides: and when both sides are of equal strength, it is the side with the better tactics that will win.'

How many All-Ireland finals have been decided on that basis I wonder?

There was a wonderful book about team management in all its aspects written a few years ago by Tim Healy from Cork but resident in Bray, Co Wicklow which was called 'Can You Manage?' It was all about football and hurling team management which I would love to have had available to me 40 years ago as it was packed with practical, useful material. Incidentally, Tim became a valued member of the Football Review Committee (FRC) last year.

Needles to say I never mentioned, let alone discussed, such books with my UCD or other players. To be talking about sports psychology in the 1970s with footballers would certainly mean men with white coats being called for immediately. Instead I digested what I had read and absorbed from that some things that firstly were practical to use with Gaelic players and secondly that helped me challenge the various players I was involved with to change things, if required, so that their play would improve. Too often players are not challenged to change their previous habits but are allowed continue making the same mistakes throughout their careers. Because many players at county level are naturally very talented some may be unwilling to change on the basis that they believe they are good enough. This is a fatal mistake particularly in the modern game where styles of play change rapidly and even rules change so that the player who is stuck in his ways and refuses to co-operate with change can be a nuisance for the team manager.

So I always went to great lengths to approach players individually and explain to them exactly what things I wanted to change, outline the reason why, the benefits that could accrue and then encourage them to work on these changes. In virtually all cases like this I was able to help the player concerned to improve his game and thereby improve the overall effectiveness of the whole team. I have watched many good managers achieve great success with players in more or less the same way.

I regard good communications as one of the most important components of being a GAA manager. When I was growing up communication between the trainer of the club team and the players was minimal. The trainer called out the team, like the great Larry McGann, often written on the back of the cigarette box, and roared a few exhortations of support, made some raucous remarks about the opposition, especially if they were from the adjoining parish or 'a crowd of townies', told the players to be very wary of that particular referee, 'remember what the so-and-so did to us last year in the county semi-final', banged the table a few times, if there was a table, and roared 'Out ye go lads and don't let your own parish down'.

That worked for the best part of 100 years in the GAA but then young lads became better educated, started playing other sports and realised there were better ways of preparing for matches. Since I was supposed to be a writer it was expected that I could put a few words together that might help to encourage and inspire and I did work hard at getting the correct messages back to players especially on the big occasions.

I had the advantage of usually being the only person speaking to the team and I always tried to have as much knowledge as possible about the opposing team – bearing in mind that there were no DVDs or other recording devices around then. It is always difficult for a person in charge of a team before a big game to get the right balance between relaxing players so that they can actually take in what they are hearing and stirring up their passion levels so that their motivation will be very high as they leave the dressing-room. We are told that the old banging on the table, kicking out the dressing-room door routine before it is opened and other violent facets of emotional upsurges are largely gone nowadays but I doubt it. It is a tradition in the GAA that dressing-rooms are critical before big games and I have no doubt that every manager in the country is carrying on that tradition at least to some extent.

As I said earlier getting the balance between calmness and passion is the problem and it is one that a great many managers at all levels are incapable of achieving.

I developed a formula of my own based on research, studying the games at different levels and watching opposing managers as opposed to relying on a reputation as a famous ex-player. The university competitions and the Dublin club games were an ideal training ground and experimentation base because between them, they provided a great cross-section of football from dealing with and against top county players to organising intermediate and junior teams in the Dublin leagues and championship. It was an apprenticeship that was often hard and frustrating but as time went by, I grew in confidence with wins in Sigerson Cups, Dublin championship and even All-Ireland club championships. So I was not exactly an innocent abroad when I got a phone call from Offaly chairman Fr Heaney asking if I would take over the Offaly football team.

Since I was fortunate enough to have been in charge of seven Sigerson winning teams, four Dublin championships, two All-Ireland club championships, three Leinster senior and two U-21s titles as well as one All-Ireland title, I feel entitled to propose that not being an inter-county star should be no barrier to being a successful team manager. Another even better example of this is Sean Boylan who managed no less than four Meath All-Ireland winning teams and when he was appointed in 1982 all the Meath people were saying was ' What are they doing with a hurling fella in charge of the Meath football team?'

Communication ability, man-management skills, the cuteness of a politician, thick-headed perseverance, a ruthless streak, respect rather than abuse of county players and an awareness of their personal problems are just some of the requirements of being a manager and nearly all of these can be acquired without being weighed down with county or club medals. Technological aids to football coaching were only emerging in Ireland in the late 1970s but being aware of that, I persuaded the Offaly players in 1978 to organise some fund-raising so that we could provide a Sony Portable VTR Camera and related equipment. This allowed us to record all our games on black-and-white video tapes and that was sort of revolutionary at the time. I found it a huge help if only to convince certain players that they were in fact doing some things wrong and also that these things could be corrected. That machine cost almost £1500 at that time which is the equivalent of around €8,000 in today's money, and there was no sponsorship in those days and very few 'Sugar Daddies' in Offaly GAA either but it more than paid its way before we all moved on to more intricate technology in the eighties.

The fact that most county and club team managers are being well paid for their efforts means that some seek and get the position purely for the money. Many of these have been proven failures in the past 20 years but the lessons are still not being learned.

I have watched county teams spend about €2 million over a five year period paying a manager and spending large amounts on team preparation only for the team to be in a worse state at the end of it than when they started. Hopefully this sort of illogical approach is beginning to dawn on some of these middle of the road counties and they will change their ways.

What is required is a co-ordinated approach to the games from the age of 12 upwards with schools of excellence and managers of underage teams being carefully selected with a fairly high level of expertise required. This should bring continuity in a county as to the style of football suitable for it through the efforts of managers who control the various underage groups from U-14 to senior grades. Chopping and changing of inter-county managers every couple of years is very counter-productive as each new manager starts from scratch rather than building on the teams who are already working to a definite pattern.

The fact that most inter-county managers still do not have even a basic coaching certificate is ridiculous and I am glad to say that the FRC managed to get a motion passed that would require all county managers to have a coaching certificate for the 2016 season. This is long overdue.

Chapter 7

My Time As Dublin U-21 Manager

I T will come as a bit of a surprise to many people, but especially die-hard Dublin GAA followers, to learn that I was once the manager of a Dublin football team. In 1972 I ended up being in charge of the Dublin U-21 team – how that happened I am still not exactly sure. I was the UCD delegate to the Dublin Senior and Junior Board in those days and UCD were Dublin U-21 county champions at the time.

I have an idea there were very few candidates for the job that Spring, maybe none at all, as all inter-county football was at a very low level in Dublin and time was running out because they were due to play Meath in the first round of the Leinster championship in Dunshaughlin. Also I think in those days Dublin GAA people had divided views on the merits of inter-county U-21 competition at all as had several other counties since the U-21 All-Ireland competition was only set up in 1964. Indeed Dublin had to wait until 2003 before they won the title for the first time when they beat Tyrone.

I remember we did some training sessions in Parnell Park before the game, which took place on April 9, 1972. Meath won a low scoring game 0-7 to 0-4 after Dublin had led at half-time by 0-3 to 0-1.

Included in that Dublin team were players who went on to win All-Ireland senior medals just two years later such as Robbie Kelleher, David Hickey and Anton O'Toole. Also on the panel was the Dublin and UCD player Pat Duggan from Kilmacud. The full Dublin team was; E. McEneaney; B. Finn, Joe O'Neill,

L. Larkin; M. McManamon, Robbie Kelleher. J. Broe: L. Sweeney, David Hickey; Anton O'Toole, Pat Hickey, P. Levins; F. Hutchinson, D. Clarke, A. Kearney. Maxie McManamon is the father of current Dublin 'super-sub' Kevin, Pat Hickey is a brother of David and Joe O'Neill is a brother of Dr Pat.

I suppose I could always say I taught those subsequent Dublin senior players everything they knew about football but I might be pushing my luck a bit too much on that one! A certain Mr Heffernan had a bit to do with it also.

And Kildare were looking for me too. Kildare-mad Michael Osborne was a main man in the county fund-raising operation for the football team. He rang me out of the blue to ask me if I would be prepared to meet him and a few others with a view to taking over the Kildare football team.

The day he rang me was one of the few times in my life that I was sick in bed from an infection and not feeling great. I told Michael to come back to me in a few days and I would talk to them. However later that week I heard on the radio that Mick O'Dwyer had been given the Kildare job. I often wondered what would have happened had I not been out of action that week. Kildare fans will probably be saying it was their lucky break!

Chapter 8
UCD Time And The Living Is Easy... Sort Of

WHILE I was involved with the UCD football club in the 1960s and '70s life for students was very different to what it has been over the last 25 years. As far as GAA players were concerned the biggest practical difference was that most students from the country stayed in Dublin at the weekends as opposed to modern times when country students can be seen heading off home by train, bus or car at Friday lunchtime.

It was the presence of students at weekends that allowed clubs like UCD to prosper because the country lads were mad about football and as the numbers at UCD kept increasing, with the arrival of Donagh O'Malley's so-called 'free education', there was demand for more football competitions. In my time we entered teams at Senior, Intermediate, Junior and U-21 grades in Dublin competitions, which represented a huge expansion in the club and posed many logistical problems.

Dublin league games were usually played at 11.30 on Sunday mornings but some of the away venues could be far from 86 St Stephen's Green where the assembly point was. I remember once getting a junior team out to play in Howth on a February Sunday morning. Many junior games were played in the Fifteen Acres in the Phoenix Park, which was manageable even for the lads with bicycles. The UCD club had no money apart from a meagre grant from the College Athletic Union Council so students either found their own way to games or got a lift with a few graduates living in Dublin who were involved with the club such as

Brendan Devlin from Pomeroy, Co Tyrone and Paddy McDonnell from Cavan. Paddy by the way was unusual for Cavan in having won a Fitzgibbon Cup hurling medal in his time as a student as did the legendary Jim Smith who captained Cavan to their first All-Ireland in 1935.

Many GAA clubs at all levels used to like playing away to UCD simply because in the winter months there was excellent facilities on offer in Belfield with hot showers, etc that many Dublin clubs did not have in those days. The legality of many UCD players was often open to question because many never bothered to transfer from their home clubs so objections could often arise. I remember one year when UCD actually got as far as the Intermediate final in Dublin and the opposing club was taking no chances – they objected to no less than SIXTEEN different players.

Most of these were lost but two or three did stand up and UCD were duly thrown out of the competition. On the other side of the coin during the summer months when UCD might have to field a team for a Dublin league game and bodies were short many a famous inter-county player living in Dublin 'guested' for the College under a false name usually somebody who was a friend of one of the student players but to protect the guilty I will not name any names, even at this distant remit, except my good friend, the late Jap Finlay, father of current Monaghan star Paul Finlay.

Since hundreds if not thousands of students from the country spent over 20 weekends in Dublin in those days they obviously had many options for passing the time. Unlike today, spending every night in the pub was not one of them for the simple reason that very few students could afford it – despite the cheap drink at the time. One of the big Saturday night attractions was a very popular late-night venue, The Grafton Cinema, a small cinema halfway down Grafton Street that became the venue for Folk and Irish Traditional Irish music sessions that started at midnight on Saturdays.

Many famous Irish performers took part in those concerts but my own special recall would be of several provided by the then largely unheard of group called The Dubliners. This was a small theatre and the acoustics were brilliant. The Dubliners stood across the width of the small stage and sang possibly at the very best they ever were. I can never forget the late Luke Kelly with that rasping voice of his standing at the and of the row next to Ronnie Drew and belting out such songs as 'The Ballad of Joe Hill' as well as many better-known songs. We were privileged to have witnessed those shows and being part of Irish history, bearing in mind the world-wide success of The Dubliners over the subsequent 50 years. The concerts were also a great way of getting some recalcitrant students to leave the pubs too!

Luke Kelly often frequented a licensed premises in Lower Leeson Street then owned by a returned US emigrant and native of Leitrim called Pat McDermott which is now owned by a former classmate of my own Pat Hourican from Gowna, Co Cavan. This place was the unofficial HQ of the UCD club and often acted as a meeting place for games and other activities. Luke Kelly was a regular visitor to McDermotts on a Sunday afternoon where he would studiously read the The Sunday Times and enjoy a drink but he was never interested in Gaelic football!

It was interesting to recall that one of Luke's greatest ballads was 'Raglan Road' written by Paddy Kavanagh the Monaghan poet from Inniskeen. Paddy was a frequent presence in that general Leeson Street – Mount Street area and I often saw him sitting on the steps of No 2 Upper Leeson Street imbibing from a bottle and conversing with any passer-by like myself who stopped to chat. I lived for many years just a few doors down. Of course Paddy was a legendary goalkeeper with the Inniskeen team for a short while until on one hot summer's day he went over to the sideline to buy an ice-cream cone only to discover that a goal had been scored in his absence, thus ending a potentially brilliant football career!

Life in Dublin was less demanding in those days with television only a new fad and not a sign of mobile phones or Tweeters. Bicycles were the man means of transport for students but a Heinkel scooter was a big step up for me when I inherited it from my brother.

Chapter 9
Taking A Bite Out Of The Big Apple

ONE October Friday morning in 1971, I got a phone call at work from John Kerry O'Donnell in Gaelic Park, New York. Such a call was rare enough because John Kerry preferred to write letters, many of which are collector's items because of the beautiful handwriting and the flowery language he employed. The call was made around 6am New York time and during it, he asked me meet a man in the Gresham Hotel in Dublin that afternoon to discuss a matter that O'Donnell was anxious to run by me. The man in question was Michael Flannery, a native of Tipperary and a former Old IRA man who had emigrated to New York in 1927 and who was very prominent in Irish circles in the city.

An Irish-American organisation in New York had recently been set up and O'Donnell availed of the opportunity to have some fun with the GAA authorities back in Ireland with whom he was having one of his many bouts of falling out. Dublin referee Clem Foley had been assaulted some time before when officiating at a big game in Gaelic Park and the GAA banned all Irish teams from playing there for a year. O'Donnell saw an opportunity to circumvent the ban by having an unofficial team play in New York to raise funds for the new organisation.

Michael Flannery was sent over to ask me if I would be able to organise a team of county players mainly from the Six Counties to go out and play games in New York and Hartford, Connecticut with the first game to be played nine days later in Gaelic Park.

This was a typical gambit by Gaelic Park owner O'Donnell to

give the finger to the GAA authorities in Ireland. Having talked to a few people and some players I knew, we decided to proceed.

I approached it as a bit of craic as there didn't seem to be any harm in it since it would not be an official game under the auspices of the GAA. As all-expenses trips to America were very rare in those days, there was no shortage of players willing to travel and in less than a week over 20 Ulstermen and Mick Burke from Cork had landed in New York. John Kerry's glee was unconfined when he greeted the new arrivals in Gaelic Park on the Thursday night prior to the game. A few thousand people turned up for the match – they were anxious to see county players in 'The Park' again.

The following week the group moved to Hartford for a game against local opposition with another large crowd attending. So far so good... but even in those pre-mobile and pre-internet days, word eventually filtered through to Dublin that some sort of game had been played in Gaelic Park, resulting in the powers-that-be in Croke Park digging for more information. Seán Ó Siocháin was the General Secretary of the GAA at the time and the president was Pat Fanning from Waterford, a man not to be taken lightly when it came to administering GAA justice.

Reputable New York-based reporter John Byrne had written a match report for the Irish Echo in New York but stressed that he had not been given an official lineout for the Irish team and was relying on hearsay around the ground as to the identity of the players. By coincidence a Central Council meeting had been arranged for the Saturday after the arrival home to Ireland of the Ulster players and this gave Pat Fanning an opportunity to produce a fire and brimstone attack on me personally. My own brother, the late Fr Phil McGee, had been a member of the Central Council for Longford for several years but, thankfully, he had left that position by 1971.

The Sunday Independent went to town the next day, hardly surprising since at the time I was the main GAA writer for the rival Sunday Press.

'A SAD COMMENTARY ON STANDARDS OF HONESTY' was the banner heading under Tom O'Riordan's report. Fanning spoke for a full half-hour on the whole subject of connivance and secrecy on behalf of New York GAA, i.e. John Kerry O'Donnell. But the harshest words were reserved for myself although my name was not mentioned, merely referring to me as 'a Dublin journalist'.

I was ordered to appear before the Executive of the GAA to explain my actions and every player alleged to have taken part was also to be written to for an explanation. Earlier Ó Siocháin had written to all county secretaries with dire warnings for any player from their county who was known to have taken part in the trip to New York.

As it transpired, the whole thing was nothing more than a puff of smoke. The New York GAA were not involved in the game, neither was any organ of the GAA in Ireland. The trip was no more or no less than a typical sortie by John Kerry O'Donnell against the GAA authorities in Ireland with nobody other than the GAA top brass paying much attention. The players from Ulster of course were delighted with their trip, which also included a visit to Boston.

In Hartford, the famous Irish actress of the time Siobhan McKenna was performing in a play and some of us had the pleasure of meeting her. I was able to remind her that she spent a lot of her childhood's summer holidays with her relatives in my home parish, Colmcille in north Longford. She reminisced enthusiastically about visits by donkey and cart to Edenmore bog for rearing of the turf.

A few years earlier when third level GAA activity began to expand into a First-Year (Freshers) competition among the various universities, it was called the Eoin McKenna Cup which commemorated a well-know Professor in University College Galway who was Siobhan's father. Small world.

Regarding the excursion by the team to the US, nothing really happened about the whole thing afterwards; I did not appear before the Executive and no player ever wrote any letters of explanation. Normal relations between the GAA in Ireland and New York, if you could ever call them that, resumed shortly afterwards. The charity got their money, the players enjoyed their trip, John Kerry O'Donnell had a good laugh and we all lived happily ever after.

Chapter 10

Tragedy Strikes My Family – On The Double

THERE is probably no organisation in Ireland whose members represent a microcosm of Irish life in general better than the GAA. Its membership is dispersed into all parts of the country, rural and urban, represent all levels of society, rich and poor, and nowadays are rapidly becoming a multi-ethnic society. Sometimes GAA people, like most sports groupings, get so immersed in their sport that in the mind of the general public their lives are totally dominated by, say, football or hurling.

I spent a lot of time involved with the GAA from modest club affairs to the highest games activities such as All-Ireland finals and administration affairs such as the recent Football Review Committee. I was aware at the same time that 'normal' life continues alongside the GAA activity and things happen to us all that remind us forcibly of this.

I had two major personal tragedies in my life that led to the deaths of a sister and brother at very early ages and they certainly ensured that I had a sense of perspective about life in general.

In the mid-sixties my older sister, Alice, was working in the Department of Agriculture in Merrion Street, Dublin and lived in a flat in Upper Leeson Street. When I first went to UCD, I was fortunate to stay with Alice for a few years which greatly facilitated my time in UCD because that college was then based just down the road in Earlsfort Terrace, beside Stephen's Green.

I later moved into a flat in Ranelagh along with four other students who were members of the UCD club. Around midnight one night in July, 1966, I was awakened by pebbles being thrown up at my window. When I opened it up, somebody shouted at me that part of the roof in my sister's house had collapsed. I rushed down the short distance to discover sirens sounding, the flashing lights of an ambulance with several people gathered around.

The ambulance actually moved away as I arrived and I was told by a neighbour what had happened. Those flats were in one of the large Georgian houses, three storeys over basement, which were over 100 years old and apparently along the top edge of the roof, there was a row of large granite blocks. For some reason on this day one of these blocks had loosened and suddenly fell all the way down to the ground floor. My sister had been out with her boyfriend and was returning to her flat. As she climbed the six steps to the front door while he was locking the parked car, the falling granite block struck her as she was searching for the keys to the front door. She was killed by the huge impact.

This was such a freakish event that it was impossible to comprehend and immediately I went into shock and felt totally confused.

Alice was rushed to the old Richmond Hospital where she was pronounced dead shortly after arrival. I had another sister also living in Dublin and eventually we met in the middle of the night in the hospital and began to realise exactly what had happened. There were no mobile phones and very few phones of any kind in rural Ireland in those times. Both my parents were at home in Longford along with my oldest brother, Fr Phil and another brother Páid. We rang them with the bad news and immediately they set out for Dublin. I will never forget meeting them on their arrival at The Richmond around 4am to be shown the corpse of Alice.

Her death in such freakish circumstances was big news and was the lead story on the Evening Herald the next day. I was numbed by the tragedy as she had been my 'guardian angel' when I arrived in Dublin. It was the brutal nature of her death which really shattered all the family members and her many friends in Longford and Dublin because nobody in their wildest dreams could have imagined such a freak occurrence taking place.

The sadness that permeated our native place, Colmcille, Co Longford when Alice was being buried was really tangible. It was worst of all for our parents, having to watch their own child being buried. At such times GAA activity seemed so irrelevant. Alice was only 27 when she passed away. I remember clearly that her funeral in Aughnacliffe graveyard was taking place at the same time as the World Cup final was being played in Wembley, which England won against West Germany. Soccer was not as ingrained in the Irish psyche at that time as it is today and none of our neighbours, relations or friends were concerned about missing the game in order to attend Alice's funeral.

But that horrific death left an everlasting impression on me as it was the first time that death had struck home to myself and our other family members. The violent nature of the death left an indelible mark and to this day I never pass through Leeson Street without thinking of Alice and the dreadful end to her life.

It was nine years later, in 1975, that tragedy again hit the McGee family. Fr Phil McGee was ordained in Maynooth in 1953 and spent most of his priesthood in education as a teacher in Moyne Latin School and as a founding member of the new Moyne Community School.

In the GAA world he had been totally immersed in promoting underage football in Longford all his life and dozens of young lads all over North Longford have memories of being packed into his Ford car, sometimes as many as 10 or 12, to play for Colmcille around various parts of Longford.

Later he became involved with Longford GAA as minor board chairman and also served as Central Council delegate. Former

GAA Director General, Liam Mulvihill, replaced him when he retired from that position.

It was for his role in the success of the Longford county team in the mid-sixties that he is best remembered for in the GAA world. Longford had developed a good set of footballers at the time but it was obvious that some outside guidance in the form of training and team management was required to advance the team further. Together with the county chairman Jimmy Flynn, Fr Phil approached the former great Cavan star Mick Higgins and inveigled him to train the team. In 1965 Longford reached the Leinster final but lost narrowly to Dublin, in '66 they won the National League by beating the Galway three-in-a-row team and in 1968 they won their first and only Leinster final, beating Laois, before losing to Kerry by a couple of points in the All-Ireland semi-final.

However, education was becoming a more important part of his life and in addition he was a well-known speaker around Ireland on behalf of the Pioneer movement. So he more or less retired from the GAA in the early seventies to concentrate on those other pursuits. Fr Phil was a Fr Harry Bohan-type priest, always working for local communities and attending to the needs of his neighbours. He was instrumental in starting a Group Water Scheme in the area, which has thrived up to the present time, and he spent much time visiting old and sick people in the region.

On the last Sunday in January 1975, I had arrived home to my flat in Dublin rather late after celebrating UCD's victory in the Leinster club final over Ferbane from Offaly. At around two in the morning, I received a phone call to say that my brother had just died from a heart attack. He was only 47. He had been living at home in Aughnacliffe with our then widowed mother. He returned late that night from visiting yet another neighbour who was ill and he complained of being unwell himself. It took quite a while in those days to get an ambulance and he passed away on his way to hospital in Longford.

Considering the effervescent nature of the man's life and his commitment to so many aspects of local activity for many years, his death at such a young age shocked the local community and GAA people all over the country. As I was much younger than Fr Phil I thought he was nearly an old man. Now when I visit his grave and see the inscription confirming his death at 47, it dawns on me just how young he was.

We all felt bereft when Fr Phil left us particularly in his local community of north Longford. In my own way I've felt that God had decided that Fr Phil's work on earth had been completed when he passed away. He had achieved great things as a GAA official in Colmcille and with the Longford county set-up, and nothing has come near since those halcyon days of the 1960s.

Most important of all, he had succeeded in setting up a brand new secondary school on the borders of Longford, Cavan and Leitrim that has turned out to be one of the landmark institutions of its kind in the country with past-pupils in all disciplines of education now spread around the world. The wonderful set of teachers he appointed prior to the opening mostly spent the rest of their careers in Moyne Community School and at present this co-ed, multi-sports college stands out as a beacon of hope for a part of Ireland that has always been haunted by the spectre of emigration.

As an out-and-out educationalist never based on elitism, I am sure that is what pleased him most of all. And looking down from above as a GAA man, he must have been very proud when two Moyne past pupils were honoured as Allstars – Seamus Quinn from Leitrim and Dermot McCabe from Cavan. The school had opened its doors in September and he died the following January. His memory and indeed his presence have never left my consciousness to this day and never will. He and I started in this school's predecessor, Moyne Latin School on the same day, he as a new teacher and myself as a first-year pupil. I can still remember the roguish way in which he would tease the Cavan lads in relation to football, bearing in mind their previous great tradition by comparison with poor Leitrim and Longford but also being aware that the good times were rapidly eroding in Cavan.

These two tragic deaths were similar to what thousands of Irish families have encountered in their lives and there is no doubt they leave a lasting impression. The big positive is that we can be inspired by such events and they can influence our lives thereafter. The new GAA pitch in the parish of Colmcille was opened in 1982 and I was proud to be able to bring a full-strength Offaly team to play at the opening just a month before that famous '82 All-Ireland final. The beautiful ground is also named after Fr Phil. So in his case at least the memory survives.

Of course when tragedy strikes a family who have a strong GAA involvement, the role of the GAA family can be of colossal importance. In Tyrone, for instance, over the past 20 years there have been many tragic deaths of prominent GAA people such as Cormac McAnallen and Michaela Harte and the communal strength of the GAA has certainly been a gigantic help to the bereaved people. I find with GAA people that the memories of the deceased do not die with their burials nor does the practical and emotional support that the bereaved receive from their GAA comrades.

One of the most moving things that I have witnessed at many GAA funerals is how former staunch opponents, often bitter ones, rally round to show solidarity with bereaved families. This is one of the noblest traits of the GAA community and one the Association should be proud of.

Chapter 11

The Year Santa Claus Arrived in June

FOR students in Dublin in the sixties and seventies, there were various way to make pocket-money, including being a temporary postman at Christmas or a waiter in public houses at weekends. Another attractive 'nixer' at that time was working in the telephone exchange as a telephonist in Exchequer Street just off Dame St in the centre of Dublin. The work required a minimal amount of training and usually involved evening or night shifts but in relative terms the money was good. Many students who did this work became very famous people later on with one becoming a prominent government minister, and not one connected with phone-tapping or the like, I might add.

After doing an interview, I managed to get on the list and soon learned how to be a telephone operator. For the benefit of younger readers, I should explain the mechanics of making telephone calls in those day bore absolutely no comparison to what telephonic communications are in this day and age. Phone calls were divided into local calls and trunk calls. In Dublin and some other large towns, one could dial local calls from your home telephone but in rural areas one had to go through the local operator who was usually the postmaster or postmistress.

To make a trunk call say from Longford to Dublin, you had to firstly book the call with the local post office and then wait for the operator to call you back. The timing of that return call was unpredictable, often taking several hours. As telephonists, our job was to pick up the incoming call and, if possible, place the trunk call immediately if the lines were not busy. For checking purposes, one usually listened for a few moments to make sure the call was properly connected and therein lies many a tale.

Often the operator would not be able to make the connection on the spot and you would then have to call back the person and make the connection later. With these sort of connection systems it was inevitable that operators would often hear a lot more than was necessary. If you were working for five or six hours and going past midnight the temptation to listen was obvious and in particular operators with a special interest in some aspect of everyday life would use the facility.

Those operators who had an interest in horse racing had a special attraction to 'accidentally' overhearing conversations between racing people such as trainers, jockeys and owners and over time they would immediately recognise the telephone numbers and indeed the voices of these people conducting telephone calls. Friday night was the busiest night for these conversations before the weekend racing. Whenever an operator plugged in to a call there would be a click on the phone which was audible to both sides but most listeners did not realise that it had any significance.

One well-known trainer of the time, Paddie Prendergast, was a big phone user and he learnt the significance of these little ticks. On one occasion very late on a Friday night, he noticed a lot of ticking noises over a short period of time while on a call and suddenly shouted: 'Will you crowd (not actually the word he used) pull out your plugs in there because I am not even going to be talking about horses at all tonight so just leave me alone this time,' and continued about his business with his caller.

In May 1964 I was on duty in the telephone exchange on a Saturday afternoon around 6pm when I answered a caller asking to be put through to England. It was common at the time for the person calling in to give the name of the person they were calling and ask for a 'personal call' which meant that if the operator asked for the recipient and the person was not in there would be no charge for the customer. I was given the name as 'Scobie Breasley' who I instantly recognised as the leading jockey in England on a par with Lester Piggott at that time. The person calling was Mick Rogers, who I knew to be the trainer of a wonder horse called Santa Claus which had just won the Irish 2000 Guineas, a race seen as a major trial for the English and Irish derbies.

The person who answered the phone said that Mr Breasley was in the bath and asked Mr Rogers to call back in an hour. I was asked to book the call for that time which I made certain I did. When Scobie came on the phone, Mick Rogers said: 'Scobie, Santa Claus has won the 2,000 Guineas at the Curragh today. I believe he will win the Epsom Derby and I want you to ride him.'

Without a moment's hesitation Breasley said he would and that was the end of the conversation. Since this information had come from the horse's mouth, and maybe even closer, I decided to have a much larger bet than I would normally have placed first thing on Monday morning and even though the odds were not great the tip certainly was.

Santa Claus came very late with a run to snatch the Epsom Derby and a few weeks later destroyed the field when winning the Irish Derby at the Curragh.

For security reasons, mostly my own, I decided not to inform any of my colleagues about this particular phone call until after the Epsom Derby but I did let them know at that time.

Chapter 12

'Never Mind That Auld Coaching – Get On With The Game'

WHEN coaching entered into the GAA lexicon in the early 1990s, it received a frosty reception. For a start the word itself drew a lot of flak because for many GAA traditionalists coaching was going to lead to professionalism – how many times have we heard that scare story since then right up to the present day? There was no such thing as a GAA coach before then, or a manager either, instead the people who were in charge of football teams at all levels were called trainers. A comment made by Joe Lennon around that time in The Sunday Press that Kerry football was 20 years behind the times really set the battleground for the coaching battle. These words seemed to most people to be heresy but coming from a man who was part of the Down team that came from nowhere to beat Kerry in 1960 and '68 and win All-Irelands they set a lot of people thinking. Would coaching work in Gaelic football after all? Was coaching only for professional sports? Where would the coaches come from and would they have to be paid?

After he had published his book 'Coaching Gaelic Football For Champions' in the early sixties Lennon became the focal point for the subject and when he decided to start a coaching course open to all who wished to partake in Gormanston in the summer of 1964 it was clear that this was more than a passing fad. Along with Joe Lennon as instructors on the course were Derry star Jim McKeever, also a teacher, Eamon Young from Cork football fame,

Mick Ryan who was involved with schools GAA in Dublin, and Frankie Byrne, another teacher and former All-Ireland winner with Meath. I attended the very first course, which was residential for a week in Gormanston and was a great success with a couple of hundred attending from all over Ireland. Teachers at primary and secondary level would have been strongly represented which it itself was a vote of confidence for coaching but of course they were off for their summer holidays at the time anyway! Looking back on that time I can remember a large number of people who were there who went on to be in charge of teams at all levels of football. A similar course was later organised for hurling with people like Fr Tommy Maher and Des Ferguson from Dublin as leaders.

The coaching strategy in the GAA was fairly haphazard for a long time with nobody directly in charge and coaching tended to be sidetracked into other branches of the Association for a while. But in the early 1970s the emergence of third level colleges specialising in physical education and sports coaching in general began to emerge and the famous St Mary's College, London, (Strawberry Hill) was a place where several GAA players attended to gain degrees in those subjects.

To help the college out in getting experience I arranged for UCD to travel to London to play against Strawberry Hill and in 1972 St. Mary's entered the All-Ireland 7-Aside run by UCD and led by Dermot Earley the college actually won the competition. Other well-known players on that team included Sean Mulvihill (Longford) brother of Liam, Billy Cogan from Cork, Vinny Murray RIP (Westmeath) who went on to coach Clongowes Wood College rugby team, Tom Donoghue who later was the trainer of the Offaly football team that won the 1982 All-Ireland, Johnny Geraghty (Galway), Mickey Ned O'Sullivan and Jimmy Deenihan (Kerry), Ted Coakley and Kevin Kehilly (Cork), Pat Sands (Galway) and Flan O'Friel (Clare).

When these men graduated they returned to Ireland and

became the first batch of qualified Physical Education teachers and instructors with strong Gaelic football connections, which was a big advance for the whole notion of coaching in the GAA. In the early 70s, the National College of Physical Education (NCPE) was founded in Limerick and many GAA players graduated from there, so much so that NCPE were able to win the All-Ireland club championship in 1978. Among that team were Pat and Mick Spillane (Kerry), Brian Talty (Galway), Eddie Mahon (Wexford), Sean O'Shea (Longford), Jimmy Dunne (Offaly), Michael Kilcoyne (Westmeath), Richie Bell, Denis O'Boyle and Martin Connolly (Mayo), Declan Smyth (Galway) and Anthony Harkin (Donegal).

Brian Mullins had earlier graduated from NCPE now called Thomond College and part of the University of Limerick (UL) and is one of the leading sporting complexes in Europe.

The influence of this influx of GAA-orientated qualified Physical Education graduates played a major role in developing football coaching in the colleges and the wider GAA family and helped greatly in modernising research related knowledge of physical fitness and related areas. Then in 1981 Pat Daly, graduate of St Patrick's teacher training college took up a full-time appointment on the staff of Croke Park and got involved with the organisation of coaching which was still only developing in the GAA as a whole. Gradually structures were set up within Croke Park to promote coaching as a fully-fledged part of the GAA scene and when a body called the Games Development Committee was set up in 1988 coaching was a definite part of its remit under the outstanding chairmanship of Lorcan O'Rourke.

As time went by other committees were set up to deal with various aspects of football such as a Football Work Group that was chaired by Dublin's Tony Hanahoe and which did a lot of work on playing rules, which of course are always an integral part of football coaching. Gradually the GAA began to invest some serious money in coaching, always being aware of the pressure coming from other sports for which elaborate coaching had become the norm. A government financed body called the National Coaching and Training Centre was set up which also helped contribute to Gaelic football coaching.

But it was still taking a long time for some county boards to take coaching seriously by setting up proper structures to provide high-quality coaching in an organised manner. For example, there was a period in the nineties when some current county players who were unemployed were simply roped in to act as coaches with little or no training for that work. This was an unmitigated disaster in some counties and definitely did more harm than good. If there is anything worse than no coaching it is bad coaching and this happened in many places around the country. Eventually county coaches with proper qualifications began to be appointed and were paid for their work and only then did proper coaching really take off.

In the late 1990s, a few major issues were facing the GAA as regards how young children were being initiated into the GAA. For decades the Association never had to worry about a supply of young boys, and some girls then too, being taught the basics of football at an early level because in most national schools there was a male teacher who was happy to coach the children. Indeed many famous footballers would invariably recall their first introduction to football when being interviewed in later life with fond memories of the influence of their teacher at national school. The GAA was spoiled for years by having that facility. But then quite quickly the ratio of male to female teachers changed in favour of females and many schools found there was nobody to look after the young players. And at the next level, secondary schools, there was also a major problem looming large with the decline of clergy in many secondary schools and a consequent absence of teachers to train the college teams. And the earlier coaches from the seventies were now ageing and that was a further problem.

But the GAA moved to solve those problems by appointing a

batch of full-time coaches for the first time and they in turn were able to coach others and again government financial aid from the Irish Sports Council played a vital role in these developments so that these earlier problems were at least partially solved.

The standard of coaching facilities available to GAA members from Croke Park nowadays is on a par with any similar sports body in the world. Pat Daly has done a mountain of work and research over many years to leave the GAA with this wonderful facility in relation to all aspects of coaching. Nowadays the GAA implements a games-based approach to football which means that the emphasis is on the actual learning and improving and hopefully perfecting the actual skills of Gaelic football in a games environment. Certainly there is a lot of attention paid to other aspects such as diet, physical training, psychology etc. but the emphasis is definitely on playing the game, and for young people enjoying the game, because they love taking part in games.

● ● ●

At the highest level inter-county coaching, training, etc. is still very much dependent on who is implementing these procedures and there are many variations in this regard. In the past decade there is no doubt that physical preparation has become the dominant trait with ever-increasing emphasis on speed, stamina and the great new mantra of the present time, Strength and Conditioning (S&C). Whenever I am in the company of county players S&C will be sure to feature in the conversation before very long. GAA people have seen the route rugby has followed in this regard with players having massive upper-body strength as a result of full-time professional training. Some GAA managers at least seem determined to go down the same route and we have seen several examples of county players with massive frames, some clearly unsuitable for their natural body structures. If this trend continues one wonders what shape some of these players will be in when they hit 40 years of age and have retired from active sport. Only time will tell but as of now anybody who dares to question these training procedures tends to be laughed out of court and categorised as an old fogey living in the past.

Personally speaking and having been in charge of teams from many different levels from underage to third level, to club to inter-county and even up to the national team, I have always believed that the physical fitness aspect of coaching and team preparation should be only a minority part of time spent. Instead I have always concentrated on making players better as footballers through good coaching aimed at improving individual skills – after all coaching is essentially a teaching and learning operation.

Anywhere I went as a manager I tried to improve the playing ability of individual players even if that meant going right back to the basic skill level such as kicking the ball properly, tackling without fouling and improving things like a player's peripheral vision. Now all this can be slow and laborious work and I just have a feeling that many managers, particularly on the club scene, prefer now to concentrate on things like S&C at the expense of what I am talking about here.

Fitness routines, including S&C can easily be acquired and learned because they are largely common to all members of a team and anyway there seems to be an avalanche of young people coming out of some third level colleges with qualifications that seem to indicate they are world experts in these matters. Making players better through diligent personal coaching is a far more difficult task which many club managers in particular are either not capable of implementing or simply assume that the players already have all the skills necessary. How naive they are if they believe that.

The fact that we have many hundreds of managers getting paid large sums of money to take charge of teams at all levels nowadays does little for quality coaching in my view because many of these people at club level are just not qualified since the majority of them do not even have a coaching certificate. Most club managers are there because they were famous footballers in their own playing days but know little about the science or philosophy of coaching which should be a central part of being a manager, regardless of the level of football involved.

There have been and still are some horrible examples of abuse of young players by managers who seem to more concerned with inducing sacrifice among players rather than teaching the skills of the game. I have heard of secondary school students being dragged in to train in the gym at 7am before they go to class which is an abuse. From Christmas until June secondary school students should receive preference towards their studies before their football, with the latter being carried out after school hours.

Innovation is an absolute necessity in Gaelic football as it is in most major sports. Over the years in football we have seen many innovations going back to the 1920s when Mayo player Sean Lavin first started using a strange thing called a solo run when he was a student in UCD at the same time as Dr Eamon O'Sullivan. What interesting times there must have been in UCD football then.

In the 1928 All-Ireland final it is claimed that Kildare used the hand-passing style when beating Cavan and in the mid-forties Antrim made a rare visit out of Ulster to face Kerry in the All-Ireland semi-final with a game that was largely based on hand-passing. In a fairly tempestuous game Kerry stood true to their catch and kick tradition and more besides to beat off the Antrim challenge and strangely not long afterwards Antrim sent a motion to GAA Congress asking that the handpass be removed and the motion was passed.

In the 1970s, hand-passing came back with a vengeance and this time handpass goals were allowed, which meant a forward could keep going until he saw the colour of the goalkeeper's eyes before sliding the ball by hand one side of him into the net.

In recent years we saw another innovation from Jim McGuinness with the packed defence that was good enough to bring him and Donegal an All-Ireland success. As always happens when some new tactic works at a high level there are many imitators and several county team managers followed Donegal's methods, which were not that different to how Tyrone under Mickey Harte played a few years earlier.

Although lots of people in the GAA vehemently objected to innovations like these it has to be said that they are a necessity. Otherwise the game becomes static and eventually boring and while the changes are useful, inevitably the fundamentals of Gaelic football still remain as the benchmark around which other innovations can thrive temporarily. It is interesting for example that Dublin footballers have recently been playing a style not far removed from what has always been the traditional game of moving the ball quickly and utilising foot-passing as the primary means of transferring the ball. Every style of football should be welcomed because as Donegal and Dublin showed in recent times, there is plenty of scope for variation in the game of Gaelic football.

It requires sensible use of the playing rules and adjustments where necessary to ensure that the fundamentals of football are maintained but also that there is always room for innovation. Most rule changes over the past 30 years have been brought about because of the changing conditions under which the game is played. Players are much fitter, stronger and harder because of all the extra physical training they undergo. These fitness improvements lead to a faster game, more quick movement of the ball and more movement of players around the field. For nearly 100 years positioning of players in Gaelic football was static. In all Dr Eamon O'Sullivan's years as Kerry trainer that lineout was sacrosanct and when other teams began to make alterations, such as when Kevin Heffernan introduced the roaming full-forward role in the 1955 Leinster final, it was the start of breaking up the traditional formation.

It is interesting to note however that when Dublin played

Kerry later that year in the All-Ireland final the Kerry full-back Ned Roche let Heffernan go far outfield but stayed back in his traditional No 3 spot and the Dublinman did not make anything like the same impact he made in the Leinster final. When Roche was asked afterwards if he went out the field to mark Heffernan he uttered the immortal words: 'No I stayed my ground and I met him on the way back!'

Chapter 13
From The Latin School To All-Ireland Finals

MOST people I met in the GAA world for the first time ask me: 'Being from Longford, I presume you went to St. Mel's College?' This was a very famous college which has won more Leinster titles than any other school, 30 in all, as well as four All-Irelands. Former GAA Director General Liam Mulvihill is just one of many famous people to win Hogan Cup medals with this institution. But I always have to say, 'No, I did not go to St Mel's.'

Two brothers of mine attended there which was the diocesan college for Ardagh & Clonmacnois and covers county Longford and parts of Cavan, Leitrim, Westmeath, Sligo, Offaly and Roscommon.

In north Longford very close to the Cavan and Leitrim borders where I was born, there had been an education facility in the form of movable hedge-schools since around 1800 before a permanent building came along in the townland of Moyne in 1897.

The hedge schools of Ireland were mainly established to educate young men for the priesthood so Latin and Greek were always primary subjects. The school got the name of Moyne Latin School and remained by that name until the 70s when a wonderful Community School was opened catering for around 700 boys and girls from Longford, Cavan and Leitrim.

The reason I was sent to Moyne Latin school was because my late brother Fr Phil McGee had been appointed as a teacher there and he and I started our educational careers the same day. With less than 100 male-only pupils in three classrooms at that time, and no sporting facilities Moyne was a rough and ready place and the number of students who went on for the priesthood declined substantially. I was only the second person from Moyne to go on to university but secondary education in Ireland was about to undergo massive transformation around that time.

The mixture of pupils from three adjoining counties always provided plenty of scope for banter relating to football and the Cavan lads usually led the debates because memories of the glory-days of that county were still fresh in the mind by the early sixties. The famous GAA parishes of Mullahoran and Cornafean were always well represented in Moyne and in my time we had two brothers of Phil 'The Gunner' Brady, Danny and Jim, while from Leitrim there was Fergus O'Rourke, brother of Colm, whose family lived in nearby Aughavas before later migrating to Skyrne in Co Meath.

Unusually in those times, Longford was also in the GAA big time as the sixties were the best period ever for that county. They won the National League in 1966 beating the great Galway three-in-row team in the final and in 1968 won the county's one and only Leinster championship by beating Dublin, Meath who were holders of the Sam Maguire Cup and Laois before losing in the All-Ireland semi-final to Kerry by two points.

My brother was, along with trainer Mick Higgins of Cavan, one of the main organisers of those victories so football was always a hot subject in Moyne Latin School.

My only football claim to fame in Moyne was that I was kicked on the shin by Danny 'The Gunner' Brady during a kick around at lunchtime and made my first visit to Dr McManus in nearby Arva to get eight stitches inserted.

After the Leaving Cert it was decided that I could go to UCD, and I opted to study Agricultural Science. No points system in vogue back then so one could pick and choose nearly any faculty. What I did not know was that the Agriculture course included subjects like Science and Mechanical Drawing, never heard of in Moyne Latin School, and I discovered this when I went to my first chemistry practical class and the lecturer told me to set up six Bunsen Burners. What? I hadn't a clue about science and even less about mechanical drawing so that first year went by in an educational vacuum as far as I was concerned. A year later and a lot wiser I set off on a BA degree which worked out ok.

I got involved with the UCD Gaelic football club at the persuasion of Longford player Seán Murray who soon bulldozed me into becoming club secretary. At that time, UCD only fielded one team in football as was the norm in all universities. That team played in the Sigerson Cup as well as the Dublin league and championship.

After a couple of years, as the number of third level students began to mushroom in all the colleges, it was decided to set up a special body to promote third-level GAA games in a more expansive manner and the first decision was to provide a competition for first-year students.

UCD were the first winners of the final played in Croke Park following victory over Queens University. That was my first time to be in charge of a football team and in all I was involved with the UCD club for 10 more years.

UCD won Dublin titles in 1963 and '65 and again in 1973 and '74 with the latter two yielding two All-Ireland club titles against Nemo Rangers and Clanna Gael from Armagh.

Around then, St Vincent's and UCD dominated Dublin club football which unintentionally gave me a great understanding of the Dublin and Kevin Heffernan football psyche.

Chapter 14

Nothing Compares To Club Success

THE greatest thing the GAA has going for it with regard to popularising Gaelic football and bringing the sport to the masses is undoubtedly the fact that it is a two-tier organisation with inter-county and club competitions. While there are only 32 Irish counties there are over 2,500 club teams in every nook and cranny of the country and it is they rather than the county teams that are the bedrock of the Association.

While I have had the privilege of managing a successful county team and all the prestige that brings to a county and the individual players, mentors and county board officers involved, my time spent with club teams is right up there with the county experiences.

Basically, I was involved with two types of clubs, University College Dublin (UCD) and two clubs in my native county, Cashel and Colmcille. I know there are many who begrudge UCD the title of being called a club team at all and I spent many years putting up with the often stinging attacks from all types of GAA people. 'Not a real club at all', 'Why should they have a chance to play with two clubs?' 'They're only a crowd of prima donnas', and so on and so on.

I know that when I was with UCD, it was a *real* club. We fielded teams in senior, intermediate, junior and U-21 in Dublin club games and the students were able to turn out and play in the Fifteen Acres in the Phoenix Park like all the other junior teams. Dublin-born students, for historical reasons, did not have the privilege of playing for UCD and their home club as well unless that club was from a lower grade than senior. Some players fell into that category and former Dublin manager Gerry McCaul played for his home club Ballymun, then intermediate, and with the UCD senior team, winning a Dublin medal. Former Dublin player Pat Duggan from Killmacud also played with UCD and won an All-Ireland club medal. Several other Dublin players also were eligible to play for the college and Dublin star Pat O'Neill actually transferred to UCD in the normal way and had a very successful career with them.

UCD made many other contributions to the GAA as any club would have done. The club started the first official All-Ireland 7-a-side in 1971 before Kilmacud took over after about seven years. The GAA pitches in Belfield were often made available for Dublin and other counties to play challenge games or to train, as Kerry's Dublin-based players did under Micheál Ó Muircheartaigh in their glory-days in the seventies. So UCD club was indeed a genuine club and the many, many players from weaker counties who improved their playing careers while there will vouch for that. There are many different ways for a club to serve the GAA other than by measuring the number of championships won.

Considering UCD supplied so many Presidents of the GAA over the years, I believe they are perfectly entitled to be called a proper club especially nowadays when there has been a huge expansion of playing activities in all the GAA sectors under the guidance of GAA Director, David Billings. Ironically, he was a sworn 'enemy' of UCD during his playing days with St Vincent's at a time in the seventies when the two clubs dominated Dublin football. David himself played with UCD and won Sigerson Cup medals. And there's further irony as former St Vincent's stalwart, Brian Mullins, is now a very progressive Director of Sport in UCD, even though there was a time when he mightn't have been let into the place.

Getting back to club games, we served a hard apprentice with several other strong teams in the capital and St Vincent's ever present. UCD won Dublin titles in 1963 and '65 before a new set of players arrived in the seventies and won two more in '73 and '74 and then two All-Irelands in '74 and '75. There was a myth around then that UCD only won because they had a team of top-class inter-county players but this was far from being the case. In the teams that won in 1974 and '75 for instance, about half were not even on their own county teams, they were just club players. The won like other winning clubs around the country through dedication to training, discipline and motivation and they had many narrow shaves along the way. And, of course, competition for places was also extremely keen.

In the past 30 years, the standard of club competition in Dublin has improved out of all recognition as huge new clubs have started up with massive playing numbers of all ages. When I was with UCD, clubs like Kilmacud, Thomas Davis, Ballyboden and the like were only starting to expand, greatly helped by the arrival of Heffo's Army in 1974, but now they are crucial components of the massive GAA expansion in the city of Dublin. This growth is particularly noticeable on the south side of the Liffey as traditionally, the GAA was much stronger on the north side of Dublin.

Small and all as the county of Longford is, only about 30 miles from one end to the other, I had never been to Newtowncashel, in south Longford on the banks of Lough Ree, until I got a call from a man called Pat Costello. Out of the blue one day, he asked me if I would be interested in training the Cashel senior football team. That was in the spring of 1977 at a time I had just taken on the Offaly team assignment. For some reason, which I still have never understood, I told Pat I would give it a go even though I was then living and working in Dublin.

Cashel had never won a Longford county senior championship; indeed they had never even got by the first round. But they had been showing up well in recent years at underage level, winning the Longford U-21 championship in 1974 with a very young team that included recent Leinster Council chairman, Martin Skelly and Michael Casey, then 16 years of age. Casey and

Mike Kenny were regulars on the Longford senior team by 1977 while John Donlon had been centre half-back on the Longford team that won the 1968 Leinster title. Trying my hand at winning a Longford senior championship was probably the challenge that encouraged me to proceed. On a freezing cold March evening I arrived to start proceedings on a hilly field with a wind blowing in over Lough Ree that would go through you.

Having found out a bit beforehand from Messrs Kenny and Casey whom I had previously known, I realised there were a lot of brothers playing football in Cashel – an awful lot. There were four Bannon brothers for a start followed by three Kennys and three Smiths.

It was obvious I had walked into a typical GAA rural club based on a handful of families – with all that entails. Rows can easily take place when brothers unite against another set of brothers in training or over team selection. There can be outbreaks of jealousy with brothers involved. Brothers can be offended when one of their own is not selected and so on.

But on the other side of the coin having sets of brothers on your team can be a powerful influence when it comes to motivation or rallying a team when required. In Cashel, we had lots of minor skirmishes along these and other lines which I was delighted with because passion like that is crucial in developing a team. It was the same with Offaly. I was doing the training myself in Cashel and many of the players were struggling at first to cope with the intensity. Bear in mind that a lot of these lads were manual workers employed with either the ESB or more often Bord na Mona. There was a lot of turf harvesting in that whole south Longford area and an ESB Power Station in Lanesboro. So they often arrived home tired after a hard day's work and coming into train even harder was a bit of a culture shock.

But with a mixture of bribery, enthusiasm and blackguarding I got them all to row in and soon their fitness levels began to improve greatly. Then the draw for the straight knockout Longford championship was announced and Cashel were drawn against the next parish team, Rathcline, from the town of Lanesboro. This could not have been a tougher assignment because Rathcline had won the county championship the previous year and many players from both clubs shared the same workplace. You can imagine how tense the lead up to that first round game was and the stakes, and the betting, were very high indeed.

In those years many famous GAA tournaments took place around the country and one of the best of these was known as the Newtowncashel Interprovincial Tournament in which about eight of the best club sides in the centre and west of Ireland took part. It was organised by the local school principal in Cashel, Seamus Folan from Spiddal, and was important in maintaining interest in football at a high level every summer.

The chairman of the Cashel club then was Sergeant Gabriel Starkin from Kilcormac, thus maintaining another Offaly connection with the parish and I had two sensible selectors in Pat Costello and Joe Mulvihill. There was huge interest in the first round game and a very large and vociferous crowd turned up in Pearse Park. The game was intense to say the very least but referee Rogie Martin from Granard had an easy-going way about him, rarely blew the whistle and there were only a handful of skirmishes. Cashel won by a single point, 2-6 to 0-11, and that result stands in my memory as one of the great days of my career and it was the same for the Cashel people and players.

Cashel progressed to the county final where they were due to meet Longford Slashers. A problem arose when the All-Ireland U-21 semi-final between Down and the Offaly team of which I was in charge was fixed for Newry on the same day and at the same time as the county final. We tried to reach a compromise on a change of time but failed. So Cashel found themselves meeting at 3pm on the Saturday before to hear my team talk for the final. Anyway, they won the final on a scoreline of 1-8 to 1-6 amid massive celebrations and not a few tears from the old-timers in the parish who believed they would never live to see such a day. All the emotion and majesty that winning your first county final brings was now with Cashel and how the parish celebrated. Meanwhile Offaly and Down drew that U-21 semi-final in Newry but I did not get to hear the result from Pearse Park until nearly eight o'clock when Offaly were having their meal in Dundalk and eventually we got through on the phone.

I regard that achievement in helping Cashel to that first Longford title as one of my most rewarding in football because I realised what a county championship really means to a rural parish. The dedication of the players that year was phenomenal, bearing in mind they had never before been exposed to such demanding tasks in physical training and tactical preparation. They were a wonderful set of footballers and they loved their couple of pints most nights of the week as workingmen do but they still won their championship and enjoyed it.

Cashel went on to become a major force in Longford football, winning four county championships and three All-county leagues in 10 years. The community spirit engendered by that 1977 victory also inspired the entire parish elsewhere because in 1980, Newtowncashel won the overall prize in the Tidy Towns competition as the tidiest town in Ireland, although I myself cannot claim any responsibility for that great achievement.

In the mid-eighties my own native parish Colmcille, on the Cavan border, had suffered hard GAA times through emigration over several decades. They had even gone down to junior grade but eventually they progressed to intermediate status. I was asked to help out for a couple of years at that stage and I worked with a number of people, including the local GP, the late Peter Heraty. We had a lot of young players and everybody worked together to strengthen their performances and we eventually ended up in the intermediate county final against Abbeylara.

The game ended in a draw but Colmcille improved enough to win the replay amid great celebration and the club has remained senior ever since and achieved a 50-year-old ambition by regaining the senior county title in 2008. That was the first since 1958; needless to say I was not involved with that victory, except as a very partisan supporter. In this case, it was a young lad from a neighbouring parish, Gowna in Cavan, Ciaran Brady, who trained the team to success over Longford Slashers in the final. More happy days.

Between Cashel, Colmcille and UCD, I shared many rewarding times with club players and there really is nothing to match helping a club to win a county championship.

The club structure has always been the epitome of GAA activity and the pity is that in many counties club championships are being abused by county team managers who insist on an embargo on club championship games while the county team is still in the championship. This is selfish and completely unnecessary. The GAA simply has to put a stop to that because it is like cutting the roots off a tree and hoping it will still keep growing.

Chapter 15

'Could Laz Molloy Please Report To The Offaly Dressing-room?'

THERE are many ways of making your debut in a big game in Croke Park but the one that fell to Laz Molloy from Offaly was certainly unique.

In June 1984 Longford and Offaly met in the quarter-final of the Leinster senior championship in Pearse Park, Longford. It was a boiling hot day and Offaly got off to a bad start when it was discovered that somebody had forgotten to collect the team jerseys.

A moment of inspiration indicated that the local Clonguish club wore green jerseys and they were requisitioned in time for the throw-in while county secretary, John Dowling, made a mad-dash back to Tullamore to collect the correct set.

A huge crowd packed into Pearse Park that day as Longford had a very good team which was led by scoring ace Dessie Barry. With Offaly having lost their Leinster and All-Ireland titles the previous year, the home side was not without hope. My presence in the Offaly dugout added extra spice to the occasion and it turned out to be a very exciting game.

Longford seemed about to cause a surprise and win before Matt Connor, scorer of nine points, turned on the style with late scores that drew the game amid huge excitement.

The replay was fixed for Croke Park the following Sunday along with the Offaly hurlers and once again Longford put on a very impressive display. The first half was a bit of a disaster for Offaly as they conceded three goals in the absence of regular Offaly goalkeeper Martin Furling who was injured.

Before the game when I discovered that we had only one goalkeeper, I happened to mention it to an Offaly fan. He said he had been talking to Laz Molloy from Croghan, an established keeper with this club, going into the game a short while before, having played a challenge game in the city earlier.

A phone call was dispatched to the Press Box with a request to send out a message on the Public Address asking Laz to report to the Offaly dressing-room under the Cusack Stand. The bould Laz heard the message and dashed across just in time.

At half-time Longford led by 3-7 to 1-8 and as mentors, we were anxious about playing Dinny Wynne – who had come in for Furlong – as it was one of those days when an occasion gets to a player.

So we sent Laz out for the second half and he kept his net intact and needless to say got a lot of publicity for his unusual introduction to the Offaly team and the Croke Park on a big day.

Offaly managed to pull away in the second-half but not without a struggle and it took a late penalty by Matt Connor, who scored 2-5, to break the Longford resistance as Offaly won by 3-15 to 3-10.

As for Laz Molloy... well, he went on to become Offaly's regular goalkeeper for several years.

Chapter 16

Heated Scenes In Long Nights Of Allstar Selections

THE first Allstars team was selected in 1971 with the Carrolls tobacco company, whose head office was in Grand Parade along the canal near Ranelagh in Dublin, sponsoring the scheme.

Equally as important to the formation of the Allstars was the fact that the whole thing was sponsored and it was the Carrolls contributions, which really launched the concept of commercial sponsorship in the GAA.

The modest sponsorship earlier on by Carrolls for the UCD All-Ireland 7-aside was probably used as a trial run by the company and an assorted mixture of GAA media people were invited to form the first selection committee to pick the Allstars for both football and hurling.

The terms of reference were drawn up by a smaller group of the media known as the Steering Committee made up of the half dozen or so front-line journalists of the time. They included Paddy Downey (Irish Times), Jim O'Sullivan (Cork Examiner), John D Hickey (Irish Independent), Paddy Purcell (Irish Press) and Mick Dunne (RTE) with Pat Heneghan representing Carrolls and Seán Ó Siocháin and President Pat Fanning representing the GAA.

In all, there were 11 selectors at the start. Needless to say with that number of journalists sitting round the same large table, achieving any sort of consensus was next to impossible. Little wonder that the meetings lasted late into the night and many heated battles took place with various vested interests fighting for their own corners – just like any other GAA meeting really.

The northern members included Denis O'Hara (Irish News), PJ McKeefrey, (Irish News), Gerry McGuigan (Independent), Tony McGee (UTV) and Liam McDowell (BBC). Other members in the early years included Michael O'Hehir (RTE), Michael Ellard (Evening Echo), Pat Quigley (Sunday World) and Donal O'Connell (Sunday Press).

I was a mere 'gasún' at the time by comparison with most of the other selectors and I represented the Sunday Press, then the largest newspaper in Ireland. But my actual name never appeared on its pages because a long-standing custom in Irish newspapers still applied in the Sunday Press which meant that my material was submitted under a pen-name and mine was Donal O'Connell.

I think I inherited this from Brendan MacLua from Clare, a former executive officer in Croke Park who later went on to found the very successful Irish Post weekly newspaper for the Irish in Britain. The original pen-name used by the Sunday Press was Fear Cuin whose real name was Art McGann from Clare.

My late mother could never understand that when she told her friends her son was the main GAA writer for the Sunday Press his name never seemed to appear in print.

At Allstar selection meetings so heated were the discussions about some players that they had to be adjourned on several occasions to allow tempers to subside. When Paddy Downey and John D Hickey locked horns about the merits of a Cork or Tipperary hurler contesting for one position, the fireworks usually took off and in the early days as chairman, Pat Heneghan did a masterful job at keeping the peace and making sure the business was eventually concluded. There were two fundamental differences between the early Allstars teams and present day selections. Players had to be nominated in individual positions,

School days: The boys from Pulladoey National School where I started my education under the watchful eye of my father Owen, who was 'The Master'. I just managed to fit in , the last person on the left, second row (circled). It was summertime, hence all the barefoot children.

Old man Paddy: Paddy Reilly pictured in goals for New York in the 1950 National League Final against Cavan in Croke Park. The two players nearest the camera are Tom Gallagher (New York) and Phil 'The Gunner' Brady (Cavan), both of whom were sent off later in the game. Paddy Reilly was aged 46 in that final which New York won. **(SEE PAGES 225–227)**

When coaching started: An interested group of participants at the first national coaching course held in Gormanston College, Co Meath in 1964.

The pioneers: The five coaches who presided at the course (front, left to right) Frankie Byrne, Mick Ryan, Joe Lennon and (back) Jim McKeever and Eamon Young.

(SEE PAGES 44, 71, 261)

Galway's glory days: Enda Colleran lifts the Sam Maguire Cup for Galway after the 1964 All-Ireland final, having received it from President Alf Murray. Enda went on to become one of the first Gaelic football analysts on *The Sunday Game.* **(SEE PAGE 265)**

A puff of wind: Wicklow referee Eamon Moules pictured here paying close attention to Cyril Dunne of Galway taking a free in Croke Park. Eamon was involved in a controversial penalty decision when Donegal played Galway in the 1967 league semi-final in Croke Park when the wind blew the ball away and the penalty was cancelled. **(SEE PAGES 153-155)**

An dún 2 3
ráige 0 5

What might have been: Peter Nolan (right) wearing the New York jersey against Meath in 1967. In 1960 and 1961 just after Nolan, from a great Clara GAA family, emigrated to New York, a huge controversy grew up in Offaly about whether Nolan should be brought home for the All-Ireland series. In the event, one of the best players in Offaly was not and the rest is history as Offaly lost out in both years to Down. **(SEE PAGES 159–160)**

Looking the part: John Kerry O'Donnell (left), for so long the bête noir of GAA officials in Ireland, is seen here on one of his proudest days when he was Grand Marshall of the New York St Patrick's Day parade in 1970. **(SEE PAGES 67 AND 273)**

GRAND MARSHAL

Big day action:
Scenes like this were commonplace on All-Ireland day in Croke Park in the 1960s. Actually I once watched an All-Ireland final from up on that wall and just about lived to tell the tale.

All-Ireland 7-a-side:
The All-Ireland 7-a-side championship organised by UCD in 1970 and sponsored by Carrolls, led to Carrolls sponsoring the Allstars shortly afterwards.

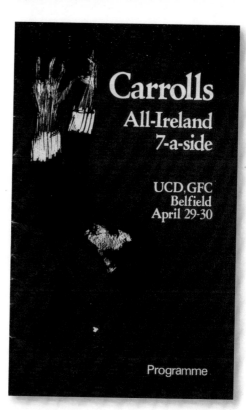

Carrolls
All-Ireland
7-a-side

UCD,GFC
Belfield
April 29-30

Programme

carrolls **GAA** allstars
1971 FOOTBALL TEAM

Stars in their eyes: This is a copy of the very first Allstars football team to be selected in 1971, when I was one of the selectors: PJ Smyth (Galway), Johnny Carey (Mayo), Jack Cosgrove (Galway), Donie O'Sullivan (Kerry); Eugene Mulligan (Offaly), Nicholas Clavin (Offaly), Pat Reynolds (Meath); Liam Sammon (Galway), Willie Bryan (Offaly); Tony McTague (Offaly), Ray Cummins (Cork), Mickey Kearins (Sligo); Andy McCallion (Antrim), Sean O'Neill (Down), Seamus Leydon (Galway). **(SEE PAGE 95)**

American dream: Pictured above is the Ulster Selection that travelled to America in October 1971, a visit that aroused much controversy. There are seven Railway Cup players included on this team. Back row, left to right: Sean Woods (Monaghan), Seamus Donaghy, R.I.P. (Tyrone), A.N. Other, J. J. Brady (Monaghan), Johnny O'Leary (Derry), Mick Burke (Cork), Ciaran Campbell (Fermanagh). Front row: Tom McGrath, (Fermanagh), Paddy Kerr (Monaghan), Kevin Teague (Tyrone), Pauric McShea (Donegal), Henry Diamond (Derry), Liam Murphy (Derry), Brian McEniff (Donegal), Peter Loughran R.I.P. (Armagh). **(SEE PAGES 57–60)**

Irish invaders: Three members of the Irish football party in 1971 who played a game in Hartford – Johnny O'Leary (Derry), Henry Diamond (Derry) and myself.

26   THE HARTFORD COURANT: Saturday, October 9, 1971

Student triumph: Brendan Lynch of Kerry (above) celebrating with colleagues after the Irish Universities won the Railway Cup for the one and only time after a replay in 1973.

Glory of the high catch: I was a keen amateur photographer many years ago and here is a fine picture of a classic high catching contest in a Longford club game in the seventies between Jimmy Flynn (9) Clonguish and John Joe Orohoe, Ardagh.

Cashel breakthrough: One of the greatest thrills of my football career was managing the Cashel club from Longford to their first county senior title in 1977 and I am pictured here with the Cashel Chairman, Garda Sgt. Gabriel Starkin, a native of Offaly. Cashel went on to win several more county championship in the following decade without any help from me! **(SEE PAGES 85–91)**

New York bound: In 1968 the UCD club, then Sigerson champions, were invited to New York to play in the prestigious Mayor Lindsay of New York charities in Gaelic Park. They also played in Boston and Chicago on the trip of a lifetime.

Financial times: In his time at UCD studying commerce, a young lad from Kildare called Charlie McCreevy was involved with the UCD Intermediate team that won the Universities championship in 1970. He is pictured here, extreme right back row, two places away from former fellow Gormanston College student Pat O'Neill of Dublin.

No ordinary Joe: In his younger days in UCD Joe Higgins, the well-known politician and Dáil Éireann member was involved with the UCD football club as Assistant Manager of the Freshers team along with Charlie Daynes from Wicklow. Yes, that really is Joe!

Best of enemies: The UCD football club has had players represented in All-Ireland finals in most of the past 50 years. In this picture we see Joe Waldron of Galway on the left, contesting with Dave McCarthy of Cork in the 1973 All-Ireland final which Cork won. Not alone were the two lads in UCD but they were actually in the same year and faculty, Agricultural Science, and were good friends.

University challenge: Irish Universities team that won the Railway Cup in 1973: Back row, left to right: Martin Carney (UCG/Donegal/Mayo), John O'Keeffe (UCD/Kerry), Seamus Killough (QUB/Antrim), Joe Waldron (UCD/Galway), Noel Murphy (UCC/Cork), Pat O'Neill (UCD/Dublin), Dan Kavanagh (UCC/Kerry), Kevin Kilmurray (UCD/Offaly). Front: Dave McCarthy (UCD/Cork), Tony Regan (UCG/Roscommon), Jimmy Stafford (UCD/Cavan), Brendan Lynch (UCC/Kerry), Paddy Moriarty (QUB/Armagh), Gerry McHugh (QUB/Antrim), Anthony McGurk (QUB/Derry).

Club honours: The UCD team that beat Clan na Gael (Armagh) in the All-Ireland club final replay in 1974: Back row, left to right: Ollie Leddy (Cavan), Denis O'Connor (Cork), Garrett O'Reilly (Cavan), Ivan Heffernan (Mayo), Frank O'Donoghue (Galway), Pearse Gilroy (Cavan), Kevin Kilmurray (Offaly). Front row: Enda Condron (Laois), Michael Judge (Galway), Benny Gaughran (Louth), JP Kean (Mayo), Paddy Kerr (captain, Monaghan), Pat Duggan (Dublin), Jackie Walsh (Kerry), Eamon O'Donoghue (Kildare).

Start of Heffo's reign: With victory all but tied up in the 1974 All-Ireland final against Galway, Kevin Heffernan went onto the field to restrain the exuberant Dublin followers lest there be a danger of the game being called off because of crowd incursion. Meticulous to the last was Heffo!

Heffo on guard: A typical shot of Heffernan on duty at Croke Park. (SEE 31–41)

The history boys of '82 who stopped Kerry's five-in-a-row march: Back row, left to right: Sean Lowry, Gerry Carroll, Pádraig Dunne, Liam O'Connor, Dinny Wynne, Liam Currums, Matt Connor, Liam O'Mahoney, Tomas O'Connor, Martin Fitzpatrick, Ollie Minnock. Front: Mick Fitzgerald, Pat Fitzgerald, Martin Furlong, Richie Connor (Capt.), John Guinan, Johnny Mooney, Brendan Lowry, Michael Lowry, Charlie Conroy. Sitting: Stephen Darby, Hugh Bolton, Seamus Darby, Aidan O'Halloran.

Long walk to freedom: The Kerry and Offaly teams parade before the 1982 All-Ireland final at Croke Park. **(SEE PAGES 13–29)**

Before the battle: The captains shake hands before the 1982 All-Ireland final. Richie Connor, left, referee PJ McGrath (Mayo) and John Egan.

Big men in action: Liam O'Connor of Offaly and Kerry's Eoin Liston contesting the ball in the 1982 final. Sadly, Liam, my brother-in-law, passed away in 2013 at the age of 58.

Leap of Faithful: Gerry Carroll jumps in the air after Seamus Darby (extreme left) scores that famous goal against Kerry in the 1982 All-Ireland football final at Croke Park.

Save of a lifetime: Martin Furlong gets down to stop Mikey Sheehy's penalty during the second-half of the 1982 final.

In full flight: Matt Connor being pursued by Kerry's Sean Walsh and John O'Keeffe as Tom Spillane watches on during the 1982 All-Ireland final.

'Don't panic Laz': This was taken on the famous day when Laz Molloy from Offaly, who was a spectator at the Offaly v Longford Leinster SFC game in Croke Park was summoned over the public address to go to the Offaly dressing room at half-time and found himself starting in goals for the second half. Neither myself or Laz look too happy at that stage but in the end Laz played very well and Offaly won. **(SEE PAGES 93–94)**

Offaly-Dublin schemozzle: I'm in the middle of a typical encounter as referee Paddy Kavanagh (Meath) keeps an eye on proceedings.

three to each position, and secondly any player who served a suspension during the year could not be considered for selection.

The present system of juggling players around into different positions is totally different and many, myself included, feel that the original method was a better one. It was a greater honour for a player to be named as the best full-back, etc in the country for that year because the competition for each position was measured that way by the general public unlike the present situation where recognised full-backs can end up playing midfield. The rules about suspension were eventually eliminated and again there are divided views on that.

Some of the biggest controversies regarding selections were not about the actual picking of the teams but rather the announcing of them. In those early days there was a gap of a couple of weeks between team selection and team announcement and some players went to extraordinary lengths to find out in advance if they were picked. The selection committee was sworn to secrecy but keeping secrets is not exactly a cornerstone of GAA activity. The efforts by players to extract information from a selector were worthy of international espionage and journalists were subjected to various ploys such as blackmail, intimidation, bribery and good old-fashioned cajoling by 'a friend of a friend of a friend'. In the end very little omerta survived and many years later the Allstars organisers got sense and announced the teams almost immediately after the selections.

The first Allstar to be selected unanimously was the Offaly wing half-back Eugene Mulligan from Rhode and the little caption relating to him stated: 'For the unchallenged depth of his football talent, sound and reliable in defence, imaginative and enterprising in attack.'

The biggest shock selection in the early years was of virtual unknown Paddy Moriarty from Armagh as a corner-forward. Paddy justified his selection and received a second award later on as a centre half-back.

Apart from the actual selections, the highlight of the Allstars scheme then was the Banquet, usually in the Burlington Hotel when all the nominees and their partners were invited as well as representatives of all county boards and prominent people in the GAA and Irish life. Searching for an All-Ireland final ticket was child's play in comparison to seeking out a ticket for the Allstars banquet where free drink for the night was a very rare treat in those times.

Overall the Allstars scheme made a huge contribution towards elevating the status of the GAA in Irish life and among the sporting fraternity in particular. It is fair to say that the Allstars alerted a whole strata of Irish people who previously had been lukewarm to the GAA to the prestigious position of the organisation in this country and even though the scheme has declined somewhat, it is still a very import adjunct to the GAA's role in society and above all it still represents excellence in the largest sports organisation in Ireland.

Chapter 17

Queen's University Says Goodbye To 'The Ban'

PROBABLY the most difficult aspect of GAA life in the last century for young people of today to understand was what was known as Rule 27, The Ban. This was a rule that forbade GAA players from playing or watching so-called 'foreign games', which included soccer, rugby, cricket and hockey. Not alone that but any persons who attended social functions, such as dances, organised by any organisation from these sports were also banned. The term of suspension was usually six months but sometimes longer and needless to say controversy was an ever-constant factor with Rule 27 and its implementation.

County Boards actually appointed vigilante committees whose duties were to attend events at which these sports were taking place and also any entertainments these sports bodies organised. The vigilante committee chairman would then report to the county chairman if any GAA members were seen involving themselves in such activities and generally suspensions would be meted out. A second offence carried a two-year suspension. No GAA club was allowed to stage a dance until the county committee had approved it.

Over the years many famous GAA players were suspended on the word of vigilante committees. A famous one in the 1950s concerned the great Tyrone player of that time, Eddie Devlin, who was a veterinary student in UCD and was selected to play for Ulster in a Railway Cup semi-final.

There was a rugby international in Lansdowne Road on the Saturday before the GAA match and Devlin was reported as being in attendance. He was immediately dropped for the Railway Cup game on the Sunday. A stern campaign led by UCD official and later GAA President Dr JJ Stuart was able to prove that he had not attended the rugby game in question. Many similar episodes like that occurred around the country. The great Limerick hurler Mick Mackey, who was also a rugby enthusiast, got around his situation by having himself elected as a member of the Limerick Vigilance Committee.

The ban was a constant source of friction within the GAA and attracted widespread public odium from non-GAA people who regarded the rule as sectarian. There was a small but dedicated band of GAA members who sought to remove Rule 27 but with little success for well over 50 years. When the 1960s arrived with soccer and rugby on television and England winning the World Cup in Wembley in 1966, the temperature went sky high in the ranks of the GAA and outside it. Nearly every time it was legal to do so there were motions at Congress asking that the rule be scrapped and the debates before, during and after such meetings were ferocious.

Floods of letters appeared in newspapers for and against with famous non-GAA sports very angry at what they saw as a slight on their Irish nationhood by the GAA. The implication that if you were a soccer or rugby player, official or supporter you were somehow less of an Irishman.

But the arrival of the 1960s ushered in a new dimension in society around the world in which the growth of youth power in third-level institutions looked anew on many old traditions, of which The Ban was just one. Younger GAA members realised too that the bigotry attached to The Ban among many older GAA officers was counter-productive and gradually prominent people began to espouse the anti-Ban cause. In addition, a growing number of young people simply ignored the rule and as more and more of them played soccer or rugby, it became impossible for the The Ban to be implemented.

The person who became synonymous with the campaign to remove Rule 27 was a Kerryman living in Dublin, Tom Woulfe, a member of the Civil Service GAA club. He rapidly became the hate figure for the pro-Ban contingent but he was made of stern stuff and stood his ground. Former Mayo All-Ireland winner Eamon Mongey also worked very closely with Woulfe behind the scenes and at that time he had a very influential column in Ireland's biggest newspaper, The Sunday Press. Going back to 1923 the GAA had a rule that Rule 27 could only be voted upon every three years but in the sixties there was a vote whenever one was due. The figures against the Ban began to grow each time and there were small signs of movement among some pro-Ban people which reflected the changing Irish society and the growing influence of young people as more and more of them went into third-level education.

Then out of the blue at the 1970 Congress in Galway, Meath put forward a motion, passed unanimously, asking that every club in the country call a special meeting to decide its attitude on Rule 27 in time for the 1971 Congress. Because the leaders of the Pro-Ban campaign had been so powerful in the recent past, little or no attention was given to the Meath motion as it was assumed that a large majority of the counties would oppose the motion anyway as had always been the case.

The motion that went before the Meath county convention came from the Dunshaughlin club and when I spoke recently to 86-year-old Patsy McLoughlin, then as now a club member, he remembered well the chain of events that led to Rule 27 being abolished. 'The original motion to have every club in the country hold a meeting to discuss the Ban came from a Dunshaughlin club meeting. A lot of us at the time were getting fed up with Rule 27 as several young lads from our club were going off playing soccer illegally and it was obvious that something had to be done. The motion was passed at the Meath county convention but not before the chairman, Fr Tully, made a very strong attack on our motion. It got through anyway and sure within the year The Ban was dead and buried,' said Patsy. 'I remember a well-known member of a nearby Meath club calling me a renegade after the motion was carried but we got over it,' he joked.

Times were certainly changing in Irish life, even in the GAA, and in the following autumn as clubs began to hold their special meetings in preparation for the various county conventions which were held in late January in those times, it became obvious that a colossal change in GAA attitudes was unfolding.

Earlier in 1971 after the Meath motion was passed at Congress, Tom Woulfe and his advisors decided to sing dumb completely until the end of the year thus creating an air of complacency among the Pro-Ban people. It was only in late October that the Anti-Ban people began to make their voices heard. Then Tom Woulfe wrote a personal letter to every local newspaper in the country and also to the Sunday Independent, outlining his case for The Ban's removal. The Sunday Press had already been covered by Eamon Mongey.

Whatever complacency the old guard had enjoyed was rudely shattered when word came through that the Cork county convention would vote to remove The Ban at the upcoming Congress. A flood of other counties soon followed and it was by then too late for the Pro Ban people to do anything.

As it transpired, only two counties, Sligo and Antrim, had voted at their conventions to retain the infamous Rule 27, an astonishing turnaround in the space of a couple of years. Having been at that Congress in the Queen's University, I remember an air of euphoria as it began to dawn on the delegates that one of the biggest decisions in the history of the GAA up to that point was about to take place.

I was by then the main GAA writer for The Sunday Press and I wrote several weeks before the Congress that the rule would go and the Sports Editor, the late Tommy O'Hara, put the largest headline I ever saw in the paper with the words 'THE BAN IS GONE'.

On April 11, 1971 at Congress in Queen's University, Belfast, ironically, it was left to arch Rule 27 supporter, President Pat Fanning to announce the end of the Rule. He did so with a gracious but rousing speech that was greeted with a standing ovation. Rather cleverly, however, he announced that there would be no vote on the contentious motion itself but instead asked merely for a proposer and seconder and specified that these should come from Armagh and Dublin, Ard Mhaca and Atha Cliath. Con Shortt proposed and when it was Dublin' s turn to second the motion, their chairman Jimmy Gray graciously asked Tom Woulfe, who was a delegate, to do so in honour of his pivotal role in having Rule 27 removed.

Shortly after that with the formality concluded it was the same Tom Woulfe who proposed a vote of thanks to President Fanning for the manner in which the business was conducted.

That was the end of the most divisive issue in the history of the GAA and it changed the face of the organisation forever. It could be said that the GAA had travelled the ultimate journey from implementing The Ban up to 1971 to seeing the Ireland and England rugby teams standing to attention for God Save the Queen in Croke Park in 2007.

To those of us who watched the bitter debates, not to mention some disgraceful suspensions against GAA members because of Rule 27, this represented the biggest change in Irish sport in our lifetime.

Incidentally, Tom Woulfe pointed out to me recently that when a Special Congress was called about six weeks later to clear up various rule formalities, the President proposed a motion that was passed which stated that the Central Council of the GAA should have the power to approve GAA grounds for use for non-GAA games. This effectively banned 'foreign games' from being played on GAA pitches. Somewhere along the line that motion got lost in translation and it was not until Rule 21 was scrapped in 2005 that the intentions of the 1971 motion came to pass.

Chapter 18
GAA's Troubled Times In Ulster

I N Gaelic football, the ultimate ambition for every player is to win an All-Ireland medal but in the Irish sporting context, it is an extremely difficult assignment. Football is a team game, which means that even though a player may be one of the best in the country, he cannot win the All-Ireland without a large number of colleagues of equal ability. To date 19 of the 32 counties have won All-Irelands but the difficulty in winning a county's first title can be horrendous and take a long, long time.

During the last 50-plus years only six counties have won their first All-Ireland: Down (1960), Offaly (1971), Donegal (1992), Derry (1993), Armagh (2002) and Tyrone (2003). I have had the privilege of watching all these historic games and there was great excitement each time the All-Ireland barrier was broken and the Sam Maguire Cup made its maiden voyage to one of these six counties. There was no first time winner in the 1950s, two in the forties, Roscommon (1943) and Meath (1949), making it a total of only eight first-time winners in over 70 years yet in the first 56 years of the GAA no less than 11 counties made the All-Ireland breakthrough.

The most productive period for first time winners was between 1992 and 2003 when four counties triumphed and the remarkable thing was that all four came from the province of Ulster. This achievement marked a transformation in the power base of Gaelic football that has left a lasting impact on the game.

In my years watching football up to about 20 years ago, most Ulster teams were regarded as weaker than teams in the other provinces with All-Ireland ambitions. Sure, there was the odd flurry of expectation such as the Antrim team of the forties and Armagh's All-Ireland appearance against Kerry in 1953. But for years after that it was a sad legacy of failure despite the gallant efforts by Armagh in 1977 and Tyrone in 1986 when both lost All-Ireland finals.

For over 30 years there were extenuating circumstances for the inability of Ulster teams to make the big breakthrough, namely 'The Troubles' as they were called that started in the late sixties. The GAA in the Six Counties went through a very torrid period in those years and only GAA people living in Derry, Down, Armagh, Tyrone, Fermanagh and Antrim can really appreciate the difficulties of day to day living there.

Since my UCD days, I had many GAA friends in the Six Counties as, at that time, a great number of Ulster GAA people tended to study in UCD. That was at a time when Queens University was the only third level institution in the north along with the teachers' training college, St Mary's.

I was also in charge of county teams that played games in all of the nine Ulster counties and over the years I heard many accounts of terrible deeds that were perpetrated against GAA clubs and individuals.

One that struck a special chord with me was the murder of Seán Browne, chairman of Bellaghy GAA club, in horrific circumstances while attending to his duties at the club. Many other atrocities were carried out against GAA people simply because, as members, they inherited the nationalist ethos that has always been a part of the Association.

I remember being involved with the Cavan U-21 team in the spring of 1988 when they played Armagh in Crossmaglen in the Ulster championship on a Saturday afternoon. It was my first time to actually experience the British Army helicopters and other paraphernalia at Crossmaglen that was so common at the time. The club showed admirable determination to retain their pitch despite everything and the fact that they did was one of the landmark achievements of The Troubles.

On that very day over in Belfast one of the most horrific events of the period took place when two British soldiers were caught in a crowd outside Casement Park and were killed in the subsequent melee. It was important for people in the Republic to actually become aware of what was happening on the ground in the Six Counties from a GAA point of view but sadly very few bothered to find out. Where I was born and reared on the Longford-Cavan border, we were very aware of The Border and all its connotations as less than an hour's drive would have brought us into the Six Counties through either Cavan or Leitrim.

In my own locality Ruairí Ó Brádaigh, who was President of Sinn Féin before Gerry Adams, and was elected an absentee Sinn Féin TD in Dáil Éireann for Longford-Westmeath in 1958, was the son of a man from Colmcille.

It never ceased to amaze me over all those years of strife how so many GAA people, including some prominent officials, could take it upon themselves to make dogmatic statements regarding The Troubles when none of them had never stood in that part of Ireland in their lives and even more sadly had no great desire to do so. Thankfully successive GAA presidents and Director General Liam Mulvihill, in particular, kept themselves fully aware of how things were developing in the context of GAA activity and they worked extremely hard to help out the various GAA units, particularly the Crossmaglen and Casement Park occupations.

Having spoken to Liam Mulvihill, I know that massive efforts were made by himself and successive presidents to alleviate the GAA problems in the Six Counties. Numerous GAA delegations to London took place but in general it was like running into a stone wall. Particularly difficult for the GAA were the various protests such as the Blanket Protest, the Dirty Protests and eventually the Hunger Strikes. Many GAA people kept saying: 'Why can't the GAA do something about these things with so many GAA members involved in the various campaigns?' Well, every possible angle was teased out in attempts by the GAA as a national body to help out and while some small successes occurred, on the major issues, the Association often found itself baulked despite fierce pressure from high-profile people like Cardinal Tomas Ó Fiach and others.

There were many flashpoints in the Six Counties over all those years and I have no doubt the tenacity in the face of oppression suffered by GAA units at the hands of the authorities strengthened their resolve to not alone keep in business during The Troubles but also to show the same tenacity in preparing teams and winning big matches when things returned to normality. The success of four first-time All-Ireland winners in just over a decade would appear to bear that out.

There were many other confrontations throughout the Six Counties in those days that attracted very little publicity outside that part of the country but were despicable events as far as GAA people up there were concerned. Searches when players were going to training on winter nights, attacks on GAA pitches, victimisation of GAA people in non-GAA aspects of life and attempts by Unionists to constantly present the GAA as merely a paler shade of the Provisional IRA. Bearing all that in mind, it was extraordinary how the GAA units not merely survived but prospered in such a climate.

I managed Cavan for four years in that period and we travelled for games all over the North including an Ulster semi-final against Derry in Omagh in 1987 when we were all delayed for hours after the game. This was due to the gate proceeds being robbed in the committee rooms of St Enda's Park. These sort of things were part of everyday life up there but largely passed unnoticed in the rest of Ireland.

When I was with Offaly, there was always a great demand from Six County county boards for challenge or tournament games because the Offaly jersey of green white and gold held special significance. We felt a special resonance on those occasions and I particularly recall a double bill, Offaly v Antrim in both codes, in Belfast and another day when Offaly came to launch the re-opening of, I think, the Dungannon GAA grounds. We had a great occasion in 1984 when Offaly played Tyrone in the Centenary Cup and the great Matt Connor gave an exhibition of his skills to a very appreciative audience. Visits to the north by teams from the south were very important in those troubled times to emphasise the essential 32-county unity of the GAA and also to give a greater understanding among GAA people in the Republic about what GAA activity was like there.

Deprivation in any walk of life often leads to higher levels of motivation leading to success later on and this has applied especially to the GAA teams in the Six Counties. As time went by into the nineties and beyond, political and military struggles began to sort themselves out and then we got a renewed vigour in GAA terms from all the units in the North. As equality for nationalists began to seep through after decades of abuse by the authorities, a whole new vista seemed to open up. GAA units began to flourish and then some money began to flow from the British government into GAA circles. Coaching moved to a new plane and the Ulster Council emerged as the most progressive province with this whole new wave of enthusiasm.

It was only a matter of time until the traditional fervour for the GAA among the clubs, schools, third level and counties would translate onto the field of play at the highest level and so it turned out with Donegal, Derry, Armagh and Tyrone all winning their first All-Ireland titles from 1992 to 2003. Coaching and general team preparation reached new heights of expertise and efficiency now that county teams in particular did not have to run the gauntlet of various security forces constantly stopping players going to training and such like.

Possibly it was the hunger to do well after such a terrible

period of failure that changed everything because we saw four successive All-Irelands going to Ulster, three of them to the Six Counties – Derry (1993) and Down (1991 and 1994) – and Donegal (1992). This was the most successful period ever in Ulster football up to that time and it changed the entire football landscape in the country.

In the following decade, the first of this century, Armagh won their first All-Ireland and Tyrone then won three. Those northern teams brought their own brand of Gaelic football to Croke Park as they had done previously with Antrim in the forties, Tyrone in the fifties and most noticeably of all Down in the sixties. With all three counties, there was greater emphasis on combination play, greater use of the low ball and more hand-passing. These changes put less emphasis on the catch-and-kick style that had dominated football for the first half of the last century and led to much debate, not to mention controversy, at the time.

When Down played Offaly in 1960 in a semi-final and replay and the final in 1961, the midfield play changed from players attempting to catch all the kickouts and other high balls to deliberately breaking the ball down in the direction of a colleague. This, when Down used it, was seen by some as 'the ruination of Gaelic football' and how often have we seen that statement over the ensuing 50 years? It was only the start of innovation that has engendered raging controversy ever since. Ulster teams were savaged, outside the province, for 'destroying the game' ever since Down arrived on the scene and until Tyrone changed all the parameters for playing the game during the first decade of the 20th century.

When Down star of the sixties and acknowledged expert on coaching Joe Lennon at that time stated that Kerry football was 20 years behind the time in a newspaper article, the intensity was really pushed up in the battle between catch-and-kick football and the changes devised by several coaches with many counties.

In his book 'A Kerry Footballer,' published in 1974, Mick O'Connell gave his first impressions of the Down style when the teams met in a Gaelic Weekly Tournament game. 'Their technique was to concentrate on the man in possession and this paid off. When an opponent had possession he was so harassed by surrounding Downmen that he was lucky to get his kick in at all not to mention placing it to a teammate.' This was a very perceptive comment from O'Connell over 40 years ago because the same comments could have been made about Tyrone and Armagh when they came to the fore in the last decade – particularly in relation to Kerry.

Kerry were beaten by Down in the 1960 final and the 1961 semi-final. O'Connell commented in his book that there was a lot of criticism of the Down style of play in that it introduced spoiling tactics. He acknowledged that Down had superior tactics that hurt their opponents more than anything else. 'If any criticism of their play was justified, it was relative to fouling, especially the pull-down. All over the field they employed this tactic and it proved profitable because it stopped any movement at source. By the time the ball was placed for a free, the Down players were again positioned to negative any advantage the opposition previously had.'

My own period of watching big-time county football coincided with the emergence of Down in 1960. It was the most dramatic debut of any county team up to then when they won their first All-Ireland. There was fierce controversy about the drawn semi-final with Offaly when Waterford referee Tom Cunningham awarded a penalty to James McCartan when many people believed it should have been a free out for charging. That was a pivotal score when Paddy Doherty converted the penalty. Had it not been scored, who knows if Down would ever have made the breakthrough as they had been beaten in the previous year's semi-final by Galway.

My late brother and I who were at the game had a small preference for an Offaly victory because wing half-back Michael Brady's family came from Colmcille.

When I got involved with Offaly football nearly 20 years later, I spoke to many of the great players of that 1960/'61 era socially and to a man they were adamant that no penalty should have been awarded. By that stage they had no reason to be partisan about the matter but not one former player I talked to would admit that the penalty was a correct decision. As they say McCartan simply got the ball and ran with it but when confronted by four Offaly backs, a frightening prospect at the time, it should have been a free out. McCartan himself has always been adamant that it was a penalty and like all controversial refereeing decisions, it is a matter for each person to make up their own mind.

Down won the replay by 1-7 to 1-5 before a then record crowd of over 68,000 and when the teams met in the 1961 final, a record crowd which stands to this day of 90,556 attended and thousands more got in when gates were broken down.

The euphoria spread across the country when Down won that 1960 All-Ireland and Kevin Mussen became the first All-Ireland captain to carry the Sam Maguire Cup across the border at Newry. It was a very emotional occasion and one people in Croke Park that day, like myself, will never forget. The victory of Down was one of the most popular ever in an All-Ireland final.

While they were joyous occasions for Down and Ulster and the process was repeated in 1968 when Down again beat Kerry in the final, the long dark shadows of turmoil and distraction descended on the Six Counties the following year when The Troubles started.

Being a member of the GAA was undoubtedly a cause for hassle and inconvenience for Ulster GAA people in the ensuing years but also being a member of a powerful nationalist body like the GAA was a source of support and encouragement in those troubled times. The fact that the vast majority of GAA games continued as usual all the time was a great source of support and even enjoyment for thousands of GAA members, players and mentors and provided a very direct link with the parent body based in Croke Park.

Chapter 19

Saluting A Drop Of The Hard Stuff

G AELIC football in this country has always been fundamentally different to rugby and soccer. From the very start, there has been an underlying element of violence in Gaelic football which is no wonder, seeing as it was only from 1884 onwards that playing rules were drawn up for the first time. Before that historians can record football contests, usually referred to as 'Caid', between neighbouring parishes that went on for days and was played by hundreds of participants.

As was quoted in one historical account dealing with the 1880s, a typical game of football could involve hundreds of players on a cross-country basis with the ball being more of an accessory than an essential. This was due to the fact that there was almost obligatory long pauses for bouts of fist-fighting and wrestling – a bit like the behaviour after discos nowadays all over the country.

The game was as much a social event as a sporting one. Some would say the game of football has not changed much from those days except that both teams have the same number of players.

Leaving aside that ancient historical role, there is no doubt that aspects of that past still influence the game. In some parts of Ireland parish rivalry can be intense to the extent that there is never a year in which we do not witness mass brawls among rival supporters and players although, thankfully, such behaviour has greatly diminished now.

At inter-county level also the contests between neighbours still arouses intense rivalry but this is nowadays regarded as central to the success of the inter-county system rather than a hindrance.

Over the past 50-odd years outbreaks of uncontrolled violence at games have largely disappeared but because the GAA organises thousands of games each year if even a tiny percentage involve violence it tends to attract media coverage to an extraordinary extent.

With regard to the actual playing of football, there is no doubt that for most of the last century, strong forceful football was a central part of the game at both county and club level. Big strong players used their physical prowess to inflict punishment on lesser opponents and the rules of the game catered for that so long as those rules were obeyed.

The people charged with enforcing the rules of fair play were the referees and for many years the main source of supply for referees came from former players. In general, this seemed to work quite well with the respect generated by the star player when he acted as referee being well accepted by players and fans. The shoulder-to-shoulder charge was always the main method of legal physical contact with an opponent but in more recent times, there has been a sea-change in the context of physical combat between players.

Modern players have adopted a range of methods to make physical contact with an opponent – much of which is illegal. This is the sort of contact that leads to bad tempers, abusive verbal contact and quite often retaliation-type fighting among players.

Whereas in previous times the physical contests were largely fair and sporting, nowadays a strong negative element has come into a lot of this contact with the sole aim of frustrating an opponent illegally. This usually ends up in a foul and a consequent stoppage in play.

Some of these foul tactics have originated from other sports but most are home grown. The amazing increase in physical fitness over the past 20 years or so means that players move faster and circulate around the playing area far more than in the past.

Dr Eamon O'Sullivan's book 'The Art and Science of Gaelic Football' had as its central point, that players should stick rigidly to the area allocated to them e.g. a wing half-back should only play in that sector of the field and not move to another part of the playing area, with or without the ball.

Indeed that was the bread and butter philosophy of Gaelic football for decades with the result that players became famous as one position performers such as a wing half-back or a centre-forward and were not expected to play in any other area.

The present day game has blown that mantra to smithereens in what is probably the greatest transformation since Gaelic football began. Nowadays all players, at county level at least, are expected to be able to play in any of the 14 outfield positions if the tactics of the team manager so demand.

It could be argued that this fluidity of movement has opened up the game and made it more exciting to watch and also because individual players now have more freedom, they are not as tightly marked as was the case in former times. This, in turn, should lead to less negative physical contact such as jersey-pulling behind the referees back by a corner-back whose job used to be: 'Stay inside that fella's jersey for the whole match', one of the many euphemisms in football which translated meant: 'Do what you like, just stop your man from playing but don't get caught.'

Many GAA followers of a certain age regret the old-style physical battles that so often were seen as the highlights of the matches – hard, tough but manly encounters that always led to great applause from the fans. Sadly nowadays such personal physical battles are rarer and rarer as tactics have taken over. This in turn has led to more cynical and certainly less manly methods of beating an opponent. Feigning injury and such like is not manly, I would rather regard it as cowardly.

In the late 1980s we saw four All-Ireland finals, including a replay between Meath and Cork which exemplified the difference between what used to be genuine physical combat on the football field as opposed to the version we see today. These games were always close, sometimes violent and there is no doubt some players did cross the line with regard to sportsmanship.

But the Meath football DNA has always dictated the direction in which their players represent the county – hard, tough, ruthless first and if there is a bit of style added on later in the game, then so be it. Several other counties, including Offaly had the same attitude in those days. The GAA public always expected that from Meath and having beaten Cork in the 1987 final by 1-14 to 0-11 based on those precepts, it represented an historic achievement for the county because they had not previously won even the Leinster title since 1970 and were conspicuous by their absence during the Dublin-Kerry glory years of the seventies and early eighties.

With Kerry then in decline, Cork took over in Munster under the managership of Billy Morgan, himself a volatile character at times, and they were back in the final in 1988 but the game ended in a draw: Meath 0-12 Cork 1-9.

And so they met for the third time in a final in the space of less than 13 months and it was inevitable the tension levels had gone sky high. Meath had a powerful team by then after a slow maturing under manager Seán Boylan and it was obvious there was no love lost between the camps. The replay soon erupted when Meath's Gerry McEntee, midfielder and spiritual leader, was sent off by referee Tommy Sugrue from Kerry in the seventh minute. This came after we had already seen a big brawl at the very start of the game and clear signs that this was going to be a battle to the death.

The tackling was certainly ferocious but with each set of players giving and taking for all their worth, what we got was a contest between old-style football warriors. Yet in the final analysis, it was the pure footballers who emerged as most decisive performers in deciding the result of the contest. For example Colm O'Rourke scored 0-3 which was instrumental in Meath winning and in addition he showed his genuine warrior status after

McEntee's dismissal by taking ownership of the Meath operation as on-field leader. He gave a masterly exhibition of leadership and team control even with 14 men. A great deal was written at the time about the behaviour of each team but this was somewhat of a generalisation because the way the Meath players and most of the Cork players played in that replay was no different to how they normally played. These were two tough teams and that is what we saw on the field. And for all the talk about dirty play and the like, it is interesting to recall that the free statistic in that 1987 replay was: Cork 21 Meath 16, which is lower than most big games in recent years including finals.

These two teams met for the fourth time in a final in 1990 but by then the balance of power had altered as Cork beat Mayo in the 1989 All-Ireland final and also beat Meath in 1990 on a scoreline of 0-11 to 0-9. I would regard these games as the last of the honest-to-God physical battles that were common over the previous 50 years if we are to believe what old-timers told me. The games looked dirty at times but still a code of manliness prevailed and it is interesting to note that very strong friendships on a personal level between the players from Meath and Cork has developed in subsequent years.

I have always regarded 'manliness' as the ultimate accolade for any sportsman but particularly a Gaelic footballer. The rules of that game cater for serious physical combat and so long as the rules are obeyed then manliness can prevail no matter how tough or hard the actual game is. Unfortunately, a lot of sports people nowadays do not understand the difference between manliness and false bravado. Physical contact is an integral component of Gaelic football and is one of its biggest attractions if practised properly and with the right attitude. But that's the rub.

Chapter 20
Changing Years – Changing Styles

THE GAA is a massive organisation. It is not an exaggeration to state that it is possibly the most representative body of people on the island of Ireland. Sometimes the power and influence of the GAA can be almost intimidating because of the massive support it engenders from all levels of society but at the end of the day, for the vast majority of Irish people, it is regarded primarily as a sports organisation which is in charge of Gaelic football and hurling and is aligned to camogie, ladies football and handball with rounders being very much a hind-tit operation.

So when I look back at the development of Gaelic football since 1960 what strikes me most is the series of changes in the way the game has been played over the decades. Major influences on the progression of football in that time have been very clear to see and provide a fascinating outline of how the game has changed.

Indeed there could not be a better starting point for this discussion than 1960 when Down had just arrived on the inter-county scene as a major force for the first time. Three people in particular organised the dramatic developments that brought Down football from next to nowhere nationally to the very pinnacle of the game in a couple of years.

Barney Carr did a lot of the actual training of the team, TP Murphy was an outstanding Down county secretary and Maurice Hayes was the driving force who took some gigantic decisions that inspired their success.

Footballers of today will be shocked, or more likely amused, to hear that one of the biggest talking points in relation to Down footballers when they arrived for the 1959 All-Ireland semi-final against Galway was that the subs were wearing tracksuits.

This development was sparked off because 'drainpipe' trousers were all the rage at the time and subs always wore their trousers while in the dugout. One day when a sub was called upon suddenly to come on he could not get his narrow trousers over his football boots and the match was almost lost while he removed his boots in order to solve the problem. It was then that Maurice Hayes decided to equip the Down team and subs with tracksuits.

The background to the two games, final and semi-final, between Down and Kerry in 1960/'61 went back to 1955 when for the first time in many years the traditional style of Kerry football, catch and kick, with players remaining in their individual positions nearly all the time, had been challenged by Dublin. When Kerry won that game it copper-fastened their way of playing football.

But in the 1960 final, Kerry were caught on the hop by the Down style and suffered their biggest loss in a final up to then, 2-10 to 0-8. The first rocket to hit Kerry was the manner in which Down set about lessening the majestic football of Mick O'Connell, then the best fielder of a ball in the country.

Sean O'Neill explains what happened: 'We had a two-fold approach; firstly we isolated O'Connell from our own kickouts by having our midfielder Jarlath Carey move out towards the side of the pitch as the kick was being taken. That left O'Connell in a dilemma of whether to go or stay. Secondly if O'Connell was under the dropping ball at midfield we broke the ball down. The Down half-backs and half-forwards knew about this and were always a yard ahead of their marker in dashing out to collect the breaking ball. James McCartan perfected this tactic against Kerry that day.'

This tactic of breaking the ball away from Mick O'Connell's grasp and isolating him from reaching Down kickouts became hugely controversial in football circles around Ireland. Some people said it was totally negative and against the spirit of the game as it should be played. Obviously Down did not agree, nor did they care as they romped to victory. The breaking-ball tactic was not the only thing Down had going for them as they had outstanding players all over the field

Down's new style of play against Kerry spread a wave of enthusiasm as teams all over the place sought to imitate their way. The great Kerry half-back of that era, Seán Murphy, summed up the new development perfectly in these words: 'The arrival of Down and Offaly in the early sixties started the gradual process of wearing down the influence of tradition which had served Kerry so well. Now Kerry were shown to be deficient in that they could not cope with a team which could catch and kick like Kerry but also had the discipline to operate tactical running off-the-ball as Down did.'

Kerry were fortunate that in the Ulster final of 1962, Cavan beat Down, but further on in 1968, Down again beat Kerry in the All-Ireland final. In fact, to this day Kerry have never beaten Down in the All-Ireland championship. The remainder of the sixties was not great for Kerry as they were outshone by the great Galway three-in-a-row team of 1964, '65 and '66 with Kerry losing the first two of those finals as they struggled to define a new way of playing football.

From 1969 to 1972 Kerry and Offaly were the dominant counties winning two All-Irelands each. The style of play had reverted to the traditional in those years with catch-and-kick predominating. A great Cork team came in 1973, having scored five goals in the opening 21 minutes of that year's Munster final against Kerry, then scored another five goals against Tyrone in the semi-final and 3-17 against Galway in the final.

This was a superb Cork football team with the very young

Jimmy Barry-Murphy the idol of the time. The style of the Cork team had advanced to a more short-passing game along with their traditional style. Another slight deviation from custom.

Then, after a period of a decade or more when there were no dramatic changes in style, came the mid-seventies and the domination of two counties, Kerry and Dublin, that lasted 13 years, 1974 to 1986, with just one interruption from Offaly in 1982. That meant those two counties won 12 All-Irelands in 13 years, Kerry eight and Dublin 4.

With statistics like that it was obvious that Kerry and Dublin had developed their own style of play with which very few other counties could compete. The key to this major changes in the game was the re-appearance of the handpass. At different time since the foundation of the GAA in 1884, the handpass had been used by individual teams but it was never regarded as a seminal event that would change the face of football history – that was until the mid-seventies.

Mick O'Dwyer pulled a crowd of kids from Kerry almost out of the hat to win the 1975 All-Ireland with the amalgamation of incredible fitness levels and the adoption of the handpass as the main means of transferring the ball. To a lesser but still significant extent, Dublin was forced to respond in kind and so we got handpass-based football for several years. At first, all handpass scores were allowed, including handpassing the ball into the net. Dublin had beaten Galway in the 1974 final playing more or less traditional football.

When the young Kerry team arrived for the 1975 final they got a shock as Jimmy Keaveney explained: 'We didn't realise how much the traditional Kerry style of football had changed in one year under Micko. We honestly thought this was a crowd of young fellows coming up from the south of Ireland to play us in the All-Ireland final but that it would be no big deal for us to put them away. But at no stage were we really in the game with a chance of winning. Kerry came at us in twos and threes running like mad. They had half-backs coming into attack and they were all moving so fast that we could not even get a stationary player to hit one of them a wallop.'

Kerry won in 1975 by 2-12 to 0-11.

Not surprisingly Kevin Heffernan set about undoing the damage of that defeat by revamping the Dublin team. This included putting in a complete new half-back line of Tommy Drumm, Kevin Moran and Pat O'Neill. When Dublin got revenge in 1976 by beating Kerry there was more dependence on handpassing by both teams and so the scene was set for their meeting in the semi-final of 1977.

The tenor of that semi-final was well described by Kerry player Denis 'Ogie' Moran: 'This game probably represented the peak of the handpass era of the seventies. It was a major factor in the incredible pace of the game. If a player went up to catch a ball in the middle of the field he had it dispatched with his hand almost before he hit the ground. If he hadn't then the player was likely to be sent flying with a shoulder charge.'

Many who were present reckon this to be the greatest game they ever saw. Over the years when it was dissected ad finitum on videos others would not entirely agree but there is no doubt it set the tone for the permanent arrival of the handpass, combined with great speed, as the definitive components of modern Gaelic football. It has remained that way ever since. A few years afterwards the GAA banned handpass goals in the face of constant criticism that goalkeepers were being made fools of.

So from time to time handpassing has been at the cornerstone of football and of course young boys have been constantly trained to use the handpass, something that in itself is not a particularly demanding skill by comparison with those of high catching or accurate long kicking.

There is still a large section of Gaelic football followers and practitioners who dislike handpassing, claiming it undermines the traditional skill. This debate continues to rage as numerous proposals are sporadically put forward by various people looking for the handpass to be limited.

The handpass oscillates in the extent of its use by county teams. After the departure of Kerry and Dublin's dominance in 1986 Cork played in three All-Ireland finals against Meath, who won two of them, and also won a final against Mayo. These Cork-Meath games were not dominated by handpassing but rather by physical force football which was a flashback to former times where men were men, as GAA people love to say. Something that covers a multitude.

These Cork-Meath games were ferocious affairs as both used a sensible mixture of footpassing and handpassing. GAA followers really enjoyed the games despite some controversial matters. These encounters seemed to indicate that handpassing was about to take a bit of a backseat but in the 1990s it was commonly used by Ulster counties, Donegal especially, but also Derry and Down who also won All-Irelands in that decade.

The biggest change in the new century was not the style of the game but the arrival of the Qualifiers and the ending of the sudden-death championship. Immediately the number of championship games increased and the season for most counties was now longer. Armagh and Tyrone also arrived to win All-Irelands and again a change of style evolved based on constant movement of players, abandonment of the traditional lineouts and emphasis on several players coming in to tackle the man in possession with the aim of taking the ball off him.

This sort of play drew massive criticism just as other developments had done in the past but it did not reach its ultimate phase until Jim McGuinness took over Donegal and gave the term 'Blanket Defence' a whole new meaning.

The prime example of this style was the All-Ireland semi-final of 2011 in which Dublin beat Donegal by 0-8 to 0-6 among outbursts of near-hysteria among football followers who saw this defensive style as the death of Gaelic football.

When Donegal won the All-Ireland the following year in 2012, the hysteria abated, however, even if defensive tactics did not fully disappear. The arrival of Dublin under Jim Gavin playing a very expansive, open game, calmed things down. But we must wait to see if 'Blanket Defence' is going to become an integral part of football or merely a flash in the pan.

In the past decade there has been a huge new emphasis on physical fitness advances in all sports and Gaelic football is no different. Elaborate training regimes are now the norm for county players and it is true to say that footballers are fitter than ever in GAA history. This does not guarantee that the quality of football is matching the fitness levels but speed and endurance are now regarded by most managers as at least as important as the skills of the game.

Football, in my opinion, is now at a crossroads on this issue and striking the correct balance between fitness and skill development and perfection will be crucial as the game moves into this decade and beyond. It will be a grave mistake if fitness becomes more important than skill perfection at county level and the managers have a crucial role to play in this regard.

Many rule changes have affected the way football is played, mostly for the better but that is not always the case. The rule to allow free and sideline kicks from the hand has largely eliminated one of the great skills of the past. Freetakers then spent countless hours perfecting frees off the ground and many players became legends with their ability to convert frees from all angles and distances.

Names like Maurice Fitzgerald (Kerry), Matt Connor (Offaly), Tony McTague (Offaly), Peter Canavan (Tyrone), Mickey Kearins (Sligo), Jimmy Keaveney (Dublin), Brian Stafford (Meath) and countless others over the years. People often went to games specifically to watch these outstanding free-takers score from off the ground.

We have only to remember the skills of rugby kickers like

Ronan O'Gara or Jonny Wilkinson to realise what the GAA has lost by largely abandoning frees from the ground. Changing that rule was a mistake because football should not abolish any of its important skills. Equally, handpassing must never be allowed to replace kicking the ball.

Chapter 21

From Kissing The Bishop's Ring To God Save The Queen

TO say the GAA has changed a lot over the past 40 years or more would certainly be a major understatement. In tandem with Irish life in general, the Association has undergone seismic change, some at its own discretion but a huge amount that was forced upon it by Irish public opinion or the pressures of changing lifestyles and social habits.

Up to the 1960s the GAA was still a strongly nationalist and Catholic organisation and these two often seemed to overshadow its role as a sporting organisation. So too was the custom of a bishop throwing in the ball to start the All-Ireland final but not before the late Kevin Heffernan nearly flattened one as the ball was thrown in for the start of the 1955 final. At that time 16 players lined up for the throw in so things were a bit crowded at throw-in time.

This was a time when team captains knelt down to kiss the bishop's ring and Faith of our Fathers rang out in Croke Park

In 1938, the GAA decided to suspend from its membership the first President of Ireland Douglas Hyde, himself a very effective promoter of the Irish language and other Gaelic cultural traditions, because he had fulfilled an official commitment by attending an international soccer game in Dalymount Park.

So powerful was the ultra-nationalist section of the GAA, mainly it must be said among the leaders of the organisation, that they still felt free to insult the President of Ireland in that manner.

For decades afterwards the nationalist streak in the GAA remained very strong bolstered in the main by the continued presence of Rule 27, The Ban, which outlawed any involvement by GAA members with what it called 'foreign games', soccer, rugby, hockey and cricket.

It might be a bit much to describe the GAA then as sectarian in outlook but there were certainly some people who leaned that way until Rule 27 was voted out at a Congress held above all places in the Queen's University in Belfast. The irony of that venue was delicious for many ordinary GAA people.

Once Rule 27 vanished, the GAA moved into a completely different phase of its evolution. No longer could comedians joke about the 'GAH' crowd' and The Ban. No longer could those who were always opposed to what the GAA stood for be arrogant in their vehement opposition and ridicule of the GAA. Moderation seemed to disperse among all the sporting bodies and Irish society was a better place thereafter.

The Catholic Church still retained its prime position as the guardians of the GAA as a Catholic sporting organisation and non-Catholics were few and far between on club or county teams. Yet that did not prevent the hierarchy in Maynooth College preventing students there from playing in All-Ireland finals because they were back studying in Maynooth in September after the holidays. The emergence of dissent in Catholic Ireland saw several famous footballers crossing the high walls of the seminary to play in matches.

As Ireland moved into the 1960s, the term 'modern' was being used for the first time in relation to Ireland and the GAA too was not afraid to make changes. Under a past President Pádraig McNamee from Antrim, the GAA produced a massive consultation document on its future which signposted the way ahead for the association and was to be a landmark of its kind for any sporting body.

Rural electrification, the arrival of television and such things often coincided with changing attitudes within the GAA, as did the coming of so-called 'free education'. Now thousands of young people, from rural Ireland in particular, were able to avail of secondary and third-level education where they competed very favourably with all the other sports available to these institutions.

The year 1969 heralded the start of what are called 'The Troubles' in the Six Counties. This period revived the more nationalistic aspect of the GAA as ordinary members and clubs around Ireland began to feel the pain that the strife up there was causing to fellow GAA members. There was a genuine feeling of frustration among GAA people that there was so little they could do to help their comrades who were under severe stress. There was total admiration for the GAA members' resilience in the face of so much hostility to people in the Six Counties who were particularly identified with the Association.

When I was manager of the Cavan team from 1984-1988, I was involved with a lot of counties and venues in the Six Counties. I sensed there was a high level of solidarity between GAA people from the Republic and those from the Six Counties. The fact that the GAA was a 32-county organisation stood out loud and clear, as indeed it must be said, was the case in other sporting bodies such as the IRFU at the time.

From the sixties onwards, the GAA began to develop its physical structures at all levels. Many of the large stadiums were upgraded and clubs began to build not just excellent playing fields but also other club facilities that gradually encouraged a wider public audience to get involved with the GAA as venues for social activities.

When we remember that tracksuits for players only arrived courtesy of the Down team in 1960, we can see how basic the trappings of football and hurling were for players in those times. The arrival of coaching as a distinct component of Gaelic football and hurling in the mid-sixties was a seminal event in the history of the GAA. People like Jim McKeever and Joe Lennon can claim a lot of the inspiration for that development even if many leading GAA administrators, including some Presidents opposed coaching on the grounds that it would eventually lead to professionalism.

In general the GAA in that period was slow to change its old habits. Games were normally only played on Sunday afternoons. Live television was confined to only a handful of games each summer. Officials were terrified that the local soccer or rugby teams might use their local GAA club grounds and their own grounds would be 'desecrated'.

But as the decades moved on another huge change in GAA attitudes emerged. That change was money. Gradually business and financial people began to realise that so powerful was the GAA in every parish in the land that it had commercial possibilities. Tentatively, sponsorship began to creep in even before the GAA had got around to sanctioning it. Local businesses began to buy sets of jersies for the parish team. Larger commercial operations began to sponsor fringe GAA events that were not strictly under the aegis of the GAA such as 7-a-side competitions. Then in 1970, cigarette company, PJ Carroll sponsored the UCD All-Ireland 7-a-side competition to the tune of £1,000 and within the year the same company were sponsoring the Carroll's Allstars and the rest is commercial history. The GAA is now taking in many millions a year from sponsorship and every GAA unit in the country is availing of commercial support.

Money has always been one of the biggest catalysts for change in the GAA and remains so to this day. The opening of Croke Park for soccer and rugby was hugely influenced by the prospect of extra millions of income for several years and that money was put to very good use by the GAA all over Ireland in many cases to help fund the building of Centres of Excellence for county boards. Money was also a factor in some of the changes in how games are played such as the introduction of the All-Ireland Qualifiers in football and hurling that broke the century-long tradition of the championships being strictly knockout.

The building of the new Croke Park was the most important development in the modern history of the GAA. It was not so much that it marked the arrival of one of the best sports stadiums in Europe but rather the statement it made about the GAA's place in Irish life. No longer was the GAA the perceived poor relation, often in the past looked upon as a refuge for culchies. It was now an organisation that came to the rescue of other sports in the national interest.

Today Croke Park stands supreme as a very successful commercial venture used regularly for high profile conferences and the like and one of the most prestigious venues for sport and recreation in Ireland despite the whinging attitude of a certain Garth Brooks in the summer of 2014. For thousands of Irish people, merely attending a big event in Croke Park, be it a GAA game or a concert, is an attraction in itself like visiting Wembley Stadium used to be for many Irish people 30 or 40 years ago.

Another huge change in attitudes towards the GAA has been the steady allocation of money from Irish governments to the organisation for various ventures, which are allocated specifically within GAA structures. This is recognition by successive governments of the important role of the GAA in fostering a healthy sporting and social environment in every parish in Ireland where the GAA operates. Such recognition has been long overdue. It is only in the last decade or so that the power of the GAA to make things happen in this country has been recognised and this has come across most clearly on the commercial side of Irish life. Even in the recent bad times companies were eager to attach their products to GAA activity with direct sponsorship at local and national level.

When I look back at the sixties and seventies when I lived in Dublin, I remember the attitude prevailing then about the GAA and it certainly was a negative and sniping one in many cases. The removal of The Ban and a few years later the arrival of Heffo's Army when Dublin won the 1974 All-Ireland transformed what a lot of Dublin people thought of the GAA and 'converts' rolled in by the thousands.

Now big GAA games are as important as rugby or soccer internationals and of course one of the biggest changes in Irish sport over the past 25 years is that thousands of the same people now attend big games in the three major sports. For years that had not been the case and rugby, soccer and GAA games were usually only attended by their own sport's supporters. This change in viewing patterns has been a huge financial asset to all three sports nowadays.

The greatest strength of the GAA today is the number of players on its books. Between football and hurling, the GAA far outweighs any other sporting body despite claims by soccer people to the contrary. Running alongside the growth in playing numbers and teams has been the dramatic increase in facilities such as playing pitches, floodlit grounds, elaborate dressing rooms, clubhouses and social centres. All these things show that in the main the GAA at local and national levels has spent its money wisely.

In most rural parishes, the GAA club is the predominant organisation as former bodies like Muintir na Tire, etc. have declined. When large funerals need to be stewarded, the GAA club usually organises it. Various meetings are held in GAA committee rooms rather than in pubs as was the case.

Indeed I regard GAA clubs nowadays as community organisations as much as sporting bodies because they cater for all sorts of people since the advent of women's football. Many women serve on club committees, even on county boards and higher bodies while children of families that have newly arrived in an area, Irish or otherwise, are quickly assimilated into the local GAA club as players at underage level.

There are of course many problems facing GAA clubs, such as

dreadful emigration among young people in most counties. Also graduates of third level colleges, including many footballers, very often have to move to Irish cities or abroad to get work commensurate with their qualifications. Companies like Google, Facebook or Paypal seldom set up business in Longford, Leitrim or Fermanagh.

If anyone wants to assess the real value of the GAA in Irish life, just close your eyes for a minute and imagine Ireland with no GAA tomorrow. Scary isn't it?

Chapter 22
Football Changes In Modern Times

EVERY year when the All-Ireland football championship is in full swing we all get engrossed in the campaign that lasts from May to late September and rarely do we pay much attention to taking a global look at how these championships transpire.

In my time watching All-Ireland finals since 1960 many dramatic changes have taken place in football, most notably the arrival of several counties who won the Sam Maguire Cup for the first time. It can truly be said that when that happens it is a seminal event in the life of any county. The whole attitude of the people to football changes, they now stand alongside the great county teams that have won before and the whole ambience of the county and its people is transformed.

In the 50-odd years since 1960, these six counties made the breakthrough to a first All-Ireland: Down 1960, Offaly 1971, Donegal 1992, Derry 1993, Armagh 2002 and Tyrone 2003. In the previous 50 years from 1910, six counties also won their first All-Irelands: Louth, Galway, Cavan, Mayo, Roscommon and Meath.

In the first 25 years after 1960 only two counties made the breakthrough, Down and Offaly, but in the second 25-year there were four newcomers, all from Ulster. So in that 50 year period, 1960-2010, the only non-Ulster team to win a first title was Offaly.

In the 25 years from 1960, Kerry and Dublin dominated that quarter century with Kerry winning 10 titles and Dublin six. Interesting too is that in the 28 years since 1986 Kerry only won six and Dublin three, which indicates a shift in power in the last three decades.

For two decades, in the seventies and eighties, Kerry and Dublin largely dominated the Gaelic football scene and are remembered in the public mind as such.

The period coincided with a new emphasis in all team sports on physical fitness and such like and it is hard to say which came first, the fitness or the handpass. At any rate, both topics dominated football for a decade with much controversy about the legitimacy of the handpass. On one famous occasion Mick O'Dwyer gave a masterclass in feigned Kerry innocence when he invited the leading referee of the time, Paddy Collins (Westmeath), to Killarney for a Kerry training session to explain the rules about the handpass. You never lost it Micko!

The power and majesty of the Dublin and Kerry teams in their prime in the 1970s set the Irish sporting scene alight and not just for GAA followers. Kevin Heffernan revolutionised the GAA interest in Dublin by winning the 1974 All-Ireland. This paved the way for massive clashes between Dublin and Kerry from then until 1981 and after a break again in the mid-eighties up to 1986.

The completiveness that existed from 1974 began to fade from 1978 onwards when an ageing Dublin team was no match for a younger Kerry side that had winning margins over Dublin in 1978 and '79 of 17 and 11 points respectively.

But as always happens in football history, trends change and in the 1980s the more traditional game came back into vogue. Handpass goals were banned and catching and kicking flourished once again where greats like Kerry's Jack O'Shea, Meath's Gerry McEntee and Liam Hayes, Dublin's Brian Mullins, Tyrone's Eugene McKenna and Cork's Teddy McCarthy among others delighted their fans with the majesty of those skills.

Eventually, 1987 spelt the end for the great Kerry team under Mick O'Dwyer after winning a staggering eight All-Irelands between 1975 and 1986, a record that is unlikely to be ever matched. Kerry then fell into one of their longest ever losing streaks and didn't win again until former great player Paidí Ó Sé managed the team to success after 11 barren years in 1997.

In the intervening years we had a most interesting period when six different counties won titles in the space of 10 years; Meath 3, Cork 2, Down 2, Donegal, Derry and Dublin one each. I remember that period particularly for two reasons: firstly the four All-Ireland encounters between Meath and Cork and secondly the arrival of two new All-Ireland winners in successive years Donegal 1992 and Derry 1993.

●   ●   ●

The Meath-Cork games were often violent affairs with old-style hard-hitting and modern play-acting on and off the ball, plenty of personal physical battles, sendings off and loads of controversy. Compared to the rather sedate games earlier in the eighties, these matches were a culture shock for many. Typical of the reaction to the replayed final on October 9, 1988 was this headline over Vincent Hogan's article in the Irish Independent the day after the game: 'Sportsmanship on its deathbed under October greyness' accompanied by a large picture of a fracas involving over 20 players and with Cork's Niall Cahalane lying stretched on the ground.

Meath, under Sean Boylan, had won the 1987 final by 1-14 to 0-11; the final was drawn in 1988 and in the replay midfielder Gerry McEntee was sent off very early in the game but Meath produced a battling display in every sense of the word inspired by the leadership of Colm O'Rourke and the result was one of Meath's greatest victories on the football field on a scoreline of Meath 0-13 Cork 0-12.

But this was a great Cork team at that time and they came storming back to beat Mayo in the 1989 final by 0-17 to 1-11. The following year Meath and Cork were back in the final and this time Cork came out on top by beating Meath 0-11 to 0-9 in another rather ugly contest which included an astonishing 69 frees and the sending off of Cork's Colm O'Neill for punching Mick Lyons, not something that was ever advisable on a football field. That Meath team was past its best by then and this was confirmed the following year when they were beaten again in the final, this time against Down in 1991.

But these were glorious years for Meath football after a barren period lasting from 1970 until 1986 during which they failed to get out of Leinster even once. They soon made up for that by playing in four All-Ireland finals, including a replay in the space of five years. After all those bitter games with Cork, normality was restored among the various protagonists in later years but Cork owed a huge amount to Larry Tompkins and Shay Fahy, two former Kildare players who transferred to Cork and were key figures in all those games.

Tompkins left Kildare following a dispute over a return air ticket to America after Kildare, for whom he was playing, were beaten in a Leinster championship game and emigrated to America. Through a rather circuitous route via Castlehaven in west Cork, Tompkins ended up playing for Cork for which Rebel football fans are eternally grateful. Not so Kildare people however.

Then the start of the nineties ushered in the rewriting of history as regards Ulster participation in the All-Ireland championship. Up to then, a period of well over 100 years only two Ulster teams had won titles, Cavan five times, 1933, '35, '47, '48 and '52 and Down three times, 1960, '61 and '68. Armagh lost a final to Kerry having failed to score from a penalty in 1953. Derry, inspired by their brilliant midfielder Jim McKeever had reached the 1958 All-Ireland final but were beaten by a Kevin Heffernan captained Dublin by 2-12 to 1-9. Next Tyrone got to their first All-Ireland final only to lose to Kerry in 1986.

Donegal did not even win their first Ulster title until 1972 when they beat Tyrone 2-13 to 1-11 amid wild celebrations in

Clones, a day I have never forgotten because of the raw emotion engendered among Donegal people after that historic victory.

But Donegal had to wait another 20 years before reaching their first All-Ireland final which they won by beating Dublin 0-18 to 0-14 amid celebrations that went on for months once the Sam Maguire Cup was symbolically carried across the county border on the Monday night. That was a powerful Donegal team captained by Anthony Molloy. Donegal drifted down the ranks after that final and it was all of 20 years before they contested, and won, the Sam Maguire Cup again.

However, waiting in the Ulster wings were Derry who had only won three Ulster titles in the previous 30 years. But inspired by Eamon Coleman and Mickey Moran, they beat Donegal in the 1993 Ulster final and in a dramatic conclusion to the semi-final they beat Dublin by 0-15 to 0-14, with wing half-back Johnny McGurk coming upfield to score a spectacular winning point before beating Cork in the final by 1-14 to 2-8. The Ulster dominance was not over yet, however, because in the following year, 1994, Down won their second Sam Maguire of that decade by beating Dublin 1-12 to 0-13.

Just when it looked as if Ulster was going to take over football, everything changed again and the next seven All Irelands were won by what might be called traditional counties. Kerry, Meath and Galway won two titles each while Dublin grabbed one as well. One of the highlights of that period was the emergence of Kildare from Leinster obscurity going back to their last title in the province in 1956, to regain the title in 1998 and again in 2000.

The catalyst for this dramatic change was none other than the great Mick O'Dwyer, who to the consternation of the GAA public at large, agreed to become manager of the Kildare team for the first time in the early 1990s. His arrival was spectacular in Kildare as the county went football mad and this was fuelled further when Kildare got to the 1991 League final only to lose to Dublin by 1-9 to

0-10. However a first-round championship defeat by Louth changed the attitude all round and after a few years O'Dwyer left Kildare. But the seeds had been sown among many Kildare GAA people and after a break he again traversed the country from Waterville to Newbridge for training.

Kildare beat Meath handily in the 1998 Leinster final and in a dramatic All-Ireland semi-final against, above all teams, Kerry then All-Ireland champions and managed by O'Dwyer's good friend Paidí Ó Sé, Kildare beat Kerry by a point 0-13 to 1-9.

It was Kildare's first All-Ireland final since 1935 and before that the days of the great Larry Stanley in 1928 when the county became the first to collect the new trophy called the Sam Maguire Cup. Seldom has there been such colour and pageant around a county prior to a final as for that 1998 game with Galway as nobody wears their hearts on their sleeves so well as Kildare GAA followers.

This turned out to be a brilliant game of football between two very skilful and talented teams but over the 70 minutes Galway thanks to players like Padraig Joyce and Michael Donnellan in particular in attack, prevailed by 1-14 to 1-10. Kildare were back to win Leinster again in 2000 but lost the semi-final, again beaten by Galway by 0-15 to 2-6. Kildare were considered unfortunate not to have won an All-Ireland in the O'Dwyer days but his period there will not be forgotten for a very long time as he revived a dormant county back to life for a few great years.

The year 2001 was an historic one in the annals of the GAA because the All-Ireland football championship, which was strictly knockout up to then, was changed. There would now be a Qualifier system whereby beaten teams would get a second chance via the back door and they would play off to produce four final Qualifiers who would play against the four provincial champions in the All-Ireland quarter-finals. This was a very controversial move and it arose from a motion presented by a Football Development Committee (FDC) of which I was a member. The motion was beaten at Congress but the then President Seán McCague asked a small group led by current Director General Páraic Duffy to respond to the many counties who had voted for the FDC proposals and from there the Qualifiers emerged.

In the first year of the new-style championship Galway were beaten in the Connacht championship but went on through the Qualifiers to beat Meath by 0-17 to 0-8 in the All-Ireland final to make history.

There are divided views, as is usual in the GAA, regarding the Qualifiers. Originally many people believed it would greatly help weaker counties to make progress in the championship as opposed to the old system which only guaranteed one game a year.

It is true that many counties did well from the Qualifiers and Fermanagh got to an All-Ireland semi-final while Wexford reached a quarter-final and teams like Limerick, Tipperary, Sligo and Westmeath and Longford among others also won several rounds in the qualifiers in some years.

But on the other hand the strong counties have been the biggest winners, of that there is no doubt. In the old days on the rare occasions when a top county was beaten by a shock result that was that but nowadays they get a second chance and rarely get caught twice. So far six All-Irelands have been won by teams coming through the qualifiers – in other words by teams that have already been beaten in the championship. These include Galway, Tyrone and Kerry.

The Qualifiers have also produced many interesting side issues such as neighbouring counties meeting in the championship who have never met before in the 130-year history of the GAA because of the provincial system. My own native county Longford for example played neighbours Leitrim and Cavan a few years ago in the championship for the first time and there has been a whole series of such fascinating encounters since 2001. The Qualifiers also gave us All-Ireland finals where the two teams were from the same province i.e. Tyrone v Armagh and Kerry v Cork, something that would have been regarded as heresy in the past.

The Qualifiers also extended the playing season for many weaker counties who would otherwise be confined to one or two games per year in May or early June. Nowadays many counties are still in the championship into late July and eight counties are still there in the month of August.

A fascinating topic for debate is working out who would have won the Sam Maguire Cup in those six years when back-door counties triumphed if the Qualifiers had never come in. Overall the Qualifiers have been a qualified success, pardon the pun, not least because of the money they bring in and also because they broke the old knockout system. But there is clearly a demand for further change in the running of the All-Ireland football championship and it will be interesting to watch developments over the next decade or so in that regard.

The greater part of the first decade of this century in GAA terms belonged to Kerry and Tyrone with Kerry winning five All-Irelands and Tyrone three. Kerry also lost three finals in the same decade which shows how dominant they were in that decade, playing in seven All-Irelands. But Kerry's success in that era was not the main topic for discussion among football followers. Instead it was the arrival on the scene of a new brand of Gaelic football that we had not witnessed before which started when Armagh beat Kerry in 2002 and was continued in two All-Ireland defeats by Tyrone over Kerry in 2005 and 2008

Armagh under the managership of former great Joe Kernan, who himself starred with his county when they lost heavily to Dublin in the 1977 final, set themselves up as a very strong physical team, one of the fittest ever seen at the time. They used their physical power to the limit and Kerry players seemed to be shocked with what they were confronted with.

Yet Armagh played to their strengths, literally, and broke no more rules than usual. Led by captain Kieran McGeeney at centre half-back, they hunted in packs to chase down space that Kerry would like to have used and they harried individual Kerry players to a level that was rare before then. Kerry were odds-on favourites and dominated the first half of the game, leading by 0-11 to 0-7 at half-time after Oisin McConville had failed to score a penalty. The Northerners had struggled in many positions but once the second-half kicked in, they gradually began to find their bearings in earnest, as is clearly shown by Kerry's fade-out, scoring only three points in the second-half to Armagh's 1-5. The crucial goal arrived in the 55th minute from McConville, the seminal score that turned the game and sent Armagh into the history books.

I doubt if I've ever seen a more dramatic last quarter to a final, as it was only in the 63rd minute that Steven McDonnell got the point that put Armagh ahead. The game lasted another 10 minutes with amazingly no score from either side and the tension around the ground was palpable. Kerry failed to score in the final 16 minutes as Armagh tightened their grip all over the field.

It was an absolutely incredible atmosphere around the stadium. Surely Kerry, with their great tradition of snatching victory in the closing minutes, would save the game? No, they didn't! Armagh had made up for their 1953 final defeat to Kerry and wrote their name in GAA folklore on a scoreline of 1-12 to 0-14. I can still recall the colour in Croke Park that day when the Armagh crowd descended from all sections of the stadium to join the presentation where joy was unconfined.

One of the really great days in Croke Park history.

Next on the agenda was the unique all-Ulster final between the holders Armagh and fierce local rivals Tyrone.

And if we thought the Armagh-Kerry final was hardy stuff, then it was child's play compared to Tyrone v Armagh. There were no less than 10 bookings, six to Tyrone and one sending off in controversial circumstances when Armagh's Diarmaid Marsden was dismissed in the 56th minute after a set-to with Tyrone's Philip Jordan.

Irsh Independent writer Martin Breheny encapsulated the

game as follows: 'It was a game that will be remembered more for the occasion than the actual game. It was always likely to be dour and that's exactly how it turned out as these two great northern rivals turned their backs on the rest of the football world to turn All-Ireland final day into a private Ulster party.'

It was a hard, tough game with many personal scores to be settled in pursuit of victory but Tyrone had the more versatile players, part of the Mickey Harte philosophy epitomised by the constant running all over the field of Brian Dooher. This carefully crafted mobility and playing out of traditional football positioning was the key to Tyrone's success and was to form the basis of their glorious period in the first decade of the century. Of course, they had a football genius to run the show on the field, for most of the game at least, in Peter Canavan, without whom Tyrone would not have won. Overall, it was obvious we were watching the full blossoming of the young men that Harte had guided to All-Ireland minor and U-21 success.

However it was in the semi-final that year that the real ructions began about the 'northern style' of football when Tyrone hammered Kerry by 0-13 to 0-6. This was one of the lowest scores ever recorded by Kerry at this level and it was caused by what became known as the 'blanket defence' – a process in which several Tyrone players were on hand to surround and harass the Kerry player in possession and prevent him from making good use or sometimes any use of possession.

This tactic, which in the main did not involve fouling, shocked a lot of GAA people but particularly Kerry and left a very sour taste in a lot of traditional mouths. Tyrone went on to take the Sam Maguire Cup for the first time and there was little point in running down their tactics. Several ways to skin a cat and all that.

It was 2005 before Tyrone met Kerry again, in the final this time, and once more they prevailed – by 1-16 to 2-10. To a certain extent, Tyrone had refined their very physical approach for this game and they were convincing winners. They played real football, hard, tough, competitive, highly motivated and totally controlled. In fact as the heading of my own article in the Irish Independent next day stated: 'Thrilling Tyrone triumph a just reward for ground-breaking blueprint' was an apt summing up of that game.

The Tyrone formula developed over many years was now intimidating opponents, including Kerry, and while critics claimed this was ruining football, the reality was that a set of brilliant footballers had been brought together under an outstanding manager in Micky Harte and they simply had all the answers to Kerry football. It was not traditional Gaelic football as we all understood it but on the assumption that the game is evolving all the time, either positively or negatively, Tyrone were fully entitled to our respect for another All-Ireland success.

This game also marked the end of one of the greatest Tyrone players of all time – Peter Canavan. That result was painful for Kerry but it was a harsh reality and was borne out by the fact that Kerry never managed to beat Tyrone in that decade in championship football. Those games represent the worst set of results ever for a Kerry team against the same opposition in the space of a few years.

Kerry always come back though and they went on to win two All-Irelands in 2006 against Mayo by 13 points and against Cork in 2007 by 10 points. Then came 2008 and another Tyrone-Kerry final meeting. Yet again Tyrone won by 1-14 to 0-14. This time the heading on my own report of the game was: 'Sheer guts closes out the deal for the Red Hand.' I also added: 'The first thing that should be said is this was a marvellous game of football, played in an excellent sporting spirit, between two of the best teams in this decade. Tyrone must be specially admired for the manner in which they clinically analysed this game and made sure that when it had to be won – in the final 15 minutes – it was they who had the confidence and sheer guts to close the deal with a staggering five successive points without reply and the amazing statistic that Kerry failed to score in that time.'

This result confirmed Tyrone as one of the greatest teams of the modern era. There had been some excuses for Kerry defeats to Tyrone in the previous two finals but absolutely none for this game.

Donegal, under Jim McGuinness, swooped in for an All-Ireland victory in 2012 that alarmed many because of the over-emphasis on defensive tactics but soon after a new Dublin manager, Jim Gavin, launched a fresh Dublin style based on all-out attack and won the 2013 final in style. This proves as always that football styles change like the Irish weather and who knows what lies ahead over the coming decades?

Long live Gaelic football, I say – in all its forms!

Chapter 23

Managers – The New Aristocrats Of Football

MANAGERS of Gaelic football teams were called 'Trainers' for nearly a century of the GAA. That all changed in the 1970s when Kevin Heffernan and Mick O'Dwyer became known as 'managers.' As often happens in the GAA, imitation took over and before long we had hundreds of managers starting with all the county teams and spreading out to clubs. Your club was nobody if it didn't have a manager.

The strange thing is that the GAA has never defined, to this day, what the role of a manager is. All other positions in the GAA have clearly defined duties but not the manager – and that's part of our problem now. Managers have never been officially part of the GAA system. Over the years they took on different roles depending on their own personalities but as time went by one overriding factor emerged clearly – the power of the manager grew and grew within GAA structures. So nowadays we have county team managers who are the most important people in the particular county

When I was involved with Offaly in the eighties and I wished to organise a challenge game against another county, I knew the name of the county chairman or county secretary to whom I could make contact to make such an arrangement.

They were all well-known people in each county who were respected by most GAA people in the area. John Dowling in Offaly, Jim King in Dublin, TP Murphy in Down, Liam Creavin in Meath, John Dunne in Galway and so on.

Nowadays I would not know the names of more than a handful

of such officials around the country – but I know the name of every county team manager in Ireland and how to contact him if I want to. It is the same with the GAA public, they know who every team manager is but few know the name of the most important officer in the county, the chairman.

And with the change in public identity of leading officers comes a change in the power structure as well. Of course chairmen and secretaries still have the same titular powers as before but managers have usurped a lot of the real power that officers had in the past.

For example county team managers have a huge say as to how club fixture-making is carried out and we have witnessed some extreme examples in recent times. In Donegal, under the managership of Jim McGuinness, senior club championship games are virtually abandoned so long as Donegal are still in the All-Ireland race and much the same applies to Dublin. And even though in each county the Central Control Committee (CCC) now has full control over fixtures arising from a motion put forward by the Football Review Committee in 2013, the county manager can still manage to disrupt them if he sees fit.

The emotional impact of a plea from the county manager to postpone club games 'to protect the county players from injury' is the weapon used by those managers who constantly want club games delayed. In reality it would appear that such managers, and fortunately they are only a minority, care little about club players but want total 'ownership' of the county players for the duration of their championship run. In some cases managers want to control the lives of county players, controlling their diets, limiting their social activities, banning them from things like using alcohol even sparingly and so on. They want professional standards applied to what are amateur players.

The biggest problem facing the GAA today is club fixtures, the inability of many county boards to draw up and implement regular programmes of club fixtures from May to September, the time of year when thousands of club players wish to play games regularly. There are many reasons why this problem exists but one of the major ones is the ability of some county managers to upset fixtures schedules.

To the best of my knowledge hardly any managers, county or club, have a written contract from the relevant GAA body to control and manage the way managers operate. They are in reality unlegislated for within GAA structures. At least at county level one would imagine that such a written contract, outlining what the manager can or cannot do regarding GAA affairs in the county should be mandatory for every managerial appointment. Then at least county boards would still have the power to manage their own county's affairs.

This is even more relevant nowadays when the vast majority of county team managers and virtually every club manager are getting paid by somebody or other. County managers can earn in the region of €50,000 a year in various guises and club managers can get €100 per session. With that sort of tax-free money, is it not peculiar that there are no controls over what exactly the manager's job entails?

This could never happen in the real world of commerce and business so why is it still going on in the GAA? The power of managers is immense as the GAA discovered some years ago when they made a full-scale assault on curbing payments but got absolutely nowhere because the people who were involved in these illegal payments, county board officers, were themselves complicit in the clandestine payments.

Personally, I would have no problem paying county managers if their duties were specified in accordance with GAA rules and they had a contract to spell out exactly what their powers and duties were, especially in relation to fixture-making. Another option is to employ managers as full-time coaches in a county where they could engage in coaching other managers or even other players as part of their remit. That, though, would require managers to be qualified as coaches but that's another story.

In other sports such as soccer and rugby most managers/trainers have relevant coaching qualifications. In the GAA, I know very few county managers who have any substantial coaching qualifications even though most of them are surrounded by highly qualified, often at degree level, and equally highly-paid people in their backroom teams. Strange isn't it?

The corollary of all that of course must also be admitted – that some of the greatest county team managers never attended a single coaching lecture in their entire lives. In my own case, I took part in the early Gormanston coaching courses and also one at Loughborough College in the UK one time.

Getting back to the actual game itself, there is no doubt that the arrival of managers into every parish in Ireland has been a huge boost for Gaelic football. The game now is better organised, the standard of play generally has improved and there is increased interest among supporters when a good manager is in place. Gone are the days when up to half a dozen people were in charge of the local football team, with one writing out the team on the back of a cigarette packet just as the players are about to go onto the field. Team managers have brought about better fitness levels and more discipline among club teams and players are better looked after in terms of injuries than in previous times.

In my time the GAA owes a deep debt of gratitude to many managers, especially Mick O'Dwyer and Kevin Heffernan, who by their efforts did wonders to promote football at many levels. Those people should be remembered for their role in doing that. For example, Meath went 16 years from 1970 without winning the Leinster championship but Seán Boylan took over in the eighties and eventually led the county to four All-Ireland final wins in 12 years. Managers who succeeded in breaking a losing All-Ireland sequence of around 100 years such as Maurice Hayes (Down), Fr Tom Gillooly (Offaly), Brian McEniff (Donegal), Eamon Coleman and Mickey Moran (Derry), Joe Kernan (Armagh) and Mickey Harte (Tyrone) did the GAA in general a great favour as did managers who achieved rare success with less well-off counties like John Maughan (Clare) and John O'Mahony (Leitrim) who won provincial football titles.

Special mention should go to Mick O'Dwyer, apart from his Kerry wins, because he got two other counties to win provincial titles, Kildare and Laois after gaps of half a century or more.

Currently at inter-county level, the cult of the manager is in danger of becoming too autocratic for an amateur sport. Pressure on players can sometimes be draconian, bearing in mind the other demands they have to meet in their lives. For instance a player who is married with a couple of young children and possibly unemployed or working part-time can be under very severe stress as he tries to meet the demands of time and effort required by the manager.

Third-level students at certain times of year when examinations are scheduled need understanding and consideration from managers but unfortunately some carry on regardless of players' needs. Players living away from their own county may have to travel up to 100 kilometres or more each way to attend training sessions on winter nights, which is also very demanding on top of all the other pressures they have to face in their lives.

The better managers are capable of taking all these and similar factors into consideration by making allowances while those who rule with an iron fist seldom achieve anything substantial with such behaviour.

Even though every county board now has a Public Relations Officer (PRO) officially in place, this person hardly ever speaks to the GAA public. Instead, it is the manager who does the talking and usually far too much of it as well. As we've seen on several occasions in 2014, some managers are brilliant at putting their foot in it and maybe they should all undergo a period of training in public relations before bursting forth at the drop of a hat.

The presence of so-called 'social media' has facilitated this development and on the other side of that debate there is the shameful manner in which managers and players are being abused on internet sites by anonymous contributors who are violating all the normal rules of behaviour in such matters. There seems little that can be done about this despicable conduct but it is certainly a major problem for GAA people.

Chapter 24
Refereeing Decisions Which Made The Headlines

REFEREES are discussed in the GAA almost as much as the leading players. It wasn't like that in previous times but the arrival of live television has changed everything because GAA followers feels they have the right to criticise officials at every turn, based on what they see on television. Currently, there is extensive coaching for referees on both the rules of football and their interpretation, while they have to undergo rigorous fitness tests which are closely monitored and inspected.

Talking about fitness levels, I can remember when that was never an issue even with inter-county referees. I think of Brendan Hayden, the former Carlow footballer, who was an outstanding referee in Leinster championship games or Eamon Moules from Wicklow, who was a great referee even though he always looked very well-fed.

Up to the 1960s it was the common practice for referees to be drawn from former footballers and several All-Ireland winners officiated at the highest level. Cavan star Simon Deignan, a very popular referee, was in charge of All-Ireland finals in 1950, '54 and '58 and played in the 1949 final. Meath's Peter McDermott, who always played with a peaked cap, refereed the 1953 All-Ireland having won an All-Ireland medal before (1949) and then afterwards (1954).

The legendary Bill Delaney from Laois refereed the 1946 drawn final and the 1951 final while John Dunne, who captained

Galway to All-Ireland success in 1938, refereed the Cork-Cavan 1945 final. These men engendered enormous respect as referees because of their reputations as top players but now it's very rare for a top referee to be a former player. Mickey Kearins from Sligo was one of the last as was Mick Loftus from Mayo who was in charge for the 1968 final when Down beat Kerry.

I have encountered every sort of referee under the sun during my time as manager of club teams, third-level, and county level up to All-Ireland finals. I've never been able to adequately describe a typical Gaelic football referee. The reality is that they all have their own personalities and I have seen amazing variations, interpretations and decisions by referees who, in theory at least, are all supposed to be singing from the same hymn sheet, i.e. the Official Guide of the GAA. I never got very worked up over referees when I was involved with teams. I told players that a referee was just one of the components that goes to make up a big game occasion. There were other factors such as the type and style of opponents, the condition of the pitch, the weather conditions on the day, the occurrence of injuries or sendings off, etc. It was up to the players to be prepared for these things and not to get upset over anything that took place – including the referee's actions.

That said, I have encountered many refereeing decisions that over the years have engendered enormous controversies and it's worth recalling some of them long after the arguments and rows have subsided.

When The Ball Blew Away

I remember a windy day in Croke Park at a National League semi-final between Galway and Donegal in 1967 just after Galway won their three All-Irelands in a row. Donegal were awarded a penalty but as Neilly Gallagher was about to face goalkeeper Johnny Geraghty, a gust of wind at the Hill 16 end of the ground blew the placed ball away. This was in the first half when Donegal were playing with the wind.

To everybody's surprise, but particularly Gallagher's, the referee picked up the ball and instead of letting it be re-placed for the penalty, he threw it up and the chance of a goal was lost. It was something which most people, media included, had not actually seen happen previously but in fact Eamon Moules was technically correct in his decision, even if it was unusual. Donegal lost the game by a couple of points and Galway went on to win the league final.

The Point That Never Was

A couple of refereeing decisions in the closing stages of the 1995 All-Ireland final between Dublin and Tyrone became very controversial particularly as the final margin of victory for Dublin was a solitary point, 1-10 to 0-12. In the 46th minute referee Paddy Russell called Charlie Redmond aside and appeared to have sent him off for some sort of retaliation. Redmond started to walk to the sideline but turned back and rejoined the play. He claimed after the game that the linesman told him he was not sent off. Over two minutes later when Russell was in the act of booking another Dublin player, Paul Clarke, he noticed that Redmond was still on the pitch and ran over to confirm that the Dublin free taker had in fact been sent off.

Redmond's presence was illegal because in those times sending off meant automatic suspension once the referee made the decision but whether it made any material difference to the final result is impossible to say. Tyrone county secretary Dominic McCaughey told journalist Raymond Smith after the game that it would be up to Central Council to decide but he implied that if a suspended player remained on the field for any period of time, the game should be awarded to the opposition.

Then just before the final whistle, another controversial decision occurred involving Peter Canavan when he passed to colleague Seán McLaughlin who sent over a point that levelled the game with time almost up.

THE GAA IN MY TIME

Russell disallowed the score because Canavan had played the ball on the ground in passing. But there were divided opinions, even among neutrals, as to whether Canavan did or did not touch the ball on the ground. Referee Russell made a brave decision at least with an All-Ireland final at stake but while no action was taken afterwards at administrative level, Tyrone people were certainly very aggrieved. That incident with Peter Canavan has never been forgotten while the one involving Charlie Redmond was one not seen before or since on such a big stage.

That Seamus Aldridge moment

The 1978 All-Ireland final between Kerry and Dublin featured one of the most amazing goals ever scored in Croke Park. It was brought about by two decisions from Kildare referee Seamus Aldridge – one, to award a free and the other, not to award a free.

Dublin had won the previous two All-Ireland finals against Kerry and Armagh and were hoping to win the county's first three-in-a-row of the 20th century. And things were going in their favour when after about 20 minutes of the first half they led by 0-6 to 0-1 in testing conditions of rain and wind.

Kerry eventually roused themselves to grab a goal and a point from John Egan and further white flags from Pat Spillane and Jack O'Shea. Dublin were still ahead by a point when the drama unfolded just before half-time.

Ger Power got involved in a contest for the ball with Paddy Cullen during which the 'keeper foot-tripped the Kerryman. Cullen stating afterwards that he was merely retaliating. No free ensued for that. Shortly after that the Dublin 'keeper won a harmless dribbling ball and passed it out to Robbie Kelleher not far away, Power went in to make a rather anemic tackle on Cullen by more or less reversing into him. To the surprise of everybody, referee Aldridge awarded a free against 'keeper who stood still with his hands in the air to make a gesture of protest to Aldridge as Kelleher innocently handed the ball to Mikey Sheehy.

The Kerryman spotted that the goalkeeper was off his line and he cleverly lobbed the ball into the top right hand corner of the net as Cullen, despairingly, realised what was happening and was a fraction late getting back after the ball went over his head and into the net. Strangely, when I was at the match I do not recall a lot of protestation from the Dublin players but perhaps they were in too great a shock over the extraordinary event that had taken place.

Kerry went into the break leading 2-3 to 0-6 and were set up for possibly the most devastating second half performance the county ever produced in Croke Park and certainly against Dublin. The final score was 5-11 to 0-8, meaning that Dublin only scored two points, both frees by Jimmy Keaveney, while Kerry scored 3-8, with Eoin Liston claiming a staggering 3-3 from play. Apart from many great goals in All-Ireland finals that actually decided the result of a game near the finish, the Sheehy goal must be regarded as one of the most significant ever in deciding a final even though it happened in the first half. It was the traumatic impact the brilliant finish achieved by undermining Dublin's confidence – which was proved by their abject second-half performance.

It fell to the magnificent writer, and Kerryman from Castleisland, Con Houlihan to best encapsulate the dramatic events regarding the 'Sheehy Goal' when he wrote as follows in the Evening Press on the day after the final: 'And while all this was going on, Mikey Sheehy was running up to take the kick and suddenly Paddy [Cullen] dashed back towards his goal like a woman who smells a cake burning. The ball won the race and it curled inside the near post as Paddy crashed into the outside of the net and lay against it like a fireman who had returned to find his station ablaze.'

Time flew for whistler Joe

While we all remember the glaring controversies involving referees, little attention is paid to small refereeing decisions that can be of equal significance. In the last minutes of the 2012 All-Ireland final between Dublin and Kerry, referee Joe McQuillan gave a free in to Dublin when time was almost up. As usual in the GAA up to then, nobody except the referee ever knows when exactly time is up. Stephen Cluxton, the Dublin goalkeeper, strolled over 100 metres from his goals to where the free was to be taken. He then proceeded to score the winning point. The referee allowed very little time after that and certainly did not allow for the time used up by Cluxton to arrive at the spot where the free was taken. Was McQuillan right or wrong? These subtle decisions often occur in football but are rarely given the attention that more dramatic events in a game are accorded.

Remember to toe the line!

As far back as 1976 there was a massive refereeing controversy at a Munster football final between Cork and Kerry at the then brand new Páirc ui Chaoimh. Kerry were All-Ireland champions after shocking Dublin in 1975 and Cork had most of their wonderful All-Ireland winning team of 1973. I well remember being among the crowd on the first day when the gates were burst open and about 10,000 people charged in with many of them remaining along the sideline thus creating a very volatile atmosphere all through the match.

With five minutes to go at the end of a tension-filled game, Cork were ahead by four points when Kerry's Seán Walsh had a goal attempt which was caught on the line by Brian Murphy. To the amazement of everyone the umpire waved the green flag claiming Murphy had stepped over the goal-line and referee John Moloney allowed the goal stand. A few minutes later, Cork's Declan Barron fisted a high ball into the Kerry net but Moloney disallowed it on the basis of a 'square ball' that was very hotly contested by Cork. This was a net gain of six points to Kerry and the game ended in a draw, with Kerry winning eventually by 3-20 to 2-19. I have watched many Munster finals but none as gripping as that one and the referee's decision on the Brian Murphy 'goal' was pivotal to the result. It finished off that great Cork team and they did not beat Kerry again until 1983 when just one year after the 1982 late goal by Offaly, Tadhg Murphy got a late, late goal to beat Kerry for the first time since 1974.

John Moloney, who passed away in 2006 was one of the best referees I have ever seen but he caused many raw nerves in Cork in the summer of 1976.

Since the advent of the Black Card and the official permission to referees to bring the ball forward for any kind of dissent or messing around after a free has been awarded, I have detected a lot more respect for referees which is long overdue.

In addition there is far less 'mouthing' by players at referees which is a welcome development also. Referees should be seen as at least as important as any player on the field but that has not been the case in the past.

Oh brother – Ref had two brothers on one team

I have seen many strange and wonderful, even weird things in the GAA in my lifetime but the way the final of the National Football League of 1966 unfolded ranks as one definitely in the weird category. League finals were really big events in those times and rated very close to All-Ireland finals in prestige and public interest.

Crowds of 40,000 or more even when Dublin were not playing were common. The teams competing in the 1966 league final were unusual for a start. Because it was decided in the GAA's infinite wisdom at the time to bring New York into the league equation by having them play against the winners of what was called the 'Home League Final' in a two legged contest.

In April of 1966 this 'Home' final took place between Galway and Longford. To everybody's surprise, except Longford people of course, Longford beat Galway then on their way to winning their third successive All-Ireland by 0-9 to 0-6 in Croke Park. It was also decided that the league final proper would not take place until the autumn and the first game was fixed for Pearse Park, Longford on October 2, 1966.

New York had a powerful team at that time with nearly all their players having played inter-county football before emigrating to the USA. Goalkeeper Willie Nolan had captained Offaly in the 1961 All-Ireland final against Down and his brother Peter would have been playing in that game also but for the fact that the Offaly County Board controversially decided against bringing him home from his base in New York for that final or for the All-Ireland semi-final the previous year in which they lost to Down after a replay. This is always regarded as the greatest 'what might have been' controversy in Offaly football bearing in mind that in three championship encounters between those teams the results were a draw and two one-point verdicts.

Kevin McNamee from Meath was another well-known player, as was a giant of a man from Wicklow called Brendan Tumulty. However the biggest surprise concerning who was taking part in this league final was not one of the players from either side but the referee.

He turned out to be none other that John Nolan, a fine player in his own right, who happened to be the brother of Willie and Peter Nolan who were playing on the New York team.

There has always been an air of mystery as to how this astonishing appointment was made but I had no doubt the inspiration for the decision was John Kerry O'Donnell then lord and master of the GAA in the Big Apple. And it was only recently after all those years that I found out the device that O'Donnell used to achieve his aims. As the away team New York had the choice of referee for the league final and they suggested three names for consideration to Croke Park and told them pick one. New York put in two names which for a variety of reasons Croke Park would never select and O'Donnell knew that. The other name left was 'J Nolan' and as that did not ring any bells in Croke Park or Longford, they gave Johnny the nod. Typical O'Donnell, typical Kerryman.

Strangely, the Longford people did not seem to have created a great fuss about this development although they had a very different attitude as the games progressed over the two legs.

The first game in Pearse Park passed off without any great acrimony as Longford won by 1-9 to 0-7. However when the second game took place in Croke Park one week later, the atmosphere changed dramatically. With a five point cushion from the first game, Longford were lulled into a false sense of security but from the moment the second game started, they faced a rude awakening. After a few minutes the Longford captain half-back Brendan Barden was hit by a New York player. Not alone was the culprit not sent off but he did not even receive a caution. This set the trend for the remainder of the game and a series of violent incidents took place with little action being taken by the referee.

Not surprisingly in this very hostile environment, the Longford followers got more and more agitated in the stands and terraces about what was masquerading as Gaelic football. Those New York players who had no interest in the tough stuff helped their team to make the game a keen and close contest so that at the end, after an extra five minutes had been added on in the second half, New York actually won the contest by 0-10 to 0-9 which meant they lost the league final on the aggregate score.

There were some violent scenes on the pitch after the game as irate Longford supporters sought vengeance but thankfully order was more or less restored in time for the presentation of the league cup. The reporter for the Longford Leader (not me) pulled no punches. 'There were occasions during the hour and seven minutes the referee played when some Longford players could have been seriously maimed and the series of ugly incidents would have discredited savages attempting to play football in an African jungle.'

The Longford county chairman, a most mild mannered man, Jimmy Flynn, whose brother Paddy was for many years Sports Editor of the Evening Press, did not hold back either in an interview with John D Hickey in the Irish Independent on the following Monday.

'It was the worst exhibition of blackguardism I have ever seen and the highest praise is due to the Longford players for the manner in which they tried to play their own brand of football. If anything like the conduct we saw from New York happened in our county the team that carried out that way would be suspended for life and I as chairman of the county board would see that this was carried out,' he emphasised.

John D. Hickey then contacted John Kerry O'Donnell who gave a masterclass in understatement: 'It was a rugged game and there is nothing I like better than an honest-to-goodness match.'

But despite all the aggravation on and off the field Longford had completed their target of winning the National League for the first and only time and the team was greeted with All-Ireland proportions when they returned to Longford with the cup on the Monday night.

Immediately after the game ended in Croke Park one of their more experienced players, Seán Murray, ran to the other end of the field to, as he said himself, put manners on the man who had attacked Brendan Barden in the opening minutes – which he certainly did.

The Nolans are a great GAA family from Clara, famous for their sportsmanship, and I was sad when referee Johnny passed away a couple of years ago. Willie returned to live and work in Offaly many years ago but Peter remained in the USA and now comes home every summer to his beloved Clara. The whole affair was an amazing saga and one could not imagine such a refereeing decision ever being taken again at inter-county level – unless of course another John Kerry O'Donnell comes along.

Chapter 25
The FRC: At Last A GAA Committee That Got Things Done

WITHIN the GAA community, committees do not have a great reputation for achievements. Somewhere in the archives of Croke Park there is probably a large stack of major reports launched by committees most of which achieved little or nothing.

In my time it was the custom of an incoming President to appoint a small army of committees to cover some of the important working components of the organisation such as fixtures and disciplinary matters but in addition there are numerous other committees that are filled by a new President but seem to be in place mainly because they were always there. In government circles these groups are called quangos and maybe that is how the GAA should describe them too.

When a candidate wins a GAA Presidential election, he is then faced with a lot of favours that have to be returned. Different individuals who have had the power to influence votes in a particular county now collect their pound of flesh by being put on a committee. They serve for three years in line with the presidency but many of the veterans at this system can simply move to another committee at the behest of the next President and for the same reason. And so it goes on and on... and on.

In my own time, I have been appointed to several committees, which has always surprised me because I never had any interest in canvassing for a presidential candidate and anyway I never had any significant power to swing votes towards a candidate. In the last couple of years of the last century, the then President Joe McDonagh established a very large committee called the Football Development Committee whose remit was to examine all aspects of Gaelic football and propose changes where they felt were necessary. I was invited and agreed to go on the FDC because the terms of reference involved a lot of things I was interested in and had often written about in the media.

The chairman of the FDC was Colonel Noel Walsh from Kilrush, Co Clare who had spent a lifetime promoting the fortunes of the four weak counties in Munster and eventually achieved a major coup when getting the Munster Council to vote for an Open Draw in their senior football competition.

The final report of the FDC was launched on November 4, 1999 and aroused both huge interest around the country and an equal amount of opposition, including downright antagonism.

The key submissions included a proposal to amalgamate the present league with early qualifying stages of the championship to provide a minimum of 10 games for all counties between March and June each year. Finishing positions in this competition would then provide 16 teams to go forward to contest provincial semi-finals and finals and thereafter onto the All-Ireland series.

There would be an All-Ireland series as follows:

Section 1: 11 teams, 7 from Leinster and 4 from Munster.

Section 2: 11 teams, 7 from Ulster and 4 from Connacht

Section 3: 11 teams not included in Section 1 or 2, including London.

Each section would be played off on a home and away basis with five games at home and five away between early March and late June. And at the end of the league section teams would go forward to compete in the knockout stages of the provincial championship and later the All-Ireland series.

The inter-county players were the most enthusiastic for the proposals as it gave them a fixed and shortened season thereby allowing more time for club games. Club games were to be played normally on the weeks between county games in the 11-game series as there would not be the same pressure in the larger competition so club and county games could alternate.

One of the biggest advantages was finance. Well-known financial expert, attached to Davy Stockbrokers, and former Dublin star Robbie Kelleher did a forensic projection on forecasts for finance under the new proposals as opposed to the then current national league. The NFL in those days brought in about £650,000 a year. Robbie estimated a conservative figure for the league section of the new proposal would bring in at least £5 million a year.

The debate raged hot and heavy in the media, in pubs and clubs and at various GAA meetings. A trend quickly emerged that many of the leading counties favoured the new proposal but most of the smaller counties were strongly against. Ulster in general were against any change and the Ulster Secretary at the time, Danny Murphy, did not even turn up for the launch of the proposals because he claimed as a member of the GAA management Committee, he should have been informed beforehand.

Eventually, it became clear the FDC proposals were not going to get by Congress as they were too radical for the time that was in it and too many counties wanted no interference with traditional provincial championships.

But all the hard work that was done by the FDC over a three-year period was not wasted. About 12 counties were in favour of the proposals and the incoming President Seán McCague decided that such a large acceptance of the new ideas was entitled to be heard and their views taken into account. Therefore he set up a short-term committee under Páraic Duffy to come up with proposals. I was included on that committee also and from that we got the back-door system which in itself was revolutionary as it marked the end of the straight knockout All-Ireland championship after 116 years.

Incidentally, the biggest loss for the GAA by the rejection of the

FDC ideas was the financial one as with an improving economic situation, the Kelleher projections would have been greatly surpassed.

Many leading GAA officers such as Seamus Aldridge of Kildare were absolutely scathing of Robbie's figures at a Central Council meeting but Peter Quinn, former President and an acknowledged expert on finances, broadly agreed with them.

I was disappointed with the rejection because of all the time and work spent on the project but I had no problems totally accepting the GAA's decision. It was the often devious ways in which some county board officers influenced their boards to reject the proposals that annoyed me most but then GAA democracy is a law unto itself – back-scratching is often the most important component of GAA democracy.

Having been involved in those two central committees and another one which dealt with promoting the cause of the less successful football counties, I had no ambition to attract further punishment. Then I got a phone call from Liam O'Neill from Laois, a man I was only slightly familiar with personally, asking me to chair a small committee of ordinary GAA members and over the period of one year or less having an overall look at Gaelic football. I was told to consult widely and come back with any suggestions that it was felt would be helpful in making the game of football even more attractive for players and public. He stressed that he had no major complaints about how the game was being played but maybe it was time to do some tidying up on certain aspects of it.

I slept on the idea overnight and decided to go ahead because there were a few differences between my involvements with the FDC a decade earlier and what was now to be called the Football Review Committee (FRC).

Firstly the FRC was a small body of eight members, secondly the President stressed that the FRC was to be totally independent of the GAA with no interference from officers and thirdly, the whole thing was only to last a year. So away we went and there was a strong element of shock among some GAA VIPs when I was announced as Chairman of the FRC. Seán Bán Breathnach said on the Friday night TG4 programme, as Gaeilge, that I was too old for the job, which was very encouraging.

I had to hand-pick the small committee and I decided to have national representation from the four provinces. I wanted people who were high-profile county players and managers, including people with a deep knowledge of modern-day coaching procedures.

I was also mindful of the need to cater for the views of less successful counties, and I brought in people with experience of dealing with teenage players while I knew it was vital to have on board members who were experts at modern mass media procedures.

The overall group who emerged fulfilled these and several other criteria: John Tobin (Galway), Paul Earley (Roscommon and Kildare), Killian Burns (Kerry), Declan Darcy (Leitrim and Dublin), Ciaran McBride (Tyrone), Tony Scullion (Derry), Tim Healy (Cork and Wicklow).

Seamus McCarthy (Tipperary) and David Kelly (Sligo) joined the committee at a later stage to contribute to our second report on structures and fixtures after our first report had focused on the rules side of the game. Declan Darcy withdrew at that stage to focus on his commitment as a Dublin senior football selector.

On voluntary committees such as the FRC, the key figure is usually the secretary because he has to constantly assess and summarise the activities of the group and make the myriad arrangements that go hand-in-hand with a group like the FRC and do a lot of report drafting. I was very fortunate to be told about a Mayoman called Kevin Griffin who worked as Director of Registery in UCD. He was brilliant in the role of secretary, which greatly facilitated the work programme of all the members.

The first commitment we made in the FRC was to communicate with as many people as possible who had an interest in Gaelic football and get their views on the state of the game. So we set up a website with a fairly detailed questionnaire in which we consulted rank and file GAA people. This was a great success with almost 3,200 responses received – and very informative ones at that.

After that, we committed ourselves to meeting a lot of football people face to face in every county in Ireland. To do this we handpicked 10 people from each county from a cross–section of involved people that included team managers, county board officers, young persons, referees, club people, managers, etc.

We ran eight such groups in total across the country and there we teased out a range of items and the response to that exercise was extraordinary. For the first time I saw people at these meetings speak openly and frankly about what they thought and believed. The views expressed showed the intensity there was among football people and their love and commitment for the sport. It was stimulating for me and all the members of the FRC certainly felt that way too.

I remember being at the meeting held in Toomebridge, where I was reliably informed we went in the front door in Co Derry and went out the other door through Co Antrim. The welcome we got all over the country at these meetings showed us people appreciated the fact that we were consulting with the grassroots and taking their views, north, south, east and west, into account.

Apart from the actual survey we got several hundreds emails and letters from individuals and invariably they opened their mail with a comment like: 'This is the first time I ever got the chance to express my views about football to an official GAA body.'

In addition, we also invited in representatives from a whole array of GAA bodies to have an informal chat about various topics. These included referees, GAA media people, team managers, third-level and second level people, all county board chairmen in the country and many more. I can safely say that never in the history of the GAA had such a level of face-to-face discussions taken place as the FRC carried out.

We also had detailed analyses conducted of matches across all grades and ages, with over 1,600 items of analysis done in total.

All these forms of communications provided the background by which we formed our list of proposals that were launched in December, 2013 and concerned possible rule changes. Obviously, the biggest topic to emerge was the question of cynical play which had reached serious levels in the preceding years. In our computer survey and in the letters and emails we received, it was top of the list without any prompting from the FRC. But changing a rule in the GAA at Congress is extremely difficult, particularly as it takes a two-thirds majority to change anything.

The media coverage of the actual motions etc. was very fair and there were plenty of contrasting views as you would expect. Inevitably, it is the negative things that dominate in media coverage in most walks of Irish life and that was why we got blow-by-blow accounts on a weekly basis of those counties that were allegedly going to shoot down the Black Card and similar proposals.

As the days before Congress in Derry approached the general belief was that there was no chance of a two-thirds majority but the FRC members never gave up and a superb presentation, including video, of cynical fouls presented by our members Paul Earley and Tim Healy was in the end the decisive factor.

It was still quite a shock when the electronic scoreboard flashed up the figure of almost 71 per cent in favour when the vote was cast on the Black Card motion even though only two speakers went forward to speak against it. The fact that the rule change would not come into force for a further 12 months was a crucial factor and the FRC members were adamant that there would be no trial runs either. At least twice before when the Sin Bin was tried on a trial basis, team managers made sure they scuttled the proposal. It is no secret that some of them were very annoyed when there was no trial run for the Black Card.

Opposition initially was largely confined to a small band of full-time opponents and one insignificant county manager had tweeted a derogatory comment about the composition of the committee within five minutes of the news breaking. But overwhelmingly, the team managers were prepared to wait and see how the Black Card would operate which was fair enough. As far as the general public is concerned, they seem to be largely in favour because it helps to open up the play and create more scores as the statistics for the subsequent national league and championship clearly showed. The elimination of the infamous third-man tackle in the new rules is a huge advance also as this was a cowardly, cynical and dangerous tackle that damaged young players in particular. The fans have also noticed that there is now more respect for referees with less abusive language or general hassling of the official by big-name players that had developed over many years. They are now aware they can get a black card for such behaviour, including verbal abuse towards an opponent. Putting an advantage rule into the rule-book for the first time has also worked very well and referees, as well as fans, were very anxious to have that included in the rules.

None of these changes are in themselves earth-shattering but as an overall package, they have greatly improved the image of football and struck a chord with supporters who were glad that rule changes they had cried out for were now part of the game.

The changes also contribute to attracting young players to Gaelic football which in this age of marketing of sport is a very important factor. Parents with no GAA background have been a bit scared of football because of the image of unsporting behaviour and fouling that went on but those fears are largely alleviated now. All in all, the work of the FRC and the modern communication methods used to consult with thousands of people may be considered a worthwhile effort on behalf of the members of the committee who devoted a large part of 18 months to the project.

If there are any lessons from the FRC exercise for the future it is to keep important committees confined to 10 people or less, avail of modern technology to consult or survey a large number of members and provide a proper statistical analysis of the topics under discussion rather than relying on custom, word of mouth or even rumour.

In this as in other areas, the GAA should not just move with the times but be ahead of the times.

Chapter 26

The Kerry Brand Name – As Strong As Ever

ANY person who has spent a long period of time involved with Gaelic football will be aware of one almost ever-present reality: Kerry tend to dominate public perception and attitudes to football more than any other county. Even at the quieter time of the year when there are no big GAA matches, people will still bring Kerry up in conversation. They will either compliment them on having won yet another All-Ireland or if they have hit a poor patch as they did from 1986 to 1997, you will hear people talk almost in awe about their capacity to 'come from nowhere' and grab a hold of the Sam Maguire Cup.

As is usual in the GAA, plain old logic is rarely to be seen when assessing any county and instead people base their views on things such as tradition, having a few famous players in the team, having a fearsome reputation for anything, be it stylish football, hard, tough footballers, 'desperate hard to beat' and so on. In all those categories Kerry have been the chief proponents which is why they now hold 36 All-Ireland titles which is more than one-quarter of titles won since the GAA was founded in 1884 and remember Kerry were late starters, not winning their first title until 1903.

Considering the legacy of Kerry football, it is strange that a definitive GAA history of the county has yet to be published although of course many excellent historical pieces have been written from time to time.

In my own time, I have always been aware of Kerry football, at first like many people, somewhat blinded by the mystique of their success but then looking at their recent history in a more rational way. It is hard to separate myth from reason when talking about Kerry and this has served their county football team very well over the decades. The names of legendary folk-heroes such as no other county could hope to compete with is typical of this. The iconic Kerry names roll off the tongue even by people far too young to ever have seen these men play for Kerry. Mick O'Connell rowing his boat across from Valentia Island, then setting off for training in Killarney before the bridge to the island was built and the same Micko leaving the Sam Maguire Cup behind him in the dressing-room the year he was captain of Kerry.

Legendary West Kerry players like Paddy Bawn Brosnan and classic midfielders such as Paddy Kennedy, O'Connell, Jack O'Shea and Darragh Ó Sé in modern times. And forwards to beat the band from Colm Cooper at the present time to Mick O'Dwyer, the attacking stars of the seventies and eighties and many, many more in every position on a football team.

These names, legends all, have contributed to place Kerry football in a privileged position with the general public and not even the odd incursions of newcomers like Down in the sixties, Offaly and Dublin in the seventies and eighties and Armagh and Tyrone in the past decade has done any serious damage to the image Kerry football has created. Because while many teams such as those mentioned have won brilliant All-Irelands they are sporadic, so far at least, in the context of the history of All-Irelands.

These were only temporary achievements by comparison with the consistency that Kerry managed through the last century and into the present one. It is interesting to note that since Kerry won their first All-Ireland in 1903 they have beaten 14 different counties in All-Ireland finals but in the same period they have lost finals to 13 different counties. The two counties Kerry have never beaten in finals in which they played are Down and Tyrone.

One could say that Gaelic football is in the DNA of every Kerry person and there is no doubt the game is of more significance to the lives of Kerry people than people in any other county because The Kingdom seems to be ever-present at the highest level. This is not entirely true, of course, and as I mentioned there was that long gap in the eighties and nineties and a similar one from 1914 to 1924.

But Gaelic football is woven into the fabric of Kerry to an amazing extent even though it has to be said that Kerry people are among the most critical of their own players when they see fit, especially in latter years. We all remember the late Páidí Ó Sé's comments about 'animals' and Kerry supporters not that long ago.

Why are Kerry so successful? From my time looking at them close-up, too close at times, it seems to be a combination of brilliant players at one particular time coupled with the power and tradition of the Kerry football ethos that carries them through when they have only 'ordinary' teams by Kerry football standards.

I have seen Kerry play very well in All-Ireland finals such as 2011 against Dublin and lose but have I also watched poor Kerry teams win All-Irelands. In the 1960s, Kerry did not have great teams but they still won two All-Irelands in '62 and '69. They failed twice to beat a great Galway team in '64 and '65 and Down in '60 and '68 – four defeats in the same decade which was a very rare series of losses.

Just when the doubters began to surface nationally, along came the glorious seventies and incredible series of games against a resurgent Dublin with wins in '75, '78, '79, '80 and '81 and this lasted far into the next decade with another three in a row in '84, '85 and '86. That was a magnificent eight All-Irelands in 12 years, with those Kerry teams dominated by some of the greatest footballers the game has ever seen.

It did not seem very significant at the time it happened but the goal scored by John Egan in the 1975 All-Ireland final was to mark the start of an extraordinary period of football supremacy. This critical score came as early as the third minute. A very young and inexperienced Kerry team got a vital boost to their confidence when a free sent in by Mike Sheehy was messed up between goalkeeper Paddy Cullen and Gay O'Driscoll, a rare occurrence in itself, and when a Kerry player failed to connect with the broken ball on the ground John Egan grabbed it and stuck it in the net.

Kerry went on to beat Dublin that day by 2-12 to 0-11 thus starting that remarkable period of success, interrupted only by Dublin and Offaly between 1975 and 1986.

Mick O'Dwyer proved himself undoubtedly as the greatest team manager ever because of the longevity of his Kerry management stint at such a high level and further enhanced his reputation by his later success in Kildare and Laois.

I was directly involved against Kerry teams in that period, having managed Offaly against Kerry in one All-Ireland semi-final and two finals. It was an awesome prospect facing that football machine in those contests and we were certainly glad to get away with a late, late win in 1982, which is well documented elsewhere in this book.

I had learned a lot about Kerry football long before I came in opposition with the county because many Kingdom footballers of all grades found their way into UCD. I became familiar with the Kerry football psyche from the behaviour of men like John O'Keeffe, Eamon Fitzgerald, Ógie Moran, Jackie Walsh, Donie O'Sullivan, Paudie and Eamon O'Donoghue, Mick Gleeson, Micheál Ó Sé, Mickey O'Sullivan, Vincent O'Connor and Willie Maher, all of whom played for the Kerry seniors and of course there were many other Kerry players from other grades also in UCD.

Whether I learned more from them about Kerry or they picked up more about me with UCD is a moot point but I certainly did not lose out by being close to so many great Kerry players in a slightly different environment to their usual habitat.

It would be wrong to assign only greatness, magnificence charisma and the like to Kerry football. Over the years they also produced many hard men and were well prepared to dish out punishment if they felt it was needed. Mostly though, there seemed to be a strong impression that playing the game really did come first with Kerry players with only the odd exception. Certainly, in my experience, watching and being involved against Kerry teams for half a century, I felt there was a stronger badge of honour about playing the game in a Kerry jersey than in most other counties.

Nowadays we often hear people make comparisons between Kerry football and soccer teams like Liverpool and Manchester United both of which have been very successful in their own right. I don't see this as a valid comparison because while the two soccer clubs can buy the best players in the world to help them win championships, the Kerry football team is confined to people who are natives of County Kerry. It is in that context that their record of 36 All-Irelands has to be measured.

Despite their great tradition as Gaelic football players, Kerry has never been hidebound by their past. In the 1970s when Mick O'Dwyer launched a gang of young tigers onto Croke Park to beat Dublin in 1975, many Kerry people thought their world was going to end when they saw the sort of hand-passing game that lay before them. Graveyards all over Kerry were said to be rumbling with the sounds of former great players turning in their graves at what the wearers of the green and gold were doing. Desecrating the style of Kerry football and the like.

But things settled down after the worst excesses of the handpass were curbed by rule, including banning handpass scores in the early eighties. Still Kerry were able to readjust and go on winning All-Irelands. When Armagh and Tyrone arrived in 2002, it looked as if the world would definitely end for Kerry football fans with the packed defences, multi-man tackling of the player with the ball and a lot more that was alien to Kerry football just then. Kerry regrouped, changed some part in the engine and soon they were motoring on a different route and won four All-Irelands in the first decade of the new century, more than than any other county.

This meant that in the seventies, eighties and noughties Kerry won more All-Irelands than any other county, an astonishing five titles in each of those decades despite the many variations in football styles put before them.

The Kerry GAA brand name is the greatest thing it has going for them and as those changes over the past 30 years show, that brand still shines through, regardless of the type of opposition they have to face.

Chapter 27
Leading Ireland To Victory In Australia

I WAS somewhat surprised in the spring of 1987 when invited to become manager of the Ireland compromise rules team, as it was then called, for the autumn series in Ireland that year.

As usual there was a lot of controversy overhanging from the previous series in Australia in 1986 where I was present as a journalist for the three-game series. Two very dogmatic protagonists were in action for the respective countries in those games, Kevin Heffernan and John Todd.

Todd was a very aggressive character who seemed peeved that in Ireland in 1984 although Australia won the series 2-1, he felt some Irish players had gone over the top with the rough stuff and needless to say being Aussies they were looking for revenge.

So the environment when the first game in Australia took place on October 11, 1986 in the WACA ground in Perth, (one of the nicest stadiums I have ever visited), was tense to say the least.

This was the first time the Australian public had watched one of these compromise games first hand. And they certainly got value for money as the game was speckled with some very violent behaviour from both sides right through the game which the home team won by 64–57 points. Among the key figures for Ireland were Mick Lyons (Meath), Brian McGilligan (Derry) and Pat O'Byrne (Wicklow), which gave a fair idea of the sort of team Heffernan had decided to select. But Ireland went on to win the Test Series 2-1 and were happy even if Mr Todd had described the Irish players as 'a crowd of wimps'.

I had the feeling that when it came to the next series a year later in Ireland, the GAA bosses were worried about violence reappearing and I got the distinct impression that it was my job as manager to ensure that mayhem did not take over. My Assistant Manager was Sean McCague, a future GAA President and manager with the great Monaghan team of the eighties. Ireland won the opening game in Croke Park by 53-51 points in a very exciting game and a big crowd of around 50,000 saw Australia win the second game 72-47. In the deciding third game Australia again won by 59-55.

I had been to Croke Park many times over the years up to then but I got a shock from the crowd reaction whenever Ireland got a good score because the noise was greater than I had ever heard in the stadium.

And then I realised that nearly 50,000 people were cheering for one team, something that could never happen in a GAA match where the support is usually split three ways, each team and neutrals. It certainly added to the atmosphere at those three games. The sportsmanship from both teams in those games was tolerable with no major outbursts of communal violence like we had seen in previous years and a couple of Irish players, particularly the blonde John Lynch from Tyrone, were well able to look after themselves, and a bit more.

For some reason, possibly because the Australian authorities were celebrating their centenary in 1988, the next series was not for three years until 1990. Organising that adventure was an enormous logistical task for a whole variety of people including myself and Seán McCague and physio Amy Johnson and trainer Brendan Hackett. Meath's Robbie O'Malley was the captain with Martin Gavigan as vice-captain. The tour manager was Frank Kenny from Roscommon and Danny Lynch, the GAA PRO, was also included.

Selecting a group to travel to Australia for the then compromise rules series was an extremely difficult assignment. Following the completion of three series, it became fairly obvious that it wasn't necessarily the best 25 Gaelic footballers in the country that had to be selected. For this form of football there were special requirements needed and therefore we ended up selecting players who were suitable for the new rules but were not considered among the leading Gaelic players of their time.

This caused some animosity as the summer went on because most people expected that we would pick something like an Allstar team.

Then there were the problems of club fixtures as the weeks drew near to departing for Australia. Cork and Meath were in the All-Ireland final in 1990 so their players were absolved from the preparations until the final was over and undoubtedly some players from each team lost out on the chance to represent their country because of that. That has always been a problem in these Test meetings and the pressure of club games has been the source of a lot of aggro too.

Selecting the final handful of players was a nightmare in 1990 as between All-Ireland final problems, injuries and big club games, great uncertainty prevailed right up to departure time. There were twins from Armagh, the Grimley brothers, who were in contention for selection all along and towards the end one of them was confirmed as a definite selection – don't ask me which one because I could never distinguish them. Naturally the other man was very disappointed as was his family but lo and behold on the Sunday before leaving, a player got injured with his club and the second Grimley got the word by phone to much celebration in Armagh. For the record, the same two were great characters all through the Australian trip as well as being the hardest men in the series.

That particular trip to Australia was possibly the best ever from the players point of view. For a start it lasted 22 days – the longest of any series. Then Ireland won the first two tests in Melbourne (47-38) and Canberra (52-31) so it was 'relaxation time' for the players after that before the final game in Perth, which the Aussies won (50-44)

It was the nearest to a professional football lifestyle these lads have ever got with training at 7.30am on glorious summer mornings followed by breakfast and relaxation with sometimes more training in the afternoon.

Looking at the photograph of that 1990 group elsewhere in this book, one can see the widespread of counties represented on that trip and the range in standards of counties from whom the players came. The late great Jim Stynes was a member of the Ireland panel that year, having in earlier years lined out for Australia as he lived in Melbourne and played with the Melbourne Demons. Apart from his major football contributions, he was extremely useful in guiding Irish players to the really important spots to visit in Australia including nocturnal ones which we shall not mention here.

Indeed it was not until Jim wrote a sort of autobiography in 1995 that I realised some of the antics that had gone on in the middle of the night behind my back. In particular, I am referring to a game of football played in the street in a small town called Albury where the warm-up match took place. It involved a visit from the local police but peace and harmony broke out before the morning training session arrived at 7am and some of us were none the wiser.

Jim Stynes was a wonderful person, kind, generous with his time, a very patriotic Irishman and Irish speaker and the life and soul of the Irish party in 1990. He had won a minor All-Ireland medal with Dublin in 1984 and eventually became the first real Irish star in Aussie Rules when winning the supreme individual award, the Brownlow Medal.

Jim was generous in his comments to myself in his autobiography when he wrote as follows: 'The best coaches do have immense presence and charisma, have a clear vision and are not intimidated by anyone. They value their position as coach and will not allow distractions to get in the way. McGee filled this description and was prepared to do anything to achieve the results he wanted. He laid down a strict code of conduct and even imposed curfews so that the lads would know there was a job on hands and this was no holiday until the job was complete.'

It was tragic in 2009 when he contracted cancer having by then become one of the most famous people in Australia and legendary for his charity work, in particular with young people. He died in 2012 and so revered was he in his new country that he was granted a State Funeral in Melbourne. Those of us on that 1990 trip were privileged to have known a great person like Jim. I can still see how absolutely delighted he was to play for Ireland in 1990, having as I said earlier played in this series for Australia.

By 1990, the fame of Jack O'Shea as a midfielder had even spread to Australia because of his brilliance in the various Test games. He was as good as ever on the 1990 team. I often wondered how great Jack would have been had he got the opportunity to sample Australian Rules.

Chapter 28
God Bless Our GAA Presidents

THEY come in every three years in a blaze of glory and publicity, hang around for a full year while they wait for the incumbent to phase out, start off with all guns blazing but most importantly they announce the myriad of committees who will assist in the running of the GAA over the coming three years.

Then they get two full years with no opposition from the next guy before the ritual starts all over again, a President on the way out, a President on the way in, a shoal of new people appointed to committees and the ring-a-ring-a-rosy continues.

In a way, it's all fairly harmless as far the general public is concerned but there is no doubt a GAA president attracts publicity nearly on a par with a Taoiseach. I have often wondered why that is so. After all if you asked say, 50 people to name the president of the FAI, the IRFU or Irish Hockey Union, hardly anybody would be able to answer. But at least 90 per cent would know the name of the president of the GAA. Strange isn't it?

Maybe it is because GAA presidents live in a no-man's land world where they appear to have great power but in fact have very little. GAA people often comment on the latest controversy by saying: 'Why doesn't the president go and sort that out' or: 'Why doesn't the president change this, that or the other?' Well, I have news for you out there. The GAA president has hardly any power to change anything in the GAA simply because most rules and regulations have to be passed by over 330 delegates at annual GAA Congress.

While the president is indeed a spokesman for the organisation, he has no real power to make changes. A good president can facilitate change by selecting individuals, or more commonly committees, to propose changes in the GAA and then a president can use his influence to ensure that particular item will be passed at Congress. But it is definitely not an exact science and many a president has got a cuff in the ear from Congress delegates by rejecting something that everybody knew the president wanted.

It is debatable if a GAA president should have more personal power in such a large organisation but anyway I can't see any change in that area in the near future. GAA people guard their democratic right like gold in Fort Knox and the existence of the antiquated two-thirds majority system is proof of that. Time after time motions at Congress have been passed by a simple majority, often as high as 60 per cent, only to suffer rejection by the delegates for lack of the 66 per cent margin.

The selection by incoming presidents of the various committees, there are about 40 of these or more by the way, can be a fascinating exercise to observe as regards how he makes his choices. One of his first priorities is to look after the key figures around the country who canvassed for the new man (we have yet to see a woman GAA president). People who study these things, and there are a few fanatics like that around, can work out those large counties like Cork, Dublin, Wexford, Limerick and the like who backed the incoming president and suitable appointments of stature will be allocated to those. Then there are veteran GAA politicians, lifers in the organisation, who simply have to be included on important committees such as Frank Murphy of Cork or Gerald McKenna of Kerry.

After that there will be committee members who have been canvassed by one of their friends and finally there are many new members on committees who have been personally admired by the incoming president over the years and many new faces to broaden the depth of committee members.

For example, people may be appointed because they have special expertise in areas not directly involving the GAA but who are capable of performing great service to the organisation on a voluntary basis for the coming few years. Any new president has to make sure his own county is well represented on the new GAA committees. After all, all GAA is local.

Liam O'Neill, the current GAA president, was unusual in that he did not have to seek election because his appointment was unopposed, a rare honour indeed in the history of the Association. This gave him a largely free, unencumbered choice of committee appointments.

Since the rule-change which limited county board officers to five-year periods in power, there has been an explosion of new people involved in GAA administration and this has been a very good thing. As a result, an incoming president has a far wider range of capable people from which to choose. Personally, I believe there are far too many committees in Croke Park but like political quangos in Dail Eireann, getting rid of these can be very difficult. I reckon 15-20 small committees would run the GAA perfectly well on behalf of the President and the Croke Park staff.

The other arm of authority is the permanent staff at Croke Park which has also expanded greatly in the past 25 years in response to the massive growth in GAA activity all over Ireland and abroad. When the first two full-time officials were appointed to assist the then General Secretary Seán Ó Siocháin, two Claremen Brendan MacLua who later set up the Irish Post newspaper for the Irish in Britain in 1970 and former great Clare hurler Jimmy Smyth. Nowadays, the Croke Park staff numbers reflects the expansion of the organisation in that time.

By comparison to the real world of business and commerce, it is interesting to realise that none of the Croke Park staff have any direct power-making decision, the same as the GAA President. The present Director-General, Páraic Duffy, like his predecessors has very little power to make changes other than administration matters and has no direct power to change playing or other rules. Considering that Duffy corresponds to a chief executive in a commercial or semi-state organisation, it is peculiar that he has so little power in the GAA and for a start his position should be designated as chief executive rather than Director General.

One of the great clichés in the GAA over the years has been: 'That crowd up there in Croke Park' and whatever else that means it is not as a compliment. There seems to be a sort of love-hate relationship between units of the GAA outside Croke Park such as clubs, county boards, provincial councils and the like which gives these units almost carte blanche to blame Croke Park for everything that goes wrong, or appears to go wrong, in the GAA even though the particular problem in the first instance is actually the direct responsibility of one of those GAA units itself.

Duffy and his predecessor Liam Mulvihill have always shown remarkable tolerance and patience over the years despite the constant negative vibes emanating from leading GAA officials over issues that are within their known remit to sort out. But that's democracy for you.

GAA presidents nowadays take a sabbatical from their normal careers for their period in office and are compensated by the GAA. This can mean that a president's cost to the GAA can vary enormously depending on the salary of the office holder but there is never any debate about this as it is a totally accepted practice. However, the more teachers become presidents the better for the GAA's finances and this profession represent the largest number of GAA Presidents. Of the last seven presidents, including Aogán Ó Fearghail, no less than five have been teachers.

It is debatable if the president of the GAA now in a full-time role, should have a more executive role and be permanently based in Croke Park as opposed to the present system where much of the president's time is spent on public relations and visiting GAA units in all parts of Ireland and abroad. There is clearly a great desire for the president to visit clubs and other GAA units in various parts of the country and this is unlikely to change. Whether GAA presidents should be making public pronouncements several times a week however is questionable but then there is massive media interest in the Association because of the wide range of matters it is involved in so the availability of the president is probably a good thing.

By the way, not many people know this, but there are actually five vice-presidents in the GAA. They are the chairmen of the four provincial councils and Britain, and they serve a three-year term though not necessarily in tandem with the president's term of office. These vice-presidents are undoubtedly the most unused officers in the GAA and it is extremely rare to see a vice-president filling in for the president – which seems a great pity.

In the same way that people ask who runs the country, the question is often asked – who runs the GAA? It is a major commercial operation or a semi-state body, the Director General is the person that ordinary rank-and-file GAA members regard as 'The Boss' because he is a full-time officer based in Croke Park and provides the continuity of power and control that a president lacks because of his short three-year period in office. It's a remarkable statistic that for the past 84 years of the GAA's history, there have only been four people who held the office now known as Director General. These were: Pádraic Ó Caoimh, Cork (1929-1964), Sean O'Siochain, Cork (1964-1979), Liam Mulvihill, Longford (1979-2007) and Páraic Duffy, Monaghan (2008–). Páraic Duffy's term of office expires after seven years in 2015 but he will be eligible for re-appointment should he so wish.

Each Director General in turn has presided over major changes in the GAA during their time in office which refutes the common perception that the GAA is slow to move with the times. Particularly with regard to infrastructure changes and patron facilities the Croke Park office under the Liam Mulvihill and Páraic Duffy have been the leaders in all the massive physical developments that have occurred most notably in modern times especially the complete rebuilding of Croke Park stadium into one of the best in Europe and a development that has changed the face of the GAA in Irish life.

We sometimes hear GAA people complain about the number of staff in the Croke Park headquarters but many do not realise the level of expansion that has taken place in GAA related activities over the past 25 years or more as it broadens its influence in Irish life from a sporting organisation to a commercial, social and general widening remit in Irish life.

Chapter 29

Frank Burke –
A Part Of History

I HAVE had the good fortune to meet many varied and interesting people during my time in the GAA but one who struck a very special chord with me was a man called Frank Burke. I met him as often happens by chance, when a GAA man told me about 'a very special person that you should talk to'. The man who said this to me was former Taoiseach Jack Lynch back in 1982 when we were at a small function in Dublin to honour the Offaly dual player Liam Currums who had just become the 14th players to win both hurling and football All-Ireland medals after Offaly had beaten Kerry.

Frank Burke was one of the earliest dual All-Ireland winners back in 1920 and has the unusual, possibly unique record of having won two All-Irelands in both codes. Because of the political problems around the 1916-1921 period All-Ireland finals were often delayed by as much as a year or more and in order to keep fixtures in some sort of order the GAA at the time would play finals more or less whenever they got an opportunity. So we find that from May 14, 1922 until October 7, 1923 Frank played in an astonishing five All-Ireland finals, two hurling and three football, winning two in football and one in hurling. He was also a regular on the UCD Sigerson and Fitzgibbon teams at that time and had the distinction of playing in the first of these competitions in 1912– so who said burnout was a new fad in the GAA?

Jack Lynch was a dual All-Ireland winner when Cork won the 1945 All-Ireland football final and he suggested that we should pay a visit to Frank's home in Rathfarnham and a very welcoming host he was. He came from a well known GAA family in Carbury, Co Kildare but when he was sent to Knockbeg College in Carlow he refused to play rugby which was the main sport there then and he left after a year and then went on to study in a new school, St Enda's, Rathfarnham where the Principal was Pádraig Pearse.

'Believe it or not,' Frank said, 'My first game of hurling for Dublin was in the All-Ireland final of 1917 and I only got in at the last minute because Brendan Considine, the great Clare hurler was dropped because, allegedly, he hadn't trained enough. That was my first All-Ireland medal and it was handy enough.' There was little or no publicity those times for the GAA in Dublin, no television or radio and only tiny pieces about All-Irelands in the newspapers so nobody knew anything about my dual All-Ireland status or me. Any way there were far more serious things to be doing in Ireland at that time.'

Frank not surprisingly was an admirer of Pearse and fought in the Easter Rising in the GPO in 1916. He was interned in Frongoch but was released after eight months as part of a Christmas amnesty. Pearse had promised Frank a job in St Enda's once he qualified in UCD in 1916 which was very apt as of course the principal was executed after the Easter Rising and Frank found himself principal some time afterwards

In those days GAA players based in Dublin usually played for Dublin county teams and Frank as a dual player of note had an impressive record, playing in eight All-Ireland finals where he won in football in 1921, '22, '23 and a hurling medal also in 1920 making him one of the earliest dual winners. That infamous day in November 1921 is forever known as Bloody Sunday and Frank Burke was a key figure that day as he was the direct opponent of Tipperary player Michael Hogan who was shot dead and after whom the Hogan Stand is named.

When Jack Lynch broached the subject of Frank's experience he was meticulous in his fascinating account of that dreadful day and his own ghastly experience when he lined out for Dublin against

Tipperary in a big tournament game that attracted a crowd of around 10,000. Frank recounted his fateful day with a clear memory as we listened to a piece of GAA and Irish history recalled as if it was only last week.

'It was a drizzly, windy day and on our way to Croke Park we wondered if the game would go ahead because of the incidents that took place the night before when Michael Collins had ordered the execution of a batch of British spies.

'I said to one of my friends on the tram: "There will surely be a raid somewhere today after that" but I never thought it would be in Croke Park. The referee, Mick Sammon, threw the ball in around 2.45 and soon afterwards an aeroplane flew over the ground and a red flare was shot out. The Black and Tans raided the ground and an officer on top of the wall fired a revolver shot. The ball had just come into my area of the field.

'When the aeroplane circled over the field again, the shooting started. At first the crowd thought the Tans were firing blanks but then we heard machine-gun fire. The crowd stampeded towards the Railway Wall furthest away from the shooting and myself and Tipperary's Michael Hogan, who I was marking, contested the ball and along with Dublin's Stephen Synnott we were the last players to leave the field.

'We got down on our hands and knees and started to crawl towards a small perimeter wall amid great confusion as the shooting was still going on and often within 10 yards of us. We lay crawling and started over towards Hill 16. I was very concerned not just for myself but also for a group of students from St Enda's on the Hill that I had brought to the game.

'We lay near the perimeter of the field but then I heard a cry: "I'm shot", and the crowd all rushed towards the Hill 16 end of the field. Eventually I groped my way to the dressing room in a very agitated condition as were all the other people there. An ambush like this at a football game was something none of us ever expected to happen.'

For many years afterwards there was an annual 'Bloody Sunday Game' played in Croke Park in November between Dublin and Tipperary to commemorate that fateful day and a plaque was erected with the names of both teams on a wall in the stadium. I presume when the times comes in November 2021, the GAA will suitably honour the centenary of Bloody Sunday in fitting style.

Frank Burke became a candidate in 1929 for the post of General Secretary of the GAA where he was eventually beaten by one vote by Pádraig Ó Caoimh who led the organisation from 1929 to 1964. Indeed, the election was itself dramatic as the sisters of Pádraig Pearse were anxious that Frank would be elected and their representative voted for him in the first count but in the subsequent count he felt he was not obliged to vote for Frank who therefore lost to Ó Caoimh by just one vote. That representative was none other than General Eoin O'Duffy, the first leader of the Garda Siochana and Fine Gael and later the well-known Blueshirt who fought with General Franco.

Incidentally there was another player of that era who also won two All-Ireland football and three hurling medals. But they were with different counties. Pierce Grace from Kilkenny won three hurling medals with Kilkenny in 1911, '12 and '13 and two football medals with Dublin in 1906 and '07.

In my time in the GAA, I have met many incredible people with astonishing tales to tell but few can outdo Frank Burke on account of his remarkable playing career, his role as a pivotal figure in the Irish nationalism movement of that period and his friendship with Pádraig Pearse.

Chapter 30

Violent Fall-out As Kerry And Derry Clash

WHEN I turned up to Croke Park for a National Football League semi-final in April 1973, I was not really expecting anything of great significance except for the likely possibility that Derry would have one of their rare victories over Kerry at national level.

Derry by then had the distinction of beating Kerry in the All-Ireland semi-final of 1958 but had lost to them in the 1971 league semi-final. Those were good times for Derry football and they had a team of tall, strong players with plenty of football ability. They had been consistent in Division 1 of the NFL for about five years and were very keen to upset Kerry this time.

A crowd of 12,569 got a bit of a shock when the game quickly developed into a war of attrition where physical battles dominated at the expense of skilful football and it was obvious that the referee, Paul Kelly (Dublin), then one of the leading officials in the country, would have his hands full to retain control.

The Kerry team of that time was not the greatest ever produced in the Kingdom and they struggled to cope with the power and strength of their opponents. Then after half-time disaster struck for Derry when first Chris Brown was sent off and four minutes later Tom Quinn joined him in the dugout. From that point on a tense atmosphere developed that superseded anything that was taking place on the playing field as Derry supporters descended on the Hogan Stand sideline in an angry mood at what they perceived as unfair treatment by the referee.

Eventually Kerry managed to draw level at full-time with three pointed frees by Mick O'Dwyer, Brendan Lynch and Donie O'Sullivan. The fact that even with two extra players for the final quarter Kerry were merely hanging on for dear life indicated that Derry were the better team and maybe that was what instigated the terrible events that followed as soon as the final whistle ended.

Legendary Irish Independent GAA writer, John D. Hickey, gave some vivid accounts of what he witnessed underneath the Press Box at the end of the game.

'They came at me like wild animals, not like human beings, only for the Guards I would have been torn asunder,' commented Paul Kelly to Hickey in reference to Derry supporters.

'At the end of the game such was the charge of 150 to 200 Derry supporters 'to get' the referee that the miracle of the day was that he was not seriously injured. Within seconds of the final whistle, he was engulfed by a crowd of what he described as 'wild animals' and for his deliverance we can all thank a handful of Gardai who acted with heroism and utter disregard for their own safety.

'When Kelly eventually managed to get to his dressing-room, the angry crowd attacked the Gardai and even the GAA's Director General, Seán Ó Siocáin was assaulted,' reported Hickey.

On the Wednesday night after the debacle, the Derry County Board met and issued the following statement: 'As far as the incidents after the match are concerned, the Derry board deplores and condemns them without reservation. The match itself and the referee's report are still sub-judice and therefore we can make no further comment.'

Gerald McKenna was Kerry county chairman at the time. According to newspaper reports, Kerry had decided in their dressing-room after the game to keep their mouths shut but later in the week an unknown source close to the Kerry camp made the following comment: 'Unless the right tail is pinned on the right ass we will have a lot to say – should there be any soft pedalling there will be a lot to be said.' That might be in the Kerry dialect but the message was clear.

The Activities Committee met subsequently with the following decisions announced immediately: Tom Quinn suspended for six months; Chris Brown suspended for four months, Tom Prendergast (Kerry) suspended for two months; Derry County Board fined £500. Replay fixed for April 29 in Croke Park.

Sean O'Connell and Adrian McGuckin (Derry) and Ger O'Keeffe (Kerry) were ordered to appear before the Activities Committee at the next meeting.

Derry appealed the penalties and were very concerned at the severity of the £500 fine. In today's money that figure would be €7,530 so no wonder they were unhappy. The fingering of Sean O'Connell by the Activities Committee also rankled as he was a football icon in Derry and generally regarded as an out-and-out sportsman. There was an allegation in Derry that O'Connell had been reported by a Kerry player in a letter to the AC and this also upped the tension as everybody moved towards the replay.

Derry lodged appeals to all the penalties which fell on deaf ears. On Wednesday April 18, Derry demanded an enquiry from the GAA about the whole affair and requested that it should be held in public with the media in attendance, that Derry should have the right to comment on the referee's performance, that there should be no haste in carrying out the enquiry and finally 'that no Derry player be asked to make personal statements which could in any way reflect on the reputation of a fellow Gaelic sportsman'.

That proposal got nowhere in Croke Park. While Derry people said after the game that they would never play under Paul Kelly again, they seemed content to go ahead with the replay following a marathon meeting in Bellaghy involving players and officers. County secretary Paddy Mullen announced to the media: 'That meeting could not have gone more smoothly and everyone was in agreement that we play the game. There was never any question of us pulling out and we are treating the match like any other.'

There was no mention, just five days before the fixture, of Paul Kelly as referee.

As things moved towards the replay date, April 29, rumours started to circulate that Paul Kelly was going to be dropped for the replay to alleviate Derry's resentment which had been greatly heightened by the suspensions and the fine but there was no official indication whatsoever of that.

A meeting took place on the Friday night in Croke Park before the replay between the Activities Committee and a group of officers from Derry led by county chairman Patsy Breen when the decision to appoint Paul Kelly emerged as the main stumbling block. Derry maintained that they had been led to believe that Kelly would be replaced for the replay but no one was too sure what GAA official had ever stated that.

At around 1am on Saturday morning, the Kerry Chairman, Gerald McKenna, received a phone call from a leading Croke Park official asking if Kerry would agree to a change of referee for the league semi-final next day. The answer from Kerry was a definite 'no'. A short time later Derry said they were leaving the meeting and withdrawing the Derry team from the game, having consulted with the team manager Harry Cassidy. The news just about made the deadlines for the Saturday morning newspapers, to the consternation of the GAA world at large.

It is interesting to record the description of these events as published in the Derry GAA history published in 1984.

'Then, in quick succession referee Paul Kelly sent off both Chris Brown and Tom Quinn, decisions which, in the eyes of all Northern people present were blatantly unjust. Despite this shock the remaining 13 Derry players played out the last quarter of the game in heroic fashion and denied Kerry what looked like being an easy if tarnished victory. Then inexcusably, as the final whistle blew some spectators broke onto the pitch to vent their fury on the referee. After a brief skirmish with the Gardai order was restored but the scenes had been captured on television and were highlighted on the main evening news.

The Activities Committee decided to make an example of Derry. Derry were fined £500 and thee were suspensions for Tom Quinn and Chris Brown but also Sean O'Connell who was dealt with not on the basis of the referee's report, but as a result of a letter written by a Kerry player. Football fans in Derry were incensed by what they saw as one-sided and vindictive treatment but the county board decided that for the good of the Association, they should swallow their feelings and go ahead with plans for the replay.

On the Friday night before the date for the replay appeals were being heard by the Central Council. Although some diminution of the sentences had been hoped for, none was forthcoming. The straw which finally broke Chairman Patsy Breen's back, however, was the announcement in contradiction to earlier indications which he had been given, that Paul Kelly would be re-appointed to referee the match. At that stage he said that Derry would not be playing and left the meeting.'

That meeting on the Friday night before the scheduled replay was the final decision and the GAA awarded the match to Kerry who went on to beat Offaly in the National League final.

●　　●　　●

It was a sad end to a very unsavoury situation and the drawn game remains only one of two such events that I can recall where a team refused to lineout for a big replay. The other one was in 1987 when Dublin and Cork drew in the NFL quarter-final in Croke Park. Both teams went to their dressing-rooms but Cork togged in and headed for the train at Heuston Station. Dublin knew extra time was required but found no opposition when they took the field. They lined out on their own, the referee threw the ball in, it was passed to Barney Rock who scored a 'brilliant' goal in front of a cheering Hill 16 audience. Since there was no player to kick the ball out the game was abandoned. Cork claimed: 'Nobody told us about extra-time.' Cork were thrown out and decided not to appeal and Dublin went on to beat Kerry 1-11 to 0-11 in the league final. One of the most bizarre endings to a big game in Croke Park for many years.

Chapter 31

The Ballsbridge GAA/Soccer Fiasco

S described in detail in another part of this book The Ban, otherwise known for over half a century as Rule 27 in the Official Guide and which forbade GAA members to play, attend or promote soccer, rugby, cricket or hockey which were classified by the GAA as 'Foreign Games' was eventually scrapped at the GAA Congress in Belfast in 1971.

But just 20 years later readers of the Irish Independent were surprised to see a banner headline in their sports pages in December 1991 under the heading of Donal Keenan's article which read: 'THE BAN IS BACK! – Dark Ages return as GAA bars all contact with soccer'.

The genesis of this story emanated from a decision by the Clanna Gael-Fontenoys GAA club which is based in the Sandymount area of Dublin to play a unique double bill of games in the RDS in Ballsbridge in December 1991. This event was to mark the centenary of the club and was to feature a GAA game between then All-Ireland champions Down and Dublin as well as a big soccer game between Shamrock Rovers and Bohemians in a League of Ireland game.

From the moment the event was announced the GAA at the highest level went on full alert. It was clear that Croke Park was somewhat caught on the hop and soon began a rearguard action to prevent the GAA game taking place. The GAA's Management Committee overturned a previous decision that would have allowed the game to take place. Strictly speaking, there would have been nothing to stop the game going ahead as the venue, the RDS, was not owned by the GAA and was seen as a multi-sport venue but Shamrock Rovers were the tenants that particular soccer season.

Dublin County Board seemed to have no problem with the games going ahead and a lot of promotional work had been undertaken by the GAA club, not just in Dublin but around the country as well. The GAA had originally lain down strict conditions for the event – it wanted full control of the fixture, assurances that the games could not be a double bill while requiring full control over the finances including gate receipts and sponsorship. The GAC initially said the GAA game could not go ahead because the RDS was not vested in the GAA but that was later resolved.

When word of these developments spread through the media, there was a very hostile reaction within Dublin GAA and beyond as it appeared to the general public that this was all part of a smokescreen to prevent a GAA and a soccer game taking place at the same venue – despite the fact that the RDS grounds did not belong to either GAA or soccer authorities. The arguments raged on until eventually the GAA issued the statement that scuttled the project with the key words being: 'The Central Council have decided that games played on the same bill as a soccer game will not be allowed.'

As often happens some newspapers were blamed by Croke Park for inaccurate reporting as the GAA desperately tried to cover up what seemed to even ardent members as a massive public relations cock-up. Eventually that particular GAA game did not go ahead but the soccer game did.

The PRO in Croke Park at the time was the popular Danny Lynch, a native of Dingle. He had his own personal doubts about the whole affair as he outlined in an interview some years later on his retirement as follows:

'I was told on one occasion to claim it was called off because the players would need injections as the RDS had been used for showjumping.

'Imagine the impact that would have had on the GAA around the country. We'd be telling young lads they couldn't go down to the local field because horses or sheep had been in there. It was a very difficult time for me because I was left to explain something for which no reason had been given.'

A storm of controversy blew across the sporting landscape and, as the GAA's official spokesman, Lynch felt the brunt of the anger and confusion. He considered resigning and returning to the Civil Service, but his wife Carmel advised him against quitting on a single issue.

'She was right. Others were to blame for the mess, so why should I leave a job I was otherwise enjoying?' he said.

That whole episode left a bitter taste particularly with many prominent GAA people from around the country who felt embarrassed by a decision that had not been properly thought out and clearly did not represent the views of ordinary GAA people at the time. Thankfully, something like that could not happen today, or could it? There are still flashpoints around the country when ground-sharing between GAA and soccer or rugby are on the agenda so maybe there is a need for more precise up to date rules and regulations to prevent further rows and dissension.

Chapter 32
Clare's First Munster Title In 71 Years

ONE of the worst beatings any football county got in the senior championship in the past 50 years was the day when Kerry scored 9-21 against Clare's 1-9 in the 1979 Munster semi-final in Milltown Malbay. Even though Kerry were in their pomp at the time it was still a humiliating result for Clare football which although often referred to as a 'hurling county' has a very strong football involvement in many parishes and over the years produced many excellent players.

The problem for Clare footballers, along with Waterford, Limerick and Tipperary, was that they were constantly overshadowed by Kerry and Cork in Munster particularly in the many years when the draw was seeded in such a way to virtually ensure a Munster final between those two counties.

Then along came a man called Lt Colonel Noel Walsh from Miltown-Malbay who served 20 years or more as a Clare selector and also was a long-term member of the Munster Council. His GAA ambition was to get an open draw for the Munster championship and after years of failure, this actually happened in 1990. That decision by the narrowest of margins and against the wishes of Cork and Kerry laid the path for one of the greatest shocks in championship history when Kerry played Clare in the 1992 Munster Final at the Gaelic Grounds in Limerick before a crowd of 24,015.

Apart from the open draw, the other major contributing factor to what happened that day was the Clare manager, John Maughan. He was a star colleges player with Carmelite College,

Moate and played with distinction with Mayo before his career was halted in mid-stream by a serious knee injury. As a young man he ventured into managership with Clare in 1991 and thus became the latest of many members of the Defence Forces to get involved with team management. Not surprisingly discipline and motivation, key figures for success in sport, were high on Maughan's agenda which in itself represented a sea-change for many Clare footballers.

By the time Clare arrived in Limerick on July 19, 1992 to face the might of Kerry, the manager had worked wonders in convincing the players that, yes, it would be possible to beat Kerry if things went according to plan. New levels of fitness and stamina had been achieved to match Kerry, who themselves were in transition after the glorious periods of the seventies and eighties when they won eight All-Irelands under Mick O'Dwyer. Now it was one of O'Dwyer's protégés, Mickey Ned O'Sullivan, who was in charge of The Kingdom.

Clare's last appearance in a Munster final was way back in 1941 and their only Munster title was back in 1917. The only Kerry star of those recent glory days still playing that day was the great Jack O'Shea, then in his 17th season.

Things got off to a bad start for Clare when playing with the wind they got a penalty in the fifth minute when Noel Roche was pulled down but Gerry Killeen's penalty was well saved by 'keeper Peter O'Leary. Kerry went two points ahead and Clare nerves were tingling on a knife-edge, as many of their fans feared the worst. But they found their feet then and scored three unanswered points from Colm Clancy, Tom Morrissey and Padraig Conway to settle Clare down. Gerry Kelly played at full-back and took on Jack O'Shea in the new position for him at full-forward and where he coped with Jacko much better than any opponent normally did.

A lead of 0-7 to 0-6 seemed inadequate bearing in mind the wind advantage Clare had enjoyed. However, Maughan's speech to the troops at half-time played a big part in ensuring that Clare's motivation was reinforced in spirit and body. They were ready for battle to wipe away the failure of 75 years. In a tight third-quarter, Maurice Fitzgerald snatched a couple of Kerry points and then there was a long spell of attrition with no scores until the 48th minute when Colm Clancy scored a powerful goal. The pivotal score of the game arrived in unusual circumstances as described by Irish Independent reporter, Cliona Foley, at the time.

'A long ball looked to be rolling wide over the end-line but at the last minute full-back Anthony Gleeson picked it up to clear it. Then he was hit by a thundering shoulder from Killeen which sent him flying over the end-line for a '45'. From that kick Martin Flynn broke the ball down in the square and substitute Martin Daly scrambled it across the line to give Clare a five-point lead with 13 minutes remaining. Typically Kerry responded better than at any time in the game but time was now against them. Yet they cut the lead to three points but then Jack O'Shea hit the post with a 20-metre free. Backed by a ferocious Clare following the players kept their heads and Gerry Killeen completed a massive personal day's work with two late points to leave the final score: Clare 2-10 Kerry 0-12.'

Wild scenes of excitement and pure relief ensued all over the stadium as the Munster Cup was presented and on radio, Clareman Marty Morrissey uttered the immortal GAA words: 'There won't be a cow milked in Clare tonight'.

Noel Roche, one of Clare's greatest ever players, then aged 32, who went on to play for Ireland v Australia ten times in his career, told the Evening Press on the Monday: 'We were meant to start a tour of the county on Sunday night but we never managed to get outside the door of the County Hotel in Ennis. There were grown men unashamedly in tears as the players celebrated a famous victory.'

Clare went on to meet Dublin in the All-Ireland semi-final but while they played very well, they were beaten on a score of 3-14 to

2-12. Donegal beat Dublin in the final but Clare had scored 18 points against Dublin, the same score as Donegal got in the final.

•   •   •

Apart from the historic Clare result that day in Limerick July 19, 1992 also marked the end of the inter-county career of the all-time great Kerry footballer Jack O'Shea, who announced his retirement immediately after the final whistle. Generally acknowledged as one of the best half-dozen midfielders in the history of Gaelic football Jack, from Cahirciveen, won seven All-Irelands as a midfielder and captained the Ireland team in Australia in 1986 managed by Kevin Heffernan. One of the most sporting players ever to play the game and very accessible to the general public and the media, Jack will rank as one of the all-time greats of Kerry football where he is most often set alongside Paddy Kennedy and Mick O'Connell as the greatest of all Kerry midfielders.

Chapter 33
Glorious Day That Changed Leitrim Forever

O F all the teams that made inter-county football breakthroughs in the last half-century, the achievement of Leitrim in winning the Connacht championship on July 24, 1994 must rank as one the most amazing.

One has to identify the background to that momentous event before appreciating the extent of what happened. Leitrim had, and still has, the smallest population in the country and in 1994 it was well below 30,000.

For a century it was a county ravaged by emigration and it was a truism rather than a joke when it was often claimed that you could field a stronger Leitrim county team made up of emigrants in New York and Boston than the team that was available in the home county.

Leitrim did have one near-glorious period in the late fifties when the county played in four Connacht finals against Galway, then one of the leading counties in Ireland having won the 1956 All-Ireland by beating Cork.

That Leitrim team was dominated by Packy McGarty who often stood single-handedly, Cuchulain-like, in front of marauding Galway players and who played for his county from 1949 to 1971. But the nearest Leitrim got to beating Galway was the 1958 Connacht final where the final score was Galway 2-10 Leitrim 1-11.

Some time later that year, it is claimed, the Galway county

chairman Fr Paddy Mahon and secretary John Dunne went to visit McGarty and presented him with a new Leitrim jersey – to replace the one that had been torn to shreds by Galway opponents in their efforts to control Packy McGarty.

But there was never enough Packy McGartys on any Leitrim team so another 30 years or more passed by and the smallest county suffered many heavy defeats. But in the indomitable nature that is always in the DNA of Leitrim people be it in sport, business, education or the arts, the county kept coming back, and back, and back.

In the early 1990s things were at a low ebb and they went for help to a Cavanman called PJ Carroll who worked as a typesetter with the Anglo Celt in Cavan. PJ was a larger than life character who was simply mad about football and had trained several clubs in different counties with great success. A Connacht U-21 title won in 1991 was the first real sign of something big might happen for Leitrim senior team but there had been too many false dawns over the years to be confident of that.

PJ set about restoring morale in the Leitrim football set-up and his rampant enthusiasm began to pay results as the team became very motivated and began to improve steadily. Over a four-year period the profile of Leitrim improved greatly and interest in football in the county grew and grew. Then when Carroll left, the county chairman Tony McGowan pulled a masterstroke by going to meet John O'Mahony about the prospect of taking over Leitrim. Immediately a whole new buzz developed in the county with the knowledge that a solid base for a good team had been developed and the presence of a manager like O'Mahony could be expected to keep things on an upward cycle.

The Mayoman had been in charge of his native county in the 1989 season bringing them to the All-Ireland final where they lost to Cork and after that the Mayo County Board decided they no longer wanted him.

He analysed the situation in minute detail and in every aspect before finally deciding to give it a go. There had been some good displays from Leitrim minor and U-21 teams in the immediate years beforehand so expectations were high. In the 1993 season, Leitrim made a huge psychological breakthrough when they beat Galway in the Connacht championship for the first time in about 45 years. In the semi-final Leitrim lost by two points to Roscommon but it still marked significance progress and John O'Mahony kept the momentum going as they prepared for the 1994 campaign.

By that time he realised that the biggest problem facing Leitrim was that their players, despite their improvement, simply did not know how to win big championship games. There are many other weak counties even today who are in that position but the manager took steps to sort the problem out by bringing in a psychologist, or as they called him in Leitrim a 'shrink'. This man did not come from a sporting background, more from the business world, but he worked very hard on individual players and the team and after much grafting, he did actually get substantial results, which greatly helped the Leitrim team.

When the Connacht championship draw was made Leitrim saw they would probably have to beat Galway, Roscommon and Mayo all in the one season, which certainly seemed a tall order and had never been achieved by Leitrim.

O'Mahony immediately lifted and challenged the players by telling them this was a great draw for Leitrim because it would show the country that they could match any of the top teams in Connacht regardless of tradition. A notable development some time earlier had been the arrival of Declan Darcy, son of a Leitrim man, Frank Darcy, from Aughawillan.

Although born and reared in the Ballsbridge area of Dublin 4, Declan started playing underage with his father's home club and remained that way into the senior grade. He starred with Leitrim U-21s and became a natural leader and captain of the senior team for 1994. Another outsider to join the Leitrim set-up was Jason Ward whose father came from Aughnasheelin but then lived in Dublin. A new parentage rule had just come into the GAA whereby children from parents from low population counties like Leitrim could declare for the parent's native county. Jason lived in Dublin but spent several years with Leitrim and was a very important member of the panel in 1994.

The game against Roscommon was played in Hyde Park, Roscommon before a huge crowd and Leitrim were in flying form in the first half which they largely dominated and led by 1-8 to 0-5 at the break. But Leitrim had a very poor championship record against Roscommon in the past so no Leitrim supporter was taking anything for granted – and how right they were.

Roscommon largely took over after the break and confined Leitrim to a meagre two points in the second half. As a nerve-wracking, for Leitrim fans, second half began to wend towards the final minutes, scores were level at 1-9 to 0-12 and for the fans at least all the old fears about playing Roscommon began to surface. But this set of players were made from stern stuff and George Dugdale shot for a point about 20 yards out from goals but it skewed narrowly wide and that seemed to be that. But hold it. Referee Brian White (Wexford) who was right beside the action noticed that a Roscommon defender had touched the ball as it went wide, over-ruled the umpire's wide signal and awarded a '45'. Without the slightest hesitation, Declan Darcy placed the ball and sent it flying between the uprights for what turned out to be the winning score. A historic victory had been achieved as it was the first time Leitrim had beaten Roscommon in the championship for 27 years, and in their own Hyde Park as well.

Three weeks later Leitrim were in Carrick to face Galway, boosted immeasurably by their victory in the previous game. This game ended in a draw with the replay in Tuam and again the doubters were out in force.

Another titanic struggle for Leitrim took place but they eventually triumphed by a single point. By this stage the fans were living in dreamland, Roscommon beaten, Galway beaten in a replay in Tuam and now the big one, a Connacht final against the kings of Connacht football Mayo managed by the legendary Kerry footballer Jack O'Shea with Leitrim managed by a Mayoman.

What an enticing prospect that was. In the lead-up to the final, fixed for Hyde Park on July 24, 1994, the county of Leitrim went mad. Flags, banners, painted cars, painted sheep, the lot as the county discovered a new world of expectation, excitement and publicity never before experienced. Emigrants from all over the world began to make plans for being home for the final, the media descended on the county and one of the central figures in that area was the captain of the only other Leitrim team to win a Connacht championship back in 1927, Tom Gannon.

As often happens in huge games like this, the Connacht final itself was not exactly a brilliant game and Leitrim fans got a terrible shock when a mix-up in the defence saw the concession of an own-goal in the first minute of the game. Bearing in mind Leitrim's deplorable history of losing to stronger teams over the years, this left fans almost distraught but the players kept their heads, realising there was plenty of time to recover, and took the game to Mayo thereafter.

By half-time, Leitrim were ahead by 0-5 to 1-0 which gave a fair idea of the ineptitude of the Mayo attack. When Leitrim rattled over five points in the third quarter with only one in response from Mayo, they looked home and dried, even though it was a wet day in Hyde Park at that stage, but whether it was complacency or nerves at the prospect of actually winning the Connacht title, some Leitrim players seemed to get distracted and conceded scores which all led up to a close enough finish before referee Michael Curley blew the whistle for full-time and Hyde Park was immediately transformed into a wonderland – for Leitrim people who had thought they would never live to see this day after a 67-year wait.

The scenes when Connacht chairman PJ McGrath, himself a Mayoman of course, presented the Brendan Nestor Cup will never, ever be forgotten by Leitrim people in the 27,000 attendance. Never had so many Leitrim people been in the same place at the same time in history. Emigrants came from the four corners of the earth to share in this day and when 95-year-old Tom Gannon mounted the rostrum as the captain and only survivor from the 1927 team to join Declan Darcy in holding the cup aloft, it was a moment that only a great sporting occasion can provide and was deeply emotional for Leitrim people.

And for every joyful face in the crowd at that time, there were also tears of joy as well. The shared lifting of that cup by Gannon and Darcy was a symbol of the harrowing struggle that had been the story of Leitrim football going back to 1927 when Michael O'Hehir's father was the trainer of the team.

Being from the neighbouring county Longford, I had many personal interests in Leitrim's progress as I was born no more than a few miles from the Leitrim parishes of Carrigallen, Cloone and Aughavas. My secondary school, Moyne Latin School, had about 30 per cent of its pupils from Leitrim. In those days, Leitrim was always regarded as the poor relations regarding county football but all that changed in 1994. Many famous footballers from other counties had strong family links with Leitrim and the locals often looked on with envy as such players went on to win All-Ireland medals.

These included Colm O'Rourke who originally lived in Aughavas, Pat O'Neill and Kevin Moran. Between emigration and migration Leitrim for over a century was one of the worst hit in terms of population decline, which left many parish clubs struggling to survive. Now the population has stabilised over the 30,000 mark, but it's still the smallest in Ireland. That 1994 Connacht victory proved to be a turning point in the economic and social life of Co Leitrim thanks to the boost to morale in the county that it provided. There was a new air of confidence among Leitrim people that has remained to this day.

Shortly after that victory, a huge wood-manufacturing

operation called Masonite arrived in Leitrim giving great employment, a magnificent new hotel was built along the Shannon in Carrick-on-Shannon and several other industrial developments took place in subsequent years. Leitrim as a county had arrived on the map having been largely ignored by the rest of Ireland previously. I know of no other county that gained so much materially from a huge GAA achievement as Leitrim did after winning that 1994 Connacht final.

I regard the occasion of that Leitrim victory as one of the greatest days I have ever been fortunate enough to attend and I know there was a wave of joy and appreciation for Leitrim players, John O'Mahony and county board officers like Tommy Moran and Tony McGowan not just in neighbouring counties but all over Ireland.

And needless to say the very popular Leitrim song, 'Lovely Leitrim' made famous by the late Larry Cunningham was the new anthem in the county for weeks afterwards.

Chapter 34
Who Killed The Railway Cup?

PEOPLE of my vintage still retain a fondness for the Railway Cup as the interprovincial competition was called when it was set up in 1927. The name came from the donation of the trophy by Irish Rail of the time. We recall the glory days of the competition when crowds of up to 40,000 turned up for the finals in Croke Park on St Patrick's Day. There were many factors which made the Railway Cups so popular in their first 50 years such as providing the great stars of the game the opportunity to compete with and against their peers from the various provinces.

The biggest function it served was that it acknowledged in a very practical way outstanding players from weaker counties and provided them with a big stage to show their talent. The semi-finals were always played in different provincial venues and that allowed the public to see first-hand the big stars of the day from the top counties playing in local stadiums.

Transport was not as convenient then as it is now and many followers of football rarely if ever went to Croke Park for the big games unless their own county was playing. The Railway Cup provided the opportunity to see the great players in action locally in the four provinces.

In addition, with no televised GAA games until the 1960s, being able to watch the star players in action first hand was a huge attraction. The Railway Cups soon developed a niche following each culminating in the St Patrick's Day double-bill in Croke Park.

Ulster's first victory in 1942 was regarded as a seminal event in that province's history and was seen as a major breakthrough.

Whenever a player from a weaker county won his first Railway Cup medal. it was seen in the same light. Jimmy Hanniffy from Drumlish became the first Longford player to win a medal in 1945 amid great rejoicing and other notable players who enjoyed fame when they collected Railway Cup medals over the years from weaker counties include: Gerry O'Reilly (Wicklow), Vincent Tierney (Longford), 'Peenie' Whelan (Carlow), Jim Rogers (Wicklow), Mick Cahill (Tipperary), Packy McGarty (Leitrim), Brendan Barden and Padraig Gearty (Longford), Mick Carley (Westmeath), Noel Crowley (Clare), Harry O'Neill (Antrim), Nace O'Dowd (Sligo) and Paddy Casey (Offaly) to name just a few. For many of these former players, their most-prized possession is their Railway Cup medal.

It was in the 1970s that the first signs of decline appeared in the competition, hastened by the arrival of live televising of the games. This was the time when the All-Ireland club championship began and when that competition's finals were staged on St Patrick's Day in Croke Park, it was a killer blow. In the early seventies a Combined Universities team was added to the four provinces in a bid to improve the interest. Paddy O'Hara was a genius of a football coach and trainer who over the years was involved in coaching nearly every county team in Ulster and left an indelible mark on every one of them. He had been a star player for Antrim in their brief moment of glory when they won the 1946 Ulster championship before losing to Kerry in very controversial circumstances. He was in charge and I was a selector with him for the three years when the Universities took part in the Railway Cup. In 1974 the Universities team went on to win by beating Connacht in a replayed final in Athlone on Easter Sunday and the cup was presented by GAA President Donal Keenan, himself a former UCD footballer who led that college to their first Dublin senior championship in 1943.

My next involvement with the Railway Cup was when I was manager of the Leinster team in the 1980s. It was something I found very enjoyable because we had such a great selection of quality players. But the closest we got to actually winning the competition was in 1983 when we reached the final in a replay in Breffni Park against Ulster and lost by 0-24 to 2-10 on St Patrick's Day. There was a great crowd and a fine atmosphere that day when Ulster were managed by Brian McEniff and Art McRory who had a wonderful record with Ulster teams that time. I always remember from that game the performance of Tommy Dwyer from Carlow who stood about 6' 7" tall and caught some mighty high balls.

On the down side of my Railway Cup involvement I remember the semi-final against Connacht in 1982 when the final scoreline was Connacht 0-8 Leinster 0-2. The forward line for Leinster that day included Offaly duo Matt Connor and Brendan Lowry, Seamus Fitzhenry (Wexford) and Tom Prendergast (Laois), all top players and obviously all four had a bit of an off day.

Most people now assume that it is time to put the Railway Cup competition to death once and for all. Personally, I am not so sure about that. After all we have here a long-standing competition involving up to 100 of the best footballers in the country, the vast majority of whom are anxious to be selected for their provinces and take part in this straight knockout competition.

Now that the GAA has gone so heavily into commercial ventures, there's scarcely a week when we do not have a press reception to launch schemes or announce new sponsorships or some other sales venture that often has very little to do with actually promoting the game of football. And here we have the marketing potential of the leading footballers in Ireland with a competition that could be adapted to a modern setting and made attractive for spectators and players.

For a start, the Railway Cup games could be played under lights in a carefully selected town with a strong GAA following for football such as Omagh, the new Casement Park, Newry, Parnell Park, Tullamore, Castlebar, Pearse Stadium, Kerry or Cork venues among others. The games could be the centrepiece of a major weekend festival of football, music and other entertainment and plain craic. Admission to the games, or at least the two semi-finals should be free. And surely a substantial sponsor would be interested in a project if this was properly marketed. When we see some of the mickey-mouse GAA competitions that are being currently sponsored, it would be very surprising if a re-vamped Railway Cup could not be viable for sponsorship. And who knows, even the GAA's new friends in Sky Television might be interested in covering the games live.

That wonderful Clare football man, Martin Donnelly, has already invested a lot of money in keeping the Railway Cup games alive and would probably be interested in a new approach also. It could be a nice competitive break too for the players without the usual pressures of big time county games and the original perk for players from less successful counties getting national recognition and playing for and against the biggest names in the game still holds true.

So before the GAA bins the Railway Cup, let's see what the options are for a revival to suit modern living, sporting and social habits.

Chapter 35

Cork Hit Five In 21 Minutes Against Kerry

'**F**ANTASTIC! That was the only word that can even begin to sum up this incredible Munster final played before a huge attendance of 29,859 at the Cork Athletic Grounds yesterday that must betimes have reduced partisan fans into a state of apoplexy yesterday.'

This was the opening paragraph of the report on the 1973 Munster final written for The Irish Press by Pádraig Puirseal and even though he was a well known novelist in his day Padraig was not known for flowery writing of this type. So what inspired this Kilkenny native to wax so lyrical on this particular game?

Padraig spelled it out like this: 'Cork scored a staggering five goals within 21 minutes of the start of the game. Cork were leading by 16 points with only 25 minutes gone and still 13 points ahead at half-time.

'I have vivid memories of that game played in terrible wet conditions and I have never seen so many Kerry players and supporters so scared as they were at half-time that day. They had good reason too!

'We had a magnificent fightback by Kerry in the second half that by the end of the third quarter had cut the Cork lead to just five points before Cork arose from their slumbers to rattle over a few more points and end the game nine points.'

Apart from the dramatic events in the game itself it is worth pointing out the disparity between the teams in advance of the game with Kerry having won the National League but Cork had been lucky enough to avoid relegation from Division 1. But playing with a ferocity that defied both the very wet conditions and the presence of so many Kerry stars on duty Cork went for the jugular straight away and after a softening up process that found many Kerry players wanting, no less than four goals were scored in about six minutes.

The first had come after five minutes when Dinny Long hit in a long free that bounced of the bar and in the ensuing scramble the ball was bundled into the net. About 15 minutes later with Cork in full control the hammer blows arrived like bullets fired from a gun. Jimmy Barry-Murphy broke down a high ball to Jimmy Barrett who goaled. Then Billy Field converted a penalty when a panic-stricken Kerry full-back line hauled down a couple of Cork forwards. Within 60 seconds Dave McCarthy hit a high ball that came off the upright to Jimmy Barry-Murphy and he had a simple task to net number four. Three minutes later Kevin Jer O'Sullivan intercepted a Kerry passing movement on his own 21-yard line, kept going almost to the Kerry 21-yard line and then chipped the ball into the goal area where Jimmy Barrett fisted it to the net. Cork 5-3 Kerry 0-2. It was hard to know which set of supporters was in the bigger state of shock because such a situation had never happened before in the long series of contests between Cork and Kerry.

Although not having one of their better days the Kerry mentors at last began to think on their feet and first moved corner forward Jackie Walsh to midfield to assist John O'Keeffe and Mick O'Dwyer went to centre-forward with Liam Higgins coming in from the bench. Only a minimal improvement resulted from the changes at that stage and by half-time the score was still scary for Kerry fans: 5-4 to 0-6.

Early in the game Kerry had moved their regular full-back Paudie O'Donoghue to left full in order to mark Ray Cummins who had moved to that position instead of his usual No 14 slot. Jimmy Barry-Murphy was then at full-forward where he was marked by Jimmy Deenihan but that move seemed to leave gaps in front of the Kerry goals which brought those five early goals. In the second half O'Donoghue reverted to his normal central role and the Kerry defence began to get some sort of confidence but the damage had been done by then

Cork of course have always been notorious for shooting wides but in the second half they gave an exhibition of score missing possibly in the knowledge that all they had to do was contain Kerry from scoring much and their own huge lead would see them through. In the end it did. But that Cork scoring extravaganza was no flash in the pan because in the All-Ireland semi-final they scored 5-10 to crush Tyrone by 15 points and hit another huge score of 3-17 to beat Galway in the final by seven points

Of all the teams that would have been expected to complete the All-Ireland double in 1974 Cork must have been odds on to do so with that barrage of scoring – 13-39 in the final three games of the All-Ireland championship was a truly astonishing tally. They did retain their Munster title but lost in the semi-final to Dublin who went on to beat Galway in the All-Ireland final

Cork had a fabulous selection of top-class players under the direction of coach Donie O'Donovan, a very shrewd football man who was way ahead of his time as he showed by the manner in which his moving of players dismantled the Kerry full-back line in the first half that led to those five goals and it really is a mystery how they failed to win another title.

Billy Morgan was one of the best goalkeepers we have ever seen, Barry-Murphy and Cummins were two brilliant dual players in the full-forward line and Declan Barron was a fabulous player at centre half-forward. Kevin Jer O'Sullivan became a defensive legend but all the players were high grade performers. And it is important to stress that this was a very strong Kerry team on duty that day in The Athletic Grounds. Over half of them won All-Irelands in 1969 and 1970 although the great Mick O'Connell watched the game on the terrace as he had retired after the replayed 1972 final against Offaly. But some young players also surfaced in that final who were to create their own reputations later that decade under the managership of Mick O'Dwyer such as John and Ger O'Keeffe, and John Egan.

Incidentally the UCD club were well represented in that Munster final of 1973 with Dave McCarthy of Cork and Kerrymen John O'Keeffe, Paudie and Eamon O'Donoghue, Mick Gleeson, Donie O'Sullivan, Eamon Fitzgerald and Mickey O'Sullivan all present or former players with the Dublin college.

Chapter 36

Oh, Come Back Paddy Reilly...

ONE of the integral components of discussion when football people congregate at weddings, funerals or after-match socialising is statistics. A whole army of people in the GAA thrives on accumulating facts and figures about players, matches, referees, scorelines, Allstar winners and many other topics which are a huge factor in the world of Gaelic games.

When I worked as a sub-editor with The Irish Press in the sixties, hardly a night would go by without the phone ringing requesting the answer to a question raised in some discussion or other which the 'debaters' could not agree upon. It was noticeable that two reasons predominated for these questions: the first was to settle a bet and the second arose around closing time in the pubs when debates like these tended to reach a climax.

I have never ceased to be amazed at the depths to which GAA people will search to accumulate information and keep it in their memories. That task was a very difficult one of course in the pre-television days and before the internet, Google, Twitter, etc were so far away in the future to be unimaginable. Nowadays all such information can be got in seconds which must be a great relief to the few sporting sub-editors left working in our newspapers.

When it comes to incidents that took place a very long time ago, there is still scope for uncertainty and surprises for those who seek out such items. A few years ago I came across a subject matter which I retained in my head, a rare occurrence at any time, because I thought it might allow me to have at least have one sticky question that the vast majority of sports fans would be unable to answer.

To test out that theory I put the question to the great Jimmy Magee, the original Memory Man and even he was stymied. He came back to me a few times as his curiosity got the better of him and eventually I gave in and took him out of his agony.

As often happens when we seek to find out information of times long gone by, there can be a follow up story to the incident which is even more interesting than the question itself. This is one of those situations.

In the 1950s there were a lot of famous inter-county footballers based in the greater New York area, a product of the rampant emigration of those years. New York GAA and John Kerry O'Donnell sought to have a proper outlet for New York teams. It was decided to play the winners of the National League, to be called the 'League Home Final' in Ireland and the winners would then play New York in what was described as the League Final proper. A strange decision but then it was New York after all.

In 1950 Cavan, who had played in the previous three All-Ireland finals including the famous Polo Grounds final in New York in 1947, won the Home Final after beating the then All-Ireland champions, Meath.

New York came over to play Cavan on the last Sunday in July in Croke Park before an attendance of 31,872. There were many notable players on the visiting team who had already made their name in Ireland, such as Bill Carlos who won All-Irelands with Roscommon in 1943/44 and Pat McAndrew of Mayo. John Kerry O'Donnell was the trainer of the team which must have been an interesting experience.

After what was described as a tough, rugged game, New York won by 2-8 to 0-12 for their one and only league title.

Cavan had two goals disallowed and near the finish Tom Gallagher from New York and Phil 'The Gunner' Brady from Cavan were sent off. As reported in the Anglo Celt at the time 'both men walked off the field arm-in-arm on the best of terms'. Those were the days.

So confident were the GAA authorities that Cavan would win the game they decided to make two different sets of medals for the teams in advance of the game. The first set, for the losers, were made in the shape of a map of Ireland and were clearly meant for New York.

But led by their captain Mickey O'Sullivan from Kerry, they went back to the US with the cup and trophies while the Cavan players were presented with medals in the shape of maps of Ireland. These certainly were unique medals for the second most important competition in Gaelic football at the time.

At last, this all brings me to my special question: Who was the oldest player to win a national football league medal? Well, his name was Paddy Reilly and he played in that 1950 NFL final at the age of 46. But no, he was NOT playing for Cavan despite the name but for New York and kept his net intact although up against a number of All-Ireland winning forwards. Paddy was actually born in 1904 in North Wall in Dublin and went to America in 1927 where he played with several different teams in New York, including Cavan. He died in Connecticut in April 1992 aged 88.

Chapter 37

Here's The Rub, Lads

UP until the arrival of qualified physiotherapists in the 1970s, it was customary for GAA teams to have masseurs to give players a 'rub' and attend to injuries during the course of a game. Very often these men – it was invariably males only that time – had served in the Defence Forces where they would have received some form of physical education knowledge or at least enough to impress players and mentors who really knew no better. For many years UCD availed of the services of a Wexfordman named Barney Crosbie, who was a keen advocate of poteen-based mixtures.

The concoctions these masseurs had in their various bottles were varied and often exotic and they normally kept their contents a closely guarded secret. The chief ingredient for many of then was poteen and not just any old poteen. No, this would usually be first-run poteen, which meant it was the first distillation of the corn mixture that was used to make the illegal brew. For people who wished to actually drink poteen there would be three runs, which meant the stuff was distilled three times. First-run poteen could be very strong indeed, strong enough to strip paint off a wall in cases.

UCD played St Patrick's Training College one June Friday evening in a Dublin U-21 final and among those on the UCD team was Jimmy Fay from Cavan, who was a medical student. It was a particularly warm evening and thirst was a major problem. UCD won the game and when the presentation was over the players rushed to the dressing room for a drink. First in was Jimmy to grab what he believed was a bottle of water which stood in the centre of the dressing-room table.

He had gulped down nearly half the bottle before he realised something was wrong. The liquor he was gulping was actually a bottle of first run-poteen which the masseur, Barney Crosbie, had left behind at half-time. Poteen looks exactly like clear water so the mistake was understandable, even for a medical student. In theory drinking a large swig of poteen should leave you severely shaken but they were hardy lads in Cavan those times, particularly if you came from Castlerahan. Jimmy Fay went on to play for Cavan and practised as a GP in Kilnaleck. Sadly, he passed away at a young age a few years ago.

Chapter 38

From Special Players To Special Needs

I'VE been fortunate over the years to have been involved with Gaelic football players from various backgrounds – many of whom were elite sports performers. These varied from club players, to third-level elite squads and all the way to the pinnacle of All-Ireland winning teams. I also had the opportunity to be involved with six Ireland teams that competed in Ireland and Australia with the Australian Rules top players in those days.

For someone who was never in danger of being classified as an elite player myself, this has been a great experience and very informative. I am fascinated to observe the mindset of famous players at all levels and their own personal levels of motivation and satisfaction when they did well.

In latter years, however, I became involved with another set of people who have presented me with an equally fascinating scenario of personalities as the famous and elite mentioned above. When my daughter, Linda, entered St Christopher's special needs school many years ago it led to my involvement with a world that I had previously never encountered and scarcely knew existed.

St Christopher's Services is situated right in the centre of the town of Longford on the old Dublin-Sligo road and is based in a premises that was formerly the residence of the prison governor in the time of the British regime. It is located on Battery Road which gets its name from the fact that there were two British army barracks, one at either end of that road in the past. In fact, one of those barracks was based where the current GAA headquarters, Pearse Park, is now located.

St. Christopher's was founded in a prefab in a Longford backstreet just 50 years ago by four local people who saw a need for special attention to be given to people with special needs. As any person who lived in rural Ireland at that time will recall, people with special needs, physical or mental, were usually hidden away from society in the past or sent away to secure premises, such as asylums, from which they hardly ever returned. They were yet another section of Irish society that was ignored by state authorities and left at the mercy of bureaucrats who often cared little for the welfare of such people.

But those four brave people REALLY cared and with absolutely no resources other than that prefab, they set about changing things in their part of the world. A long and arduous campaign evolved over the years culminating in the present outstanding buildings and facilities that are among the best in this country. Sadly in recent years, government finance has been very severely cut in St Christopher's with a consequent decrease in some services. It's very hard to understand how clients of special needs premises are punished in this way when we consider the wastage that we constantly see in other areas of public expenditure. And I'm not forgetting the exorbitant wages some public office-holders get in state or semi-state organisations.

All forms of special needs are now catered for at St Christopher's and for 20 years or more now I have been actively involved in various capacities, most recently as chairman of the Board of Management of the primary school section of the complex.

I can safely say that nothing that I have ever been involved with in sport in former times has affected me so much as my involvement with St Christopher's and I stress that I am only peripherally involved by comparison with the wonderful people who work full-time there. I am constantly struck by the achievements of the clients there who do extraordinary things despite the often very serious setbacks they have inherited. Not surprisingly participation in sport is absolutely central to the vast majority of people in St Christopher's because it is there that they can best express their abilities and simulate their heroes in sport. Music is the other great facet of their lives that seems to bring a special response also. The levels of ability may vary enormously depending on their own special needs but their level of participation does not. Their enthusiasm, their dedication to their favourite sport and the gracious way in which they accept victory or defeat is really humbling.

And this is the comparison that strikes me every time I visit the place. There are no complaints after a defeat, the referee is never blamed, and there is always a sense of appreciation after every single event or contest from the performers. The person in charge of sport in St Christopher's is Una Flynn from Ballymahon and watching her fervour for this most difficult of tasks I often ask myself is there a more dedicated sports coach/teacher in the whole of Ireland than she. To watch her change young special needs people from total inability to participate in sport when they arrive in St Christopher's to transforming them to ride bicycles, swim lengths of the local pool, and of course engage in football is truly astonishing.

All I can say is that I doubt if I would be capable of managing what Una achieves and I am sure the same would apply to many of the leading hurling and football team managers around the country. Patience is the key to all of this for special needs people involved in sport and Una Flynn certainly has that in spades. I have no doubt there are probably hundreds of people like Una Flynn in this country but how often their great work is overlooked in favour of the more flashy managers in all sports that constantly hog the media headlines.

I always feel humbled when I visit St Christopher's and see what people with special needs can actually achieve under often very restrictive conditions. A local schoolteacher Liam Madden in Newtownforbes voluntarily organises a large crowd of special needs people to partake in swimming in the local pool every Monday night and bowling on Thursday nights and the bowling in particular is often participated in with All-Ireland type fervour.

Our daughter, Linda, if she has a good night at the bowling rink, will be very quick to tell me: 'I was on fire tonight!' with all the enthusiasm of a footballer scoring the winning goal in the county final. Liam organises the Special Olympics in this area and is a hero for all the participants. There are many other volunteers who improve the quality of life for people in St Christopher's and such people are the unsung heroes of Irish life in my opinion. Nearly every parish in county Longford has a branch of the St Christopher's organisations and each year they raise a lot of money to provide extra facilities, outings etc, for the clients there. St Christopher's is one of the best known organisations in Co Longford.

The classic expression people use when they visit establishments like St Christopher's is: 'It gave me a whole new perspective on life' and indeed that is true.

That is why I am always delighted to see famous GAA players getting involved in visiting these establishments as both they and the clients are beneficiaries. Indeed GAA players have been exceptional in getting involved with special needs people once the initial almost fear is got over by the visitors.

I have no doubt many famous players learned to appreciate how fortunate they are to have the ability to perform such wonderful skills in their own sport when they see and are amazed with what special needs people can achieve under what are often very severe restrictions physical and mental restrictions.

The arrival to prominence of the Special Olympics has been a huge eye-opener to the general public of the capabilities of people with special needs. It was certainly an eye-opener for me when I began to visit St Christopher's Centre in Longford and made me very humble to have been so fortunate in what I managed to achieve as a football team manager with elite athletes.

Chapter 39

A Farewell To Liam O'Connor – A Gentle Giant

THIS is an edited version of the oration given by Richie Connor, Captain of the Offaly All-Ireland winning team of 1982, at the graveside of his cousin Liam O'Connor, and my brother in law, in Aglish graveyard, Co Waterford on December 2, 2013 aged 58. Liam was the first member of the Offaly panel from the famous 1982 All-Ireland final to pass away.

"Liam was born on September 23 1955 in Eneghan, Walsh Island. Thirty-two days later a mile down the road in the townland of Monevane, I was born. Our mothers were sisters and our fathers were brothers. With that background it was natural Liam and I played a lot as children together many years before playing together in GAA venues from Croke Park to Gaelic Park, New York. From an early age athletics was Liam's sporting forte and in one year at the Offaly schools sport he won medals for Long Jump, High Jump and would you believe the Pole Vault. My sole medal was in the 200 metres.

In those years there was very little schools or underage football in our part of Offaly and there was no significant colleges football in Portarlington where we attended secondary school. When I later went to Ballyfin College, Liam took little interest in football and he did not play minor or Under-21 for Offaly. Whereas I was consumed with football at that time, I felt Liam had little interest pursuing a similar path. However that all changed in 1974 when

Walsh Island won the Offaly U-21 championship and Liam at six foot four was one of the most committed players – a sign of what was to come.

The Walsh Island football revival grew dramatically and the club won six-in-a-row Offaly SFC titles and two Leinster club titles between 1978 and 1983. Liam was one of only two players who played in every game in all those competitions. In 1972, Willie Bryan, a first cousin of Liam and I, collected the Sam Maguire Cup for Offaly so football fever was running high in our parish then. By then Liam was regarded as a workman-like player and honest but lacked the sparkle that attracted county selection. But he showed with Walsh Island that he was a vital member of a team and when the need was greatest in a game Liam could always be relied upon when the game was tight and men who stand up were needed.

But by sort of chance Liam got his big break in 1979 when I had been full-back for Offaly but got injured before a Leinster championship game against Laois, our greatest rivals. Liam was named full-back where he would be opposing the great Laois player, Bobby Millar, who himself sadly passed away some years ago at a young age. I was asked by Eugene McGee to sit behind the goals and 'keep an eye' on Liam and run on with advice. I never had to go near him. Bobby had a quiet game and Offaly won.

By 1981, Liam was the established full-back for Offaly where he played his best football in the biggest and most pressurised games. We played in two All-Ireland finals winning one and Liam was pitted against the great Eoin 'Bomber' Liston at his peak in those games. I would safely say that Bomber was never as quiet over those 150 minutes of football as he was in the two All-Irelands. In the 1982 final itself most people will remember the long crossfield kick that was perfectly measured and weighted to find Seamus Darby stealing in behind Tommy Doyle and which gave Darby very little to do. As welcome and important as it was this was not typical of Liam's play as he rarely crossed even his own 50-yard line.

Personally, the incident that most typified Liam's football qualities happened midway through the second half when Offaly were under the Kerry cosh. A through ball was falling kindly for the great John Egan as he sped towards the goals. It seemed that John, who sadly himself has passed away also, was going to get onto this ball in full flight and we all know what that meant. But from nowhere Liam committed himself, sprinted across and had the strength to ensure the ball was spilled away from danger – no mean feat with the likes of John Egan around. I doubt if any other player on our team would have the same speed and strength to complete that task.

Off the playing field, Liam was always a prankster and he enjoyed a good laugh of which there were many over the years. As a player however, Liam was quiet. Quiet in the dressing room and quiet on the pitch. In fact it was often days after a game that we learned he had a broken finger or a sore jaw. Liam just kept playing doing all he could to help win the game. And so it was when life dealt Liam a hard blow over the last year he found himself in a particularly tough game. But he didn't complain.

When Padraig Dunne and I visited him in his home a couple of months ago he was in the second half of his biggest game, playing against the wind and 10 points down but he was not giving up nor was he complaining. It was only in the last few days when the inevitable result was staring him in the face that he conceded and accepted the reality with dignity.

Liam, you were a gentle giant who didn't know your own strength. You were a great team player, you were a worthy All-Ireland and Allstar winner and on behalf of the Walsh Island and Offaly teams that we were part of I say goodbye and may your soul rest in peace here in Aglish, a place and a community I know you grew to love.'

Chapter 40
My Life In The Papers – National And Local

NEWSPAPERS have always been an important part of my life, not just in the context of my GAA activities but also as part of working life. In my time, I have seen some gigantic changes to both the production of newspapers and the style of presenting news, sport and other material in the various papers. When one visits a library and looks back at newspapers of 50 years ago, the change in the whole character of the business is amazing. At the present time the newspaper industry faces its greatest ever challenge as it attempts to compete with internet publishing which in many cases threatens the very existence of traditional newspapers.

My first involvement with the papers was in the mid-sixties with a weekly GAA paper called 'The Gaelic Weekly'. This publication was sort of an unofficial voice for the GAA but in reality it was first and foremost a commercial concern that had to pay its way. While the GAA did give some financial assistance in the early years to the paper, there was always a grudging element about it that saw the paper clinging on for existence.

My first experience in writing for a newspaper was a couple of years earlier when I was involved with the student paper in UCD under the editorship of none other than Vincent Browne. This was very much a 'pulling the divil by the tail' operation in those times but I was involved with the GAA club in UCD and my first writing assignment, believe it or not, was to cover the annual rugby Colours Match which took place on a Wednesday afternoon in November between UCD and Trinity College, Dublin. This was a rather pale imitation of the Oxford–Cambridge game in England.

I had never even attended a rugby game at this stage and The GAA Ban was still in existence. I managed to write enough about the rugby game to pass the editor's approval but that was the end of my rugby writing career.

'The Gaelic Weekly' started in the late fifties following on another GAA publication called 'The Gaelic Sportsman' and lasted to 1968 by which time it had changed to a monthly paper. The theory was that with all the GAA people involved in business, etc. there would be a ready advertising supply for the weekly paper. However that was not the case and it was always a struggle as the cost of running what was, in effect a national paper with circulation in the 32 counties, was enormous.

Many famous people wrote for the paper including former players such as Jack Mahon from Galway and Tony Wall, the Tipperary hurler. Career writers like Owen McCann and many others also contributed columns. In the early sixties, 'The Gaelic Weekly' founded what were called the Cuchulainn Awards – a sort of precursor of the Allstars scheme and these were incredibly popular until they died out in 1967.

I was a general writer and production person for the paper and it gave me a good grounding in the basics of newspaper production. I got a major break in my budding writing career in the early seventies when a vacancy arose for the lead GAA writer in The Sunday Press, then the largest newspaper in Ireland. A man called Art McGann had written that GAA page since the foundation of the paper in 1949 under the pen-name of An Fear Ciuin. When he left in the mid-seventies, he was replaced by Brendan MacLua who was an Executive Officer in Croke Park, the first such appointment, along with his fellow Clareman the former hurling star, Jimmy Smith.

MacLua was a very forceful writer, also under a pen-name because that was the rage at the time, and he also wrote a brilliant professional boxing column in The Irish Press every Friday under the pen-name of Seán O'Neill.

Then MacLua, along with a London-based Waterford-born Accountant, Tony Beatty, decided to set up the first Irish newspaper in Britain in 1970 called The Irish Post. This paper played a vital role for the Irish diaspora in the UK and was particularly important during the period of The Troubles when it gained enormous prestige mainly because of the outspoken writing in defence of the Irish community by Brendan MacLua under his own name and also under various pen names, most notably 'Frank Dolan' which had a huge following during all those troubled years.

MacLua suggested to the Sunday Press people that I would be very suitable to replace him and that is what happened. I had a pen-name as well – Donal O'Connell – and so I came from nowhere in journalism to be suddenly writing the GAA page for the largest paper in the land with a circulation of 475,000. The great Michael O'Hehir also wrote a column for the paper for many years.

I could easily have ended up in London working for The Irish Post because MacLua and myself spent several weeks before the paper's launch travelling around Britain visiting the various Irish clubs, societies etc, to promote the new paper among all the GAA clubs in particular. He wanted me to stay on in England but I decided against it. Had I gone I or Offaly 1982 would never have been heard of.

The Sports Editor of the Sunday Press, Tommy O'Hara, was one of the old-style media people and a lovely person. He was a great man for banner headlines which he used as posters for the paper in the shops. He loved doing mini-series about famous GAA players complete with those large headings. One of the biggest he used was : 'THE IRON MAN FROM RHODE' which referred to a two-part article I wrote about the legendary Offaly player Paddy McCormack as he arrived at the end of his career. Tommy wanted a dramatic headline so I provided that one and amazingly it has remained as the brand name for McCormack, and he revels in the title ever since.

Shortly after I started writing for the Sunday Press, I got one of my biggest ever exclusive stories concerning the decision of the Derry County Board to withdraw their team from the replayed 1973 National League semi-final against Kerry which took place in the early hours of the Saturday morning before the game. My story was the main item on the front page of the paper. For some reason which I've long forgotten, my own name appeared as the byline and not my more commonly used pseudonym Donal O'Connell. It was nice to get the recognition for such a big story at the time.

RTE's Seán O'Rourke had joined the Sunday Press around the same time in the news department and he didn't do too badly later on either. After many enjoyable years in The Sunday Press, the Sunday Tribune was launched in 1980 and I was offered the job as main GAA writer by the Sports Editor, Seamus Martin, which I accepted. Starting a new Sunday paper was a very challenging task but things went very well and I have no doubt the style of the sports writing was a critical factor in gathering new readers. Eamon Dunphy wrote about soccer, David Walsh was general sports writer and went on to win all the top journalism awards with the Sunday Times, having started with the Leitrim Observer newspaper.

A small but very significant column written by Eoghan Corry, then starting off in the business, proved to be very important. He was first GAA writer to give a small preview to EVERY game in the national leagues and championship. It was amazing the impact it made around the country because previously most papers only dealt with the strong counties. This was one of several innovative approaches which the Tribune people came up with and the paper achieved very good circulation figures for a good while.

It was during this period that I first encountered the great Larry

McGann and the stories of the original staunch 'Fior Gael's' life and times and this too became very popular all over the country.

I must digress at this stage to deal with another newspaper engagement that came about largely by accident. In my own native Longford the main weekly was The Longford Leader, founded in 1897, and an institution in the county. In the 1930s a new but smaller paper, the Longford News, was founded by a talented but very eccentric character, Vincent Gill. He had once been a policeman but writing was his passion and he once had material published in the famous American magazine, The New Yorker. He was in his element writing on local matters and local people, often with a very acerbic twist. For instance, under the heading of 'Town Improvements,' he once listed the names of those who had recently emigrated and on another occasion when a gap had to be filled in the front page at short notice, he printed a large black space under the heading: 'Drumlish after Dark'.

Over the years his paper acquired a small but loyal following, mostly from people in the town of Longford. In the 1970s he was in failing health and the paper struggled and eventually closed down. I got to know Vincent and I offered to help him get the paper back in business. I did so despite the presence of about a dozen cats who lived in his tiny house where his printing press was also located. I had been toying with the idea of trying to buy the paper but wasn't very serious about it and then along came Albert Reynolds, at that time an aspiring Fianna Fail TD who we all knew had the money to buy the paper. He did a deal with Vincent but admitted that he knew nothing about newspapers other than reading them.

He arranged to meet me to see if I could keep the paper going until a more long-term arrangement could be made. We met on a Christmas Day, above all days would you believe, and did a deal. The paper survived and improved and a few months later an executive from the Longford Leader, Derek Cobbe, joined the News and the paper's short-term future was secured. Albert Reynolds' interest in the Longford News was solely to promote himself in politics and how well he achieved that, eventually becoming Taoiseach in 1992. Sadly the Longford News like so many other small local papers was closed down a few years ago, having being owned at the time by Ulster Unionist politician Lord Kilcloney, also known as John Taylor.

But the Sunday Tribune closed down for a time in the middle of 1982 before resuming in 1983 and once again I found myself being asked by Vincent Browne who was the new editor of the paper, to be their main GAA writer again. Then in the late 1980s fate intervened once again when the Sports Editor of the Evening Herald, PJ Cunningham, asked me to join the Evening Herald and write my column there. PJ was a former Offaly Under-21 player during my time in charge with the Offaly senior team and won a Leinster U-21 medal in 1977 so he knew GAA affairs very well. Then when he was moved up to be Sports Editor of the Irish Independent I followed suit a short time later and I have remained there for over 20 years.

In 1982 there was an industrial dispute in The Longford Leader which closed the paper for over eight months, a lifetime in weekly newspaper terms. When a settlement was reached in November, I was appointed Managing Editor of the paper which was a full-time appointment. Getting the paper's circulation and advertising figures back to what it was before the dispute took a long time but they did recover and the paper went from strength to strength during the 22 years that I was in charge there. Being from County Longford and being well-known in GAA circles was a huge help in achieving that. I held two positions which in most other local papers would have been undertaken by two people, which meant they were very busy times for me.

Many young journalists joined The Longford Leader in my years there. In local newspaper circles, the Leader always a had a very high reputation long before I joined. For a couple of years we also had a Cavan version of the paper called the Cavan Leader and among the young lads who started working there was Damien O'Reilly, now a leading broadcaster with RTE radio where his Saturday morning programmed 'Countrywide' has a huge following in particular among the farming population. Good going for a guy who was born and reared in Blanchardstown, Co Dublin. Needless to say with a name like that he has strong Cavan connections, the Ballyjamesduff area to be precise.

Christy O'Connor, well know hurler in Clare and author of the magnificent hurling book 'Last Man Standing,' also spent some time with The Longford Leader though I doubt if that made him any more knowledgeable about hurling.

One day in The Longford Leader a big tall strap of a lad from Lanesboro arrived in more or less demanding a job and I decided to give him a try. He managed okay eventually and is now a famous television star as Midland Correspondent for RTE called Ciaran Mullooly.

Bryan O'Brien was a young trainee photographer living in Dublin but a native of Tralee and he applied for a job with The Leader. I told him, as I always did with such matters, to show me some of his work first of all and on a St Patrick's Day he travelled by bus to Longford and did the photographic coverage for the local parade in Longford town.

The moment I saw his pictures I knew we were looking at different class here and he got the job. His work was amazing and it was little wonder that after a couple of years he joined The Irish Times as a staff photographer and proceeded in subsequent years to win all the major photography prizes in the Irish media business.

There can scarcely be anything more satisfying for a journalist, including an editor, than to be working for a good local newspaper. They are full of life, cover all aspects of the county involved, cater for young and old and are generally trusted and highly regarded by the people who buy or read the newspaper. The Longford Leader would be very typical of the genre covering the entire county of

Longford but also covering important border areas in adjoining counties, Leitrim, Cavan, Roscommon and Westmeath.

GAA games between any two of those counties attracted immense coverage and were often the highlight of the sporting year in County Longford. Those neighbouring counties involved no less than three different provinces which meant of course that up to 2001 when the All-Ireland qualifiers started, Longford never played against Roscommon, Leitrim or Cavan in the All-Ireland championship. So it was over 120 years of the GAA's existence before we got a championship game between Longford and Leitrim or Cavan and indeed Longford beat both of these two when it happened a few years ago.

In GAA terms, the public in any particular county tend to rate their neighbours in terms of their standing. Cavan GAA people always regarded themselves as superior to three of the others Longford, Westmeath and Leitrim and it was hard to argue against that with their five All-Irelands and 37 Ulster titles bearing in mind that Longford, Westmeath and Leitrim between them have only won four provincial titles.

Cavan looked differently on Roscommon because of their glory days in the forties at a time when they were a match for the Breffni men, actually beating them in the 1943 All-Ireland final. In latter years, the balance between the counties has shifted quite a bit mainly because of the decline of Cavan and there is no great difference between these four counties nowadays, but the local rivalry when any pair of them meet is as strong as ever.

There is much more to local newspapers than covering GAA events and all local sports have to be covered adequately to match the explosion in sporting activity that now exists in every corner of rural Ireland.

News, court cases, special events and above all local notes are the bread and butter of local papers. Of these items, in The Longford Leader at least, the local notes are easily the most important single section of the paper. When I joined the paper, I upgraded the role of the local notes with greatly increased coverage and the name and contact number of each local correspondent was printed every week if only to give these correspondents the status in their local community that they deserved.

I was fortunate to have inherited many brilliant writers for local notes and I managed to find some more of equal quality. When a survey was carried out on the likes, dislikes, etc, among readers of The Leader, the most popular by far were those pages. Among these contributors was Cormac McGill, a schoolteacher in Leitrim who was a native of Donegal. He was a GAA fanatic, firstly in his pursuit of Donegal, where he wrote a brilliant GAA column for the Donegal Democrat under the byline 'The Follower' and also with Leitrim GAA, where for many years he was a famous adjudicator and tutor and judge for the Scor competitions. Cormac, who was the father of Croke Park Executive Fergal McGill, was a very strong nationalist and had a great love for the Irish language and often conversed with me 'as Gaeilge' especially regarding GAA affairs.

One Friday afternoon about 16 years ago we got a message that the British Ambassador was in Longford and would like to visit the local newspaper. As was our wont in The Leader nobody got too worked up about the upcoming visit. I noticed that Cormac, who was typing at a desk in the office, began to get a bit restless as the time for the visit approached. As I was passing by he whispered: 'Is maith liom dul amach' which sort of caught me on the hop before he added that he would prefer to not be on the premises when Her Majesty's Ambassador arrived. He duly abandoned his desk. He must have discussed this earlier with one of the reporters because he too decided to walk out in sympathy. That journalist, Shane MacCabe, happened to be a son of Jim McCabe who played corner-back for Cavan when they beat Meath in the 1952 All-Ireland final. When the visitor departed, normal relations in the Leader office resumed. As you can gather, the tentacles of the GAA are woven into every aspect of rural Irish society.

The bane of my time working in The Longford Leader was the threat of libel actions, something which has come to dominate the Irish media world, particularly over the past 30 years or so. Local newspapers are not immune from that nor are prominent GAA people. A few GAA presidents in my time have taken money off newspapers based on libel or defamation claims and I am sure some other prominent GAA people have done the same but they have always managed to keep these things secret.

Most newspapers will have such legal actions pending be they small or large but thankfully most never get to court and some sort of compromise is achieved. Politicians, local and national, are always on the alert for libel actions if they believe, or even imagine, their honour or their reputation has been besmirched by something written about them in a newspaper.

The most famous politician in our area was the late Albert Reynolds and we reported on his progress from a Longford councilor to becoming Taoiseach in 1992 and beyond. We never had any falling-outs with Albert but he was ever on alert for even the slightest error or even innuendo in reporting his affairs, which is fair enough.

It was clear from the start that he was never going to sue The Longford Leader, he was after all a very clever politician. Instead he insisted in having any errors or omissions he perceived be immediately corrected in the paper. Every newspaper I was involved with, national and local, had very strong GAA involvement because from the 1970s on, there was a totally different attitude in the Irish media to the GAA. One reason for that was the removal of The Ban, Rule 27, in 1971 because that removed a monkey off the GAA's back that had been disastrous for decades. The GAA then was easy meat for all sorts of cranks and plain ordinary people involved in other sports who found it very hard to like or appreciate the GAA because of the draconian nature of

The Ban and the selective manner in which the rule had been enforced over the years.

The decision by the GAA in April 1939 to remove Douglas Hyde, the first President of Ireland, from his position as Patron of the GAA because he, in his official capacity, attended a soccer match against Poland in Dublin shortly after his inauguration, did untold damage to the image of the GAA at home and abroad.

The new President was always an ardent follower of the GAA, a leader of the Gaelic League and the ultimate Fíor Gael as far as the people of Ireland were concerned. It has to be said also that from a media point of view there were many who had little time for the GAA among some devotees of soccer and rugby, though such critics were very much in a minority.

The other development that transformed GAA coverage in the media was the rise of the Dublin football team under Kevin Heffernan in 1974. For the first time really the competition between the various media outlets, newspapers, television and radio was intense thereby leading to much more coverage of GAA activities from which the GAA greatly benefitted from the seventies on. In the subsequent 40 years or so, that trend became ever more noticeable and GAA coverage today in the Irish media does actually represent the extent of GAA activity, influence and involvement with the community.

In my time writing for the various national newspapers I was regarded as something of an outsider. That is because I was somewhat removed in Longford from the inner circle of journalists who lived and worked in Dublin. For a start I was a columnist with those newspapers which is very different to being a reporter or editor. A columnist was once described to me by an American author as follows: 'He is the guy who waits 'till the battle is over, comes down from the hills and then shoots the survivors.' True to an extent but perhaps just a teeny bit over the top. And for years my late mother used to think I was actually a communist 'till some of the neighbours put her right.

A columnist does not have to concentrate on the minutiae of a game like a reporter has to do by keeping accurate statistics on all aspects of the game. Instead he or she can try to assess the overall scene and explain to people, particularly those not at the game, how the game was decided. Also it is recognised in the media business that a columnist is entitled to adapt a particular style of his or her own more so than a reporter who is expected to largely stick to facts. In other areas also I often found myself removed from the cohorts of leading GAA writers by not living in Dublin most of my life and therefore immune to that generic insult so often thrown at media people as being 'that crowd from Dublin'.

For over 25 years there used to be a function on the day after the All-Ireland final where both teams were invited to lunch and socialise with each other – at least that was the theory even if it did not always work out that way. While every Dublin-based GAA journalist of any repute would invariably be invited to these receptions, and a lot of non-GAA journalists as well, I was never issued with such an invite even though at times I was writing for the biggest newspaper in the country. I really enjoyed being able to attend two of those post All-Ireland functions on my own merit when I was entitled to attend after the 1981 and 1982 All-Ireland football finals because I was manager of one of the teams involved in those finals and they had to let me in. That was sweet.

There is no doubt that having achieved something worthwhile as a football team manager was a help in my profession as a writer on Gaelic football. At least it allowed me to refute a claim often thrown at even the best GAA writers: 'Sure what would that fella know about the game sure he was never heard of when he was playing.' The reality of course is that it is far more important for a sports journalist to be proficient at his profession of writing and analysis than his reputation as player or manager.

The development of recent years among all newspapers in Ireland and Britain to have sports performers writing columns has seriously undermined the role of full-time journalists and this particularly applies to GAA coverage nowadays. It is sad to see reputable GAA writers of long standing being downgraded in favour of a famous player whose published material has not even been written by himself but by a ghost writer. Many of the tenets of the journalism profession are set aside to facilitate these fly-by-nighters and their level of objectivity and impartiality is often far removed from what should be demanded by professional, properly trained journalists.

The arrival of a raft of new media outlets in the past decade has changed the face of old-style journalism for all time. Good writing will always stand out but the Twitter brigade and other subscribers to social media outlets have changed the face of media coverage. The fact that so much stuff is published anonymously by people not governed by the fundamental rules and traditions of print journalists is also a problem. These contributors often cause grave offence and acute embarrassment to players and mentors by their abusive comments.

Chapter 41

Honorary Degree From The National University

THIS is the text of the introductory text presented by Dr Iognáid Ó Muircheartaigh, Pro-Vice-Chancellor of the University, President, National University of Ireland, Galway, on September 20, 2007, on the occasion I was conferred with a Doctor of Laws honoris causa.

"A Sheánsailéir agus a mhuintir na hOllscoile:

Is mór an onóir domsa fear uasal, tuarisceoir den scoth, eagarthóir irise, foillsitheoir, bainisteoir fóirne peile thar cinn, agus saineolaí ar chursaí spoirt, Eugene McGee, a chur in bhúr láthair le go mbronnfar dochtúireacht oinigh air.

I hope I can be excused a personal aside before I introduce Eugene McGee this afternoon. Exactly 25 years ago from yesterday, September 19, 1982, I brought my eldest daughter, Róisín, then seven years of age, to Croke Park to see her first all-Ireland final. It was Kerry versus Offaly, and Róisín asked me which team she should cheer for. I told her 'Kerry, of course', knowing the importance of instilling basic values at an early age. All was wonderful until the final minutes, when the Séamus Darby goal dramatically ended the dream of an historic Kerry five-in-a-row.

Róisín, totally traumatised, turned to me and said: 'It's all your fault, you told me to cheer for Kerry.' She still has not forgiven me, and so it was with some mixed feelings that I accepted the honour of presenting to you Chancellor, for the conferral on him of an honorary doctorate, the manager of that Offaly team, Eugene McGee. I will return to the matter of the 1982 game later on.

Eugene McGee was born in the parish of Colmcille in north Longford, the second youngest of seven children born to Owen and Catherine McGee. His father was a national schoolteacher or 'the Master' as he would have been known in those days. Eugene had the rare distinction of being taught by his father in national school and by his brother in secondary school, the late Fr Philip McGee, a well-known GAA figure who was the last principal of Moyne secondary school and the first principal of Moyne Community School, which evolved from the Moyne Latin School, originally a hedge school and later a preparatory school for seminarians.

Eugene himself followed the family tradition of teaching for almost a year when he graduated from University College Dublin with a BA and HDip, but the attraction of journalism soon had his attention. English, he will admit, was one of his best subjects and, while at UCD, one of his first assignments was to cover a rugby match between UCD and TCD for the UCD weekly newspaper. He also wrote for the GAA weekly newspaper, Gaelic Weekly, which began publishing his articles.

After graduating from UCD he worked for the national newspapers: The Sunday Press, The Irish Press, The Sunday Tribune and the Evening Herald as GAA columnist and he worked freelance with the Longford News until his appointment with the Longford Leader.

Following a strike in the paper in 1983, Eugene became the new editor of the Leader and he was in charge of the revival of the paper which had been off the streets for the duration of the dispute. His job was to pick up the pieces and he had total editorial control. Faced with the task of making the Longford Leader the pre-eminent newspaper not just in County Longford, but in the midlands, the first step was to recover all the lost sales from the

Longford News, which he did in about six months. He personalised the paper more and brought in several technological changes. The Leader was the first provincial paper in Ireland to get agreement with the National Graphic Association over direct input, which would allow its journalists to use Amstrad computers. He also brought business and administrative changes, and in 1989 he led a management buy-out which took the paper, which was founded in 1897 by JP Farrell and had remained in the Farrell family since its foundation, out of the Farrell family completely, with himself becoming the majority shareholder and Managing Editor.

The Leader is the traditional paper in the county and that inspires loyalty in its readers. Eugene McGee's editorial policy was for the Leader to be a totally neutral paper. He also saw the paper's job as defending the local community and to speak up for the local community. The survival of the paper after the 1983 strike bears testimony to its popularity with Longford people and to the leadership and integrity which Eugene McGee has shown in running the paper.

Eugene McGee, who has given so generously to Longford, is not only known for his journalistic skills but also for his sporting achievements. He has been one of the most successful coaches and managers in Gaelic football, starting with the UCD club whom he coached to six Sigerson Cup wins as well as two Dublin championships and two All-Ireland Club titles in 1974/75. He later managed the Offaly football team which won three Leinster titles and which, as already mentioned, stopped the great Kerry team from winning the five All-Irelands in-a-row by beating them in the All-Ireland Final of 1982.

The defining moment came a few minutes from the finish when Séamus Darby scored the memorable goal which was to give Offaly a one-point victory (1-15 to 17 points) and snatch what appeared to be the Kerry team's place in history right from under their noses. He also managed the Ireland team on two occasions for the Compromise Rules International Series against

Australia, winning the 1990 series in Australia 2-1.

Eugene McGee's first book 'Classic Football Matches' was published in 1993. The book featured 30 great football games played between 1955 and 1992 and showed his great interest in and enthusiasm for Gaelic football. In 1996 his great writing skills were manifested again in 'St Mel's of Longford: A History 1865-1990', which tells the story of the diocesan college for Ardagh and Clonmacnoise since its foundation in the post-famine era of 1865 right up to 1990 and its outstanding academic and sporting record.

Eugene lives in Longford town with his wife, Marian, and children, Conor and Linda. He has been quoted as saying that the best thing he ever got out of Offaly is not the All-Ireland, but his wife! He is a man of great integrity and one of the top journalists who challenged the GAA in his sports columns on issues that others did not dare to raise, while consistently showing his interest and enthusiasm for the sport.

I had hoped that this conferral might, for my daughter Róisín and myself, exorcise the ghosts of 1982. However, I went to Croke Park again this Sunday with Róisín, and although at 32 years of age she no longer asks who to cheer for, I am pleased to say her early upbringing has borne fruit, and she arrived at the match in her Kerry jersey. And we won! But as luck would have it, Róisín nearly left the stadium before the game started, suffering severe flashbacks, when in the customary honouring of the 25th anniversary of an All-Ireland win, the aforementioned Offaly team of 1982 (amongst them the bête noir Seamus Darby) reappeared and paraded right in front of us.

Eugene McGee has been an outstanding journalist, and a great football manager and expert, and, in presenting him to you for conferral of this honorary doctorate, a Sheánsailéir, I forgive him for 1982, agus anois iarraim ort an gradam is airde atá ar fail ón Ollscoil seo a bhronnadh air, sin é Dochtúíreacht Oinigh.'

Serious Cavan men: Having finished with Offaly in 1984 I spent four happy years with Cavan and in an Anglo Celt picture, I am seen here along with Cavan selectors, Tom Dowd, Sean Farrelly, Paddy Maguire and Ray Carolan. I was the first 'outsider' to be appointed Cavan manager.

Two greats and myself: At a function of a Cavan Association in Birmingham with All-Ireland winners John Wilson and Peter Donoghue.

Medal map: This medal was presented to Mick Higgins after Cavan lost the NFL final to New York in 1950. In the shape of a map of Ireland, it had been crafted on the basis that New York would be the losers. In fact their reward for winning was Trench Coats.

Dual stars: Liam Currums (Offaly), the late Jack Lynch (Cork) and the late Frank Burke (Dublin), all dual All-Ireland winners, pictured together in Mr Burke's house in 1982. **(SEE PAGES 191–194)**

Learning process: Myself on a visit to Aston Villa, talking to the then manager Ron Saunders in the eighties, when I was studying other sports' training methods.

Academic talk: Pictured at a debate on the GAA in Trinity College Dublin in the 1980s, from left, Tom Woulfe, Joe Lennon, Jack Lynch who chaired the debate, myself, Mick Loftus and Con Murphy, the latter two former GAA presidents.

When men were men: A shot from a typical Meath-Dublin replay with the entire Meath defence, except Mick Lyons who had already been sent off, dealing with Dublin's Kieran Duff (15) and Vinnie Murphy, underneath. Meath players are Michael McQuillan, Martin O'Connell, Kevin Foley, Robbie O'Malley, Liam Harnan and Colm Coyle. How would they fare out against the current Dublin attack?

International duty: The Ireland touring part in Australia in 1990 when Ireland won the series 2-1. This was the last of the three-match series.

Back row, left to right: Danny Lynch, GAA PRO, Kerry, Noel Roche, Clare, Kevin O'Brien, Wicklow, Alan Mulholland, Galway, Keith Barr, Dublin, Jack O'Shea, Kerry, Brian Burke, Tipperary, John Grimley, Armagh, Eamon Heery, Dublin, Michael Fagan, Westmeath, Paddy Barrett, Limerick, Dermot Power, Croke Park, Paddy Collins, Referee, Westmeath. **Second row:** Ciaran O'Neill, Croke Park, Pat Comer, Galway, Mark Plunkett, Offaly, Mark Grimley,

Armagh, Pat O'Byrne, Wicklow, Eoin Liston, Kerry, Jim Stynes, Dublin and Melbourne, Bill Sex, Kildare, Val Daly, Galway, Tommy Carr, Dublin, Stephen O'Brien, Cork, Sean McCague, Assistant Manager, Monaghan. **Front row:** Brendan Hackett, Trainer, James McCartan, Down, Dessie Barry, Longford, Paul Curran, Dublin, Martin Gavigan, Vice-Captain, Donegal, John Dowling, GAA President, Robbie O'Malley, Ireland Captain, Meath, Eugene McGee, Ireland Team Manager, Longford, Bernard Flynn, Meath, Tony Scullion, Derry, Kevin Fagan, Dublin, Amy Johnson, Physio. Absent: Frank Kenny, Tour Manager, Roscommon. **(SEE PAGES 179–183)**

Extra, extra: Three months before 'The Ban' was officially voted out at Congress in Belfast in 1971, I wrote this story for the Sunday Press under my then pseudonym of Donal O'Connell. **(SEE PAGES 239–251)**

Read all about it: This was the heading on page 1 of the Sunday Press on the day that Derry refused to play Kerry in a league semi-final in 1973. This was an exclusive story that I had written when the Sunday Press was the paper with the largest circulation in Ireland.

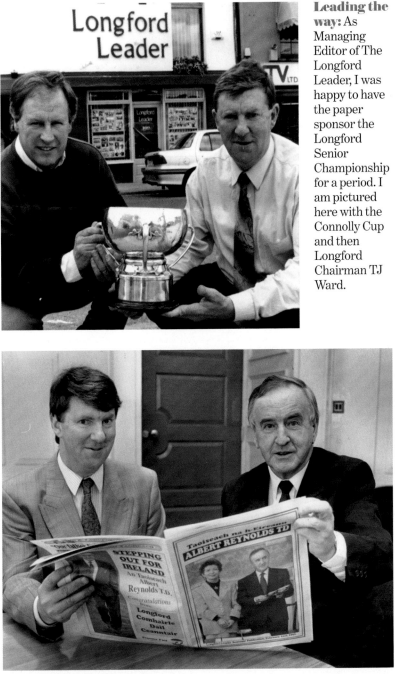

Leading the way: As Managing Editor of The Longford Leader, I was happy to have the paper sponsor the Longford Senior Championship for a period. I am pictured here with the Connolly Cup and then Longford Chairman TJ Ward.

Political interlude: At the launch of a special supplement by The Longford Leader to mark the election of Albert Reynolds as Taoiseach in 1992.

Honours even: At the awarding of an honorary degree to my brother Páid last year in St Patrick's College, Drumcondra, are my sisters Ita and Evangeline, along with Páid and myself.

Proud day: Pictured at the graduation from Trinity College, Dublin of my son Conor are my wife Marian, daughter Linda, Conor and myself.

In full flight: Our daughter Linda hard at work on her bicycle at St Christopher's Services, Longford.

(SEE PAGES 231–234)

The easiest degree I ever received: At the ceremony at the National University of Ireland after receiving my Degree of Doctor of Laws *honoris causa*.
(SEE PAGES 253–257)

Medal of honour: My late brother-in-law Liam O'Connor (above left) is presented with a medal to mark the 25th anniversary of Offaly's victory over Kerry by former GAA President Nickey Brennan in 2007.

In memory: My late brother Phil (left) was heavily involved with Longford GAA and was also in the Education and Pioneer movement. He had a ground named after him in Colmcille's, Longford (below).

Fr Phil McGee Park
Pairc an Ath Mac Aodha

Ready for action: Matt Connor (above) as a young member of the Offaly senior team. Matt always took home a supply of footballs after training so that he could practise his place kicking, with good effect as his incredible scoring records proves.
(SEE PAGES 299–302)

The bosses: Fr Sean Heaney, County Chairman and John Dowling County Secretary who were in charge of Offaly GAA when the county won both hurling and football All-Irelands, 1981 and 1982.
(SEE PAGES 275–276)

The greatest: Mick O'Dwyer is entitled to be called the best manager in GAA history because of the diverse range of his contributions across several counties. If class is a measurement of success, then Micko was the best. **(SEE PAGES 288–290)**

Unsung heroes: It is for his loyalty to his native county that I identify Declan Browne (above, receiving the Tommy Murphy Cup from Sean Kelly) as a person I greatly admire and I respect him and all the other great players, like Longford's Paul Barden (inset), whose pride in their native county was at the heart of their football career. **(SEE PAGES 265-267)**

Media stars: Liz Howard was one of the first female media people involved in the GAA and appeared on The Sunday Game in the early years after it started in 1979. **(SEE PAGE 280)**

Class act: Micheál Ó Muircheartaigh's commentaries may be gone but that voice will never be forgotten by GAA people. **(SEE PAGES 271–272)**

Jimmy's winning matches: Donegal's Jim McGuinness deserves great credit for his bravery in breaking the shackle of conservatism in football. **(SEE PAGE 290–292)**

Officialdom: Speaking at the press conference to announce the National Football Development Committee's recommendations at Croke Park in November, 1999.

The commmittee that gets things done: GAA President Liam Ó Néill (seated left) with myself as FRC Chairman, along with other members of the FRC, from left, Kevin Griffin, secretary, Tim Healy, John Tobin, Tony Scullion, Killian Burns and Paul Earley at the official launch of the First Report of the FRC. Absent from the picture was Ciaran McBride **(SEE PAGES 163–171)**

Relief: Along with FRC secretary Kevin Griffin and FRC member Tony Scullion immediately after the vote was announced at the 2013 Congress in Derry.

Pros and cons: Every other sport that was previously amateur, most notably athletics, rugby union and cricket have traversed the road to professionalism and often it was a confrontational road that caused a lot of disputes and aggravation. Were the GAA to agree to bring in some form of pay-for-play in the future, it need not be so contentious. **(SEE PAGES 311–320)**

The following article appeared in the Longford Leader in September 2007, (after I had left might I add).

'Dr McGee I presume?

Ex-Longford Leader Editor, former all-Ireland winning manager and renowned GAA commentator Eugene McGee is to get one more descriptor before his name, that of Dr.

Eugene, whose 1982 Offaly side famously denied Kerry an unprecedented fifth Senior Football All-Ireland with a dramatic last minute goal, is to receive an honorary doctorate from the National University of Ireland, the Longford Leader has learned.

And appropriately it will be a date in September, some 25 years after his most famous outing to Croke Park, on which Eugene – who lives with his wife Marian and children Conor and Linda on the Battery Road, Longford – will receive the honour.

As well as his exploits in Gaelic Games however, Eugene – originally from Colmcille – is being honoured by the NUI for his overall contribution to Irish life, particularly, according to the citation, for providing an authentic voice for a rural Irish community through his work with The Longford Leader where he was Editor for 22 years. Eugene will receive an LLD or doctorate of law from the National University of Ireland directly, which is one of the highest honours available in the state. In so doing Eugene becomes the first Longfordian to receive a doctorate from the Central Council of the National University of Ireland since the poet Pauric Colum, a fellow native of Colmcille, who received a similar award in 1951. More recently Liam Mulvihill, Director General of the GAA received an honorary doctorate from NUI Maynooth, which is a constituent college of the NUI.

Joining Eugene at the conferring ceremony in September will be Dunnes CEO and entrepreneur Margaret Heffernan, former FG Donegal TD Paddy Harte (OBE), being honoured for his work in commemorating Irish people in World War I; renowned pianist Hugh Tinney, and historian Margaret McCurtain.'

Chapter 42

Fifty Football People Who Mattered To Me

I N nominating 50 people for special mention in my book, I am not in any way classifying them in order of preference. I simply wish to acknowledge a selection of GAA people for whom I have had great respect over the years, be they players, managers or administrators. As with everything in my book these are personal opinions based on my own lifetime involved with Gaelic football. The GAA represents the most accurate cross-section of Irish life that is available and I hope these personalities adequately reflect that too.

*   *   *

M ICHAEL O'HEHIR was arguably the best-known person in the GAA for about 50 years in the last century because of his radio and television commentaries on Gaelic games from 1936 to 1985. He was also the best publicist the GAA ever had in the days before television and at a time when even radio sets were few and far between and daily newspapers were only bought by a handful of people in rural Ireland.

His actual voice was distinctive with a sharp, clearly defined sound while his own distinctive set of phrases and words such as 'schemozzle' meant he was imitated in every school village and GAA pub in Ireland for nearly 50 years. In all, he commentated on 99 All-Ireland finals and it was a cruel twist of fate, which denied him the 100th commentary because he suffered a stroke in the weeks preceding that All-Ireland.

I have always felt that O'Hehir was treated somewhat less than generously by the GAA. He should have been identified in history more clearly by having one of the stands named after him so that his name would be alive forever more in a GAA context in Croke Park. The esteem with which he was held was exemplified in 1987 when the 1947 Polo Grounds All-Ireland was commemorated in Croke Park. While the survivors of those teams got a rousing reception, it was the huge standing ovation from the large crowd for Michael O'Hehir when he was wheeled onto the pitch which dominated the day and showed the respect GAA people had for the best publicist the association ever had.

There are many great snippets of commentary from Michael which have survived in GAA folklore but I will show my bias by naming just one in relation to the closing moments of the 1982 All-Ireland final, Offaly v Kerry. 'And they look as if they were winning the way Offaly are dithering and dawdling ... and here they come. This is Liam Connor the full-back... a high lobbing, dropping ball towards the goalmouth... a shot and a GOAL, a GOAL, a goal for Offaly There was a goal in it! Oh, what a goal!'

RAYMOND SMITH was a sort of Boswell for the GAA for about 30 years in that he was the first journalist who went to the trouble of chronicling the games of football and hurling in his own lifetime in the second half of the last century. Books such as 'The Football Immortals', 'Decades of Glory', 'The Book of Hurling' and many similar titles were eagerly sought out by GAA followers all over the country. Smith, a dyed-in-the-wool Tipperary man, was an effervescent, larger than life journalist who specialised in news and politics as well as covering GAA games. He had a wonderful way of cutting through the hyperbole and silly chit-chat so beloved of sports people. Smith always got through to the leading players and administrators and his use of direct quotations was particularly effective.

For many years he filled a vacuum regarding GAA literature

until many more GAA writers began to have books published during the last 20 years or so.

JOE LENNON was the man who can justifiably claim that he introduced the concept and practice of coaching into Gaelic football just as Fr Tommy Maher did for hurling. Joe was from Poyntzpass, Co Down and had a distinguished playing career, winning All-Irelands in 1960 and '61 and was captain of Down when they beat Offaly in that 1961 final in front of the biggest crowd ever to attend a GAA game.

Joe qualified as a teacher in England before studying in Loughborough College of Education, then one of the premier colleges involved in sports education where he obtained a First Class Honours Diploma in Physical Education and then taught in Gormanston College in Co Meath.

He faced serious opposition when he broached the notion of coaching in football and most of the leading GAA officials of the day were very much against the whole idea. In 1964 he published his first book, 'Coaching Gaelic Football for Champions' and later 'Fitness for Gaelic Football'.

It was in 1964 that together with a number of other people, he directed the first national coaching course in Gormanston, something that launched the concept of coaching as an integral part of the promotion and expansion of Gaelic football. Joe is certainly entitled to be regarded as one of the key figures in the development of Gaelic football since 1960.

JAMES McCARTAN (Down) was the most important player in the historic arrival of Down as a major football force for the first time when they won the Ulster title in 1959. The following year they made history by beating Kerry in the All-Ireland final and thus brought the Sam Maguire Cup across The Border for the first time. The year after that Down completed back to back victories by beating Offaly in a close encounter.

In a team full of quality players, notably Sean O'Neill and Paddy Doherty, McCartan was the one to lead Down into battle into then unknown territory and his controversial penalty in the 1960 semi-final that earned his team a draw against Offaly epitomised the stature of the man.

SEAN PURCELL from Galway is generally regarded as among the five best footballers the game has ever seen. I was fortunate to see him play towards the end of his career and his performance in Galway's All-Ireland win in 1956 over Cork showcased his greatness. He built up an uncanny football connection with his great friend from Tuam, Frank Stockwell, and they were legendary in football folklore as 'The Terrible Twins'. Purcell played in all the pivotal positions for Galway and excelled in each of them.

JIM McKEEVER was arguably the greatest midfielder the game has seen alongside Mick O'Connell in the days when high-fielding of the ball was the supreme skill in Gaelic football. A native of Ballinascreen, he was instrumental in Derry's shock defeat of Kerry in the 1958 All-Ireland semi-final and even though they lost to Dublin in the final, Jim was selected as Footballer of the Year.

He took a leading role after his playing days in the advancement of coaching and had an immense influence over many young county players in Ulster when he taught in St Mary's Training College, Belfast for most of his career.

MICHAEL KEARINS spent most of his playing career with struggling Sligo football teams but on those years when he had decent support, his brilliance shone out countrywide. His free-taking from all angles and distances set him apart in that department but it was also matched in his ability to score from play. For many years he stood out as a beacon of hope for other great players who played for weaker counties and rarely got a chance to share the limelight. Michael had the honour of leading his county in an All-Ireland semi-final against Kerry in 1975. He was also one of the last ex-players to take up refereeing to national standards.

BRIAN McENIFF is on my list mainly because of his perseverance in driving Donegal to the ultimate prize when the county won its first All-Ireland in 1992. Brian stood out for many years as a player of national distinction when Donegal were often quite poor and did not get much recognition from the rest of the country as a football force. But he kept driving standards for Donegal to aim for and he was legendary in seeking advice from mentors from other counties who he felt could be of assistance in his own cause. It was his dedication and his sheer love for his native county that was instrumental in that breakthrough success for the county.

As manager of the Ulster Railway Cup team along with his good friend Art McRory from Tyrone he was in charge, among other wins, of a six-in-a-row series in the 1990s.

TONY HANAHOE wasn't regarded as one of the flag-carriers of the great Dublin teams of the seventies but his role in all those successes was never doubted by his own colleagues or by those who looked beneath the surface of superficiality when analysing how teams achieve success at the highest levels.

As a centre-forward, he had many similarities with Seán Purcell as his mixture of keen intellect, exceptional vision off the ball and high-quality passing ability set up numerous scores for his colleagues. As captain, he was one of the few to collect the Sam Maguire Cup twice, in 1976 and '77, and his decisive leadership qualities complemented Kevin Heffernan's own unique qualities in that regard.

BRIAN MULLINS was cast in the heroic context of Gaelic football because he was a big, flamboyant player, an outstanding high-fielder. powerful when carrying the ball and immensely strong in every aspect of his play. He was seen as the guardian angel of the Dublin team – if there was a problem to be sorted in a match he was the man do it, regardless of what was required.

It was no wonder he was a folk hero for the Dubs' followers and his ferocious competitiveness was central to everything the Dublin teams of the seventies stood for. For the fans he could take on and beat the best of the country players from any county and therefore he held a special place in their hearts. His recovery from a near-fatal car crash in 1980 simply epitomised his bravery and he became a key figure in guiding a young Dublin team to All-Ireland victory over Galway in 1983.

MARTIN FURLONG of Offaly was one of the last of the old-time goalkeepers, the sort of men who were utterly fearless at a time when football was a lot harder and more dangerous than it is today. He had a remarkable career for Offaly from when he won a minor All-Ireland in 1964 to 1985, three years after he played in his last All-Ireland in 1982.

He was famous for attacking the high ball coming into his area and also for attacking any forward who dared contest a 50-50 ball inside his own square. As a result, most forwards decided to let the hare sit and see what resulted from the dropping ball rather than contest with Furlong. As a footballer, he never looked like a top-class athlete but his timing always made up for a lack of speed.

His penalty save against Mike Sheehy in the 1982 All-Ireland final was one of the decisive moments of the game as had it been scored, Kerry would have gone four points clear and on their way. Martin was one of the relatively few players to have won All-Ireland medals 11 years apart, 1971 to 1982.

DECLAN BROWNE was a very special footballer based purely on his technical ability as a player. But he was much more than that because his inter-county playing career was confined to lining out for his native Tipperary and as everybody knows, that virtually guaranteed that he could never achieve anything substantial as the county faced the near impossible task of beating Kerry or Cork or even both to win a Munster championship medal. As a footballer the fact that he won Allstars playing with one of the so-called weaker counties shows how his greatness was fully accepted by GAA people all over Ireland.

His loyalty despite being touted by several counties over the years and given many 'attractive' offers, strikes at the very heart of what the GAA is all about – loyalty with one's own parish and county. That showed in his pride when he climbed the Hogan Stand in Croke Park and collected the Tommy Murphy Cup after a thrilling game with Wexford in which the wider GAA world really appreciated how good he was.

It is for his loyalty to his own native county that I identify Declan Browne as a person I greatly admired and I respected him and all the other great players from such counties whose pride in their native county was at the heart of their football career.

ENDA COLLERAN was a member of one of the best football teams I have seen in my time, Galway, when they won three successive All-Irelands in 1964/'65/'66. There were many fantastic players on that team but Enda Colleran was a brilliant corner back in the days when playing in that position required specific skills that are not around in the modern game.

Enda was a master of his craft and one of the few corner-backs to rely solely on skill to beat his opponent. In those times physical power rather than skill was seen as the most important component for corner-back play. Enda was also a wonderful ambassador for his county when they were in the limelight all those years. He became the first prominent analyst on The Sunday Game and with all due respects to the many famous figures that have featured on the programme since, I would regard Enda Colleran as on a par with any of them and better than the vast majority. Sadly he died a relatively young man aged 62 in 2004. Enda was selected on both the Team of the Century and the Team of the Millennium, some honour.

TONY SCULLION from Ballinascreen was one of the hardest defenders I have known who did not specialise in being a tough man for the sake of it. He was essentially a great man-marker as many an Ulster player, and Derry colleague, will vouch for but he relied on the skills of the defender's role first of all. In a team in the early eighties that had a lot of big men Tony Scullion was regarded as small in stature but like so many players of that era it seemed as if he always compensated, and more, by sheer hard work and a great sense of anticipation. But Tony has done far more for the GAA than just helping Derry win an All-Ireland in 1993. He has been corner-stone of his club Ballinascreen, starred for Ulster for a decade and played for Ireland with distinction in Australia in 1990.

Then in recent years he has worked as a full-time Coaching Officer with the Ulster Council where he is extremely highy regarded in the entire province. As a member of the Football Review Committee in recent years I saw at first hand how dedicated he is to making Gaelic football one of the greatest sports in the world and getting rid of the distasteful habits of recent years that have damaged the fabric of the game. He had the courage to face up to some difficult decisions in administration but he never flinched from doing the right thing – just as in his playing days.

PAUL BARDEN was a player I first got to know when I was involved in the management of the Longford minor team and from the first time I watched him it was clear he was a very special talent. In a county like Longford however having such talent as Paul had is not enough to make a major impact. He also must have a fairly decent set of 15 to 20 players representing the county otherwise a player like Paul is doomed to remain in the backwoods of the game usually labouring in Division 3 or 4 of the national league. And indeed that has been Paul Barden's fate for most of his career. Thankfully in the modern game great talent such as he has can be seen nationwide through television coverage which was not the case with similar players away back. The rare enough coverage Longford got on television over Paul's career did enlighten the wider GAA audience about his talent.

Like so many of the players I am describing in this section Paul is a model footballer in every sense, a brilliant forward, most unassuming and extremely dedicated to his club Clonguish and his county.

In Longford you can play for the county for a dozen years or more, as Paul has, and win next to nothing and Paul's main prize was an O'Byrne Cup medal and recognition by being named on Leinster teams. But a player like him means so much to the people of Longford by his demeanour and his brilliant football skills and because he is one of the best players in Ireland AND he represents Co Longford. Of course it is a great mystery how Paul Barden has never been selected as an Allstar even though on at least three occasions he seemed the obvious person to be named only to be passed over by a player from one of the strong counties. But Paul Barden will be remembered far longer in Longford than many players from strong counties who collected Allstars.

MICKEY HARTE is entitled to be rated as one of the best managers over the past 50 years if only because he managed Tyrone to three All-Ireland final wins. Apart from Mick O'Dwyer, Kevin Heffernan and Sean Boylan, no other manager has achieved that in this period. He is unusual in that he carefully laid the groundwork for senior success by managing Tyrone minor and

U-21 teams to All-Ireland success before taking over as Tyrone senior manager and he made maximum use of the best of those underage players to win those senior titles.

The local rivalry with Armagh was the focal point for Tyrone's period of supremacy and if it was Armagh who got their hands on the Sam Maguire Cup first in 2002 it was Tyrone under Harte who controlled Ulster football for the following almost 10 years. It was unusual as football records go for a county to win three All-Irelands over five years without retaining the title even once but the longevity at the top which Mickey Harte maintained outweighs that statistic.

Mickey Harte developed and perfected his own particular Tyrone style of football. It was strong, robust, unorthodox in positioning and heavily dependent on players showing fluidity of movement from their traditional positioning to hunting in packs when attacking and defending. The iconic pictures of five or six Tyrone players surrounding a Kerry opponent in some of these games caused much controversy but Tyrone followers never worried about that and will forever be grateful for the imagination and bravery of Harte in devising playing methods that best suited HIS set of players which after all is the ultimate test of any football manager.

DECLAN DARCY played a vital role in Leitrim's historic success when they won the Connacht senior title for the first time since 1927 by beating Mayo in the final in Hyde Park, Roscommon in 1994. The historical aspect to this victory was immense as Leitrim, a county always decimated by emigration, never seemed likely to regain a Connacht title after decades of failure and often dismal failure. But inspired by a couple of good underage teams and boosted by the recruitment of Mayoman John O'Mahony as team manager suddenly out of nowhere there appeared the prospect of a football miracle.

And Leitrim had to do it the hard way that year by beating

Roscommon, Galway in a replay and Mayo in the final when Jack O'Shea was manager. As the games went by that summer the excitement grew with each passing week and at Connacht final time the emotion among Leitrim people from the county and the thousands of emigrants who came home for the final was very tangible. Declan Darcy was not alone a great footballer but he was a natural leader and in that capacity he played a pivotal role in Leitrim's success. Amazingly, Declan was born and reared in the Ballsbridge area of Dublin 4 but he played all his club football with his father's native parish Aughawillan so he was very familiar with the roads from Dublin 4 to Leitrim.

Declan is finished playing now but he has joined the backroom team of Dublin football manager Jim Gavin where the qualities that meant so much to Leitrim in 1994 are evident in the capital nowadays.

MICK HIGGINS was a very famous Cavan footballer winning three All-Irelands; he was one of a few former players to train his own county to provincial titles four times; and he trained Longford (1968) and Donegal (1972) to their first provincial successes. He was also a leading inter-county referee.

It is almost impossible to appreciate nowadays the sporting environment into which Mick Higgins was thrust shortly after his parents decided to return from America when he was 10 years old. This was not a mere GAA star, this was a sporting icon of his time to match contemporaries such as Ring and Mackey, Jackie Kyle in rugby and Jackie Carey in soccer, national figures who transcended the bounds of their own sport and captured

Mick Higgins played in six finals, starting at the age of 20 in 1943 – including a return to his native city for the 1947 final in the Polo Grounds, New York – and finishing by collecting the Sam Maguire Cup after the defeat of Meath in a replay in 1952 when he scored 0-7 of Cavan's total of 0-9.

There were many iconic figures in Cavan in those times, whose names still are remembered, such as the great leader John Joe O'Reilly, the first man to collect the Sam Maguire twice in succession; Phil 'The Gunner' Brady, who made lads like Francie Bellew look like friendly kittens; Peter Donoghue, one of the greatest of all free-takers and Tony Tighe, Higgins' alter ego, with whom he had a telepathic understanding in attacking play.

He was inveigled to train Longford and the county reached their first Leinster final in '65, beat the great Galway team in the League final in '66 and won their one and only Leinster title in '68 beating Dublin, Offaly and Meath – then All-Ireland champions – along the way. No wonder Mick Higgins was revered in Longford!

In 1972, when Donegal were struggling to make a breakthrough, Mick came to their aid and got them to their first Ulster title, along with Brian McEniff. But there was hardly a county in Ulster where he did not provide expertise and instil confidence, at that time often lacking in Ulster, and he never looked for a penny in return.

Mick was also an outstanding referee, at times when games were genuinely tough, as opposed to the 'shapers' who think so at present. There was a legendary 'Battle of Ballinascreen' in the late 1950s when Derry played Down in the Ulster semi-final, a game that really lived up to the label. Even though Mick was training Cavan, who were awaiting the winners in the final, such was their respect for him that both counties were happy to have him.

The most modest superstar I ever met, Mick granted himself only one small boast, that he never hit a cowardly blow and never got sent off. That distinction defined his whole life and ensured that he was the most loved players of them all among Cavan people. One wonders how many of the 'greats' of the present time will be able to carry that badge of honour to their grave as Mick did.

I was fortunate to become very friendly with Mick Higgins in his later life because in the pantheon of the best 50 footballers of all time he would certainly rank very high.

LIAM CURRUMS was only the 14th player in the first 98 years of the GAA to win All-Ireland senior medals in both football (1982) and hurling (1981). He played in both finals in 1981 and could have been the first man to win the All-Ireland double in the same year had not Kerry beaten the footballers in 1981. That honour eventually went to the great Teddy McCarthy of Cork in 1990.

Liam was a natural, brilliant hurler but a 'made' footballer and it was his natural speed off the mark that made him a special player in an era when Kerry players like Ger Power and Pat Spillane were setting new standards for speed of movement around a Gaelic football pitch. Currums had many a joust with Power and it was often fascinating to observe their contests of speed in the rapidly moving play that was caused by the arrival of the handpass in the late seventies.

He will be specially remembered in Offaly for getting the opening score of that famous 1982 All-Ireland final when after about eight minutes and no score on the board from either team he took off from his wing halfback position on a solo run, kept going past several opponents and lofted over a magnificent point from about 40 yards to set the tone for Offaly's performance. The night before that final at the team talk the Offaly manager had instructed Liam Currums under no circumstance to go kicking the ball but to handpass to a colleague because kicking was not exactly his strongest point. But lo and behold, off he goes to score that spectacular point and the manager said then 'After seeing Currums kick a point like that Offaly can't lose this match!'

MICHEÁL Ó MUIRCHEARTAIGH the rightful heir to the great Michael O'Heihir, this native speaker from west Kerry remarkably transcended the arrival of television, the internet and Facebook to still become the most liked and listened to sports commentator in Ireland for over 30 years. His biggest asset, as with all great sports commentators, was his voice, crystal clear and sharp and of course he added in that special facility of being totally bi-lingual and his interjections as Gaeilge even at the heat of battle in a big championship match was so accepted even by listeners who did not understand Irish that it was accepted as part of the Ó Muircheartaigh package of brilliant language expression.

His knowledge of the people involved in GAA games was phenomenal and much of that was gained by his never-ending visits to every corner of Ireland to carry out GAA events of all kinds but especially to schools at all levels. His ability to be universally popular in an age when media people are usually polarised, particularly GAA media people, was truly amazing and you hardly ever heard a harsh word said against the man.

But what made Micheál so good for so long was his feel for the games and the players. He regarded himself as an integral part of every game and not just because he visited dressing rooms before the games but because of his natural affinity for GAA games and of course the Irish language. His ability to stitch in messages to GAA connected people from San Francisco to Lyreacrompane and from Outer Mongolia to Hackballscross while commentating in the heat of a Munster hurling or All-Ireland final was breathtaking at times and his tales of greyhound and other sporting exploits marked him out as the definition of a true Irishman in the best sense of the word. Irish sport, and particularly the GAA were very fortunate to have Micheál Ó Muircheartaigh to adorn the English and Irish language with such brilliance on behalf of GAA games and already since his well deserved retirement he is sorely missed by thousands of GAA people. The commentaries may be gone but that voice will never be forgotten by GAA people.

SEAMUS DARBY will never be forgotten as long as Gaelic football lives on and that is mainly because of his historic goal in the 1982 All-Ireland final. The goal changed the course of GAA history by preventing Kerry doing what has still never been done, winning five successive All-Irelands. But it is a mistake to regard Darby's achievement as just a one-goal wonder. People forget he is one of a fairly small number of players to have won senior All-Irelands at 10-year intervals as did his fellow Offaly colleagues of 1982, Sean Lowry and Martin Furlong. Easy to forget also that in the 1982 Leinster final Seamus Darby scored 1-3 against Dublin but he missed the semi-final because of injury.

Often forgotten also is the quality of that goal as the conditions were very poor with wind and rain at the time and he had very little time after he collected the ball from the late Liam O'Connor to act before Kerry defenders descended on him. If there was ever a definition of pressure in sport that was surely it. The actual strike was also high quality because it rose up through the flight and actually went over the head of Charlie Nelligan the Kerry goalkeeper who was a very big man. Thankfully the DVD is there to show the brilliance of that particular kick under the most demanding of circumstances.

Inevitably it is the score that changed football history that will be attached to Seamus Darby's name forever more and it is great to see that he has long ago got accustomed to his historic achievement and is not allowing his life to be dominated by it. While the team ethic is everything in sport generally an achievement such as Darby's on September 19, 1992 still gives the player concerned the right to have immense personal satisfaction and pride because of that momentous score.

JOHN KERRY O'DONNELL would have probably revelled in being described as a Maverick within the GAA system for the best part of 50 years. He lived most of his life in New York and was a native of Gleann na Gealt near Camp in County Kerry. In the 1940s, when the GAA centre in The Bronx was in danger of being lost to the GAA, O'Donnell was involved in retaining the ground and for 60 years or more he and his family controlled Gaelic Park.

He became a wealthy man from his own business operations and he became the most important person in the GAA in New York. He played a leading role in the staging of the 1947 All-Ireland between Cavan and Kerry in The Polo Grounds.

As time went by John Kerry began to get more involved in connections between the GAA in New York, under his control largely, and the GAA back in Ireland. He organised annual charity games called the Cardinal Cushing games whereby he selected small groups of leading hurlers and footballers to play exhibition games in New York and Boston. Later again games began to take place between the New York teams and teams from Ireland and by 1952 these had reached the level of New York playing the winners of the National League ether in Ireland or New York.

O'Donnell always regarded New York as a sort of independent body not officially part of the parent GAA in Ireland thus leading to many rows over various matters and running battles with the Central Council which he reveled in. But in those days the thrill of getting a free all-expenses trip to play football or hurling in America was a powerful attraction for players and officials and O'Donnell knew that. He was able to manipulate his way to achieve things for New York that no county in Ireland managed to do. He once got nominated by Kerry and Longford to stand for GAA president but got a very poor vote. Famously for the League final of 1966, he managed to have a brother of two of the New York players, the Nolans from Offaly referee the two-leg matches. Hard to believe, but true!

Often in GAA and other matters O'Donnell was generous to a fault but he also ruled New York GAA with an iron fist. Without his initiatives, it is doubtful if Gaelic Park would have survived and for decades it was the focal point for Irish emigrants to meet every summer and autumn Sunday. Many an Irish couple traced their marriage in NY to meeting in Gaelic Park. Countless fundraising events took place there and numerous teams and other groups from Ireland travelled to New York on fundraising expeditions which John Kerry O'Donnell usually facilitated. A hard man but a fair man best describes the maverick GAA person that was John Kerry O'Donnell.

FR SEAN HEANEY AND JOHN DOWLING Since this is a personal book, I have no hesitation in including these two men as very special to me. As chairman and secretary of the Offaly County Board in the years I was involved in that county they presided over the most successful period that Offaly ever had, winning All-Irelands in hurling and football. These were hectic times for Offaly GAA teams in the late seventies and early eighties highlighted by they winning their first hurling All-Ireland in 1981.

For a small county like Offaly which was split geographically that time about 50-50, between football in the north of the county and hurling in the south, managing the county board at the time was not easy. Club games had to be fitted in, and were, even though in 1981 Offaly had both teams playing in All-Ireland finals. The necessary finance had to be organised to train the teams and of course striking a balance between hurling and football was always something these two men had to be conscious of.

John Dowling had been a long-serving county board officer before I arrived and as a fairly conservative one he was probably wary of me as I had no experience of county football. It was Fr Heaney who approached me to go to Offaly and in fairness to Dowling he gave me full co-operation even though some of the ideas I was introducing to Offaly were not to his liking initially. But he had an overriding desire to do what was best for the Offaly teams and gave me every assistance as indeed he did with Dermot Healy in hurling who was brought in from Kilkenny. Taking in two outsiders at that time for two fairly high-profile team assignments was a risk for both Fr Heaney and John Dowling and not surprisingly there was some criticism from the locals. But they were strong individuals and the combination of their collective knowledge of the county and the intense desire in he county for success allowed Fr Heaney and John Dowling to lead from the front and this was the key to their great success in charge of Offaly GAA along with several other top-class county board members. It was no coincidence that John later went on to be a very competent President of the GAA itself having earlier been chairman of the Leinster Council and of course he was also one of the most outstanding referees in both codes ever seen.

In fairness, Offaly had a history of 'outsiders' being in charge of their county teams going back to 1960 when the great Peter O'Reilly from Dublin trained the football team that contested three All-Ireland semi-finals and a final against Down. When Offaly footballers won their first minor All-Ireland in 1964, the basis of their subsequent All-Ireland victories of 1971/'72 Fr Tom Gillooly from Westmeath was trainer and he was also in charge for those two senior All-Irelands.

Those were great years for the GAA in Offaly and for their dedicated supporters in both codes. The steady hands of Fr Sean Heaney and John Dowling were critical in ensuring that all the various components required for All-Ireland success at organisational level and the setting of high standards all round were ever present in County Offaly while I was involved with the Faithful County.

TOMMY MORAN was Leitrim county secretary for many years including the glorious period that culminated in 1994 when Leitrim won the Connacht senior final for the first time since 1927. He was a very efficient county board officer but he was much mor than that. Leitrim is a very small county with the smallest population in Ireland, under 30,000, and a consequent small GAA population also. In addition some of the best football talent in County Leitrim has consistently emigrated to find work and the old saying that Leitrim could field a stronger football team based in New York than in Leitrim was not entirely untrue. Emigration has been ever-present in Leitrim like no other county in the country.

It was in that context that Tommy Moran, a national school teacher, played such an important role in the GAA in the county simply by being an optimist, a wonderful public relations person for the county and always presenting the positive image of Leitrim even when things were dire from a GAA point of view as they often were. In a county like Leitrim a person like Tommy Moran fulfills a very important role because he stands up there to defend his county and to instil self-confidence and belief in the face of despair.

Leitrim, despite its logistical problems is now a thriving GAA unit with clubs in every parish and lots of young players emerging at underage level. Success is measured in different terms in Leitrim to Kerry, Dublin or Galway and it is a debatable point as to which are the most successful counties in promoting what the GAA stands for, the glamour counties with unlimited resources of man and women power and financial resources or a county like Leitrim who are constantly forced to operate under miserly conditions. Tommy Moran would no doubt opt for his native county in that regard and it is hard to disprove him. Tommy also had time to become a top-class referee at inter-county level and of course he is a top-of-the-range MC at public events in the county and is also a member of the Connacht Council. But above all he is a great ambassador for county Leitrim and when your county is not very successful on the playing fields this is very important.

ART McRORY'S name will not roll of people's tongues like happens with Mickey Harte or Peter Cavavan in some parts of Ireland but Art's role in the modern-day lofty position which Tyrone enjoys nationally should never be underestimated. Through the education system in the Six Counties he was ever present as a promoter of all that is best in the GAA and on the inter-county front he was in charge of numerous Tyrone teams of all age-groups over many years.

Along with Brian McEniff of Donegal he formed the most successful Railway Cup management team of all time for over two decades and I know that players from that province really looked forward to working with Art McRory and regarded it as a major perk to be involved with Ulster.

Art went very close to guiding Tyrone to their first All-Ireland title in 1986 when they lost to Kerry and again when they had a heart-breaking one point defeat to Dublin in a very controversial finish involving a dubious foul awarded against Peter Canavan in the 1995 final when Art was joint manager with Eugene McKenna. He has spent over 30 years working at the coalface of Tyrone football and I am sure many county and ex-county players are very grateful for his guidance during their formative years when he worked for the GAA in Vocational Schools system, a system that has served Tyrone football very well over the years.

On top of all that Art McRory is a very friendly gentleman and presented a great image for Tyrone football when manager. When teams assume greatness as Tyrone footballers have it is important to remember the people who laid the groundwork for those achievements and Art McRory is certainly in that category. I had the pleasure of working on the Football Development Committee, 1997-2000 where he was a very astute contributor on the structures of the football championship.

He was always mad about greyhounds too, but that never did a GAA person any harm!

DR MICK LOFTUS from Mayo was an outstanding player, All-Ireland referee and President of the GAA 1985-1988. He was one of the very few leading GAA officials prepared to stand out against sponsorship of alcohol companies in the GAA when he steadfastly opposed the Guinness sponsorship of the All-Ireland hurling championship. As county coroner for Mayo for many years Mick experienced at first hand the tragedy of drink driving and other alcohol related deaths and was prepared to stand out from the rest of the GAA on this matter of principle.

For many years he refused to attend the All-Ireland hurling final because of the alcohol connection and he was much admired for his stance. Many other prominent GAA people privately agreed with that stance but did not have the courage to stand up and say No. That sort of courage on matters of principle is rare in the GAA where officials prefer to hide behind the rule-book as their excuse for avoiding making unpopular decisions. Dr Mick Loftus was a magnificent exception to that.

JOHN MAUGHAN from Mayo as a team manager did not get to win the Sam Maguire Cup even though he went desperately close to doing so in the 1996 draw and replay with Meath. But he was a manager ahead of his time with new ideas for training and coaching and his own flamboyant appearance on summer sidelines in shorts. His greatest achievement was managing Clare to beat Kerry in the 1992 Munster final, which in the context of weak counties operating in the All-Ireland championship was an extraordinary result.

Along with his fellow Mayoman John O'Mahony who managed Leitrim to a Connacht title in 1994 he provided new hope for all those less successful counties with small football catchment areas and at that time there was hope that these significant results might kick-start a similar revival among other such unsuccessful counties. Alas, this did not turn out to be in the intervening years at provincial level although Kildare, Westmeath and Laois did win Leinster titles after very long gaps and in Westmeath's case for the first time.

Maughan was a well-liked manager with players and public and still is because he was able to enjoy the big games and always seemed at ease with what he was doing or saying even in defeat and there were few harder defeats than the drawn final against

Meath when only a ball hopping over the crossbar after a long kick from outfield by Colm Coyle prevented Mayo taking the Sam Maguire Cup. John's attitude to the game was in contrast to some big-name managers nowadays who always seems to be living on the edge.

L IZ HOWARD was one of the first female media people involved in the GAA and appeared on The Sunday Game in the early years after it started in 1979. Her background as a GAA person was very strong as her late father Garrett Howard won All-Ireland hurling medals with Limerick and Liz herself became very active in camogie as a player with Tipperary, Clare and Dublin and later on as administrator at all levels. She was elected President of the Camogie Association in 2006.

Her first official involvement with football and hurling was as PRO of the Tipperary County Board. She worked with the then Leinster chairman Liam O'Neill and president Nickey Brennan to set up a three-year trial series that saw the camogie All-Ireland finals played on the same programme in Croke Park as the U-21 hurling final which was a major departure at the time.

When Liz Howard became the first and only female contributer to The Sunday Game there were many raised eyebrows among some of the more conservative GAA fraternity but her ability im the role soon stifled any opposition. She had an important management role with Aer Lingus in Ireland and the United States and she was one of the promoters of the No Name Club which sought to encourage a sensible approach to alcohol consumption.

It is interesting to note that in the intervening period since Liz Howard worked on The Sunday Game very few females have graced the studio of that programme in connection with Gaelic football.

N OREEN DOHERTY was the first female to be elected a county board secretary which was a major breakthrough in the politics of the GAA. She was appointed in 1996 and served for 14 years while in 2005 she was appointed to the new position in the county of full-time administrator.

Since Noreen made that bit of history many females have joined the administrative system of the Association such as Kathleen O'Neill who is the Kildare county secretary. All over Ireland there are GAA clubs where females hold important positions which is in keeping with the progress of women in nearly all sports in this country.

The next big step in the GAA could be regarding referees and we wonder who will be the first female referee to take charge of an inter-county game in any grade. And when it happens how will, those tough, hardy males respond? Something to look forward to in the coming years!

DENIS (DINNY) KELLY was not very famous in county Offaly but he was very well known and liked in Raheen GAA club in the county where he lived in Alderborough near the very pretty village of Geashill in north Offaly. Dinny who worked as a gardener, spent most of his life promoting Gaelic football among underage players, driving them to matches, helping out with the training and generally making sure young lads were inspired to play football and hopefully wear the famous green, white and gold jerseys of Offaly down the road.

The great work undertaken by people like Dinny Kelly and many others in the Raheen club over the years brought its reward when the late Larry Coughlan joined the Offaly team that won All-Irelands in 1971 and '72. Ten years later when Offaly beat Kerry in the 1982 final Raheen had John Guinan in the half-forward line and Martin Fitzpatrick as a sub. It was John Guinan who made way near the end of that game to allow a certain Seamus Darby to some in as a sub and score a famous goal.

Dinny started ringing me up on and off about 1979, just for a chat about football and it was clear to me just how much the game meant to him. And when the two Raheen players joined the panel around 1980 Dinny was in cloud nine, he was so proud that his own parish would be represented in most of the big county games including the biggest game of all. Dinny was always positive about Offaly football and even when we lost a big game he would be on the next day to offer support and remind me that Offaly are not called 'The Faithful County' for nothing. There was never a harsh comment from Dinny about players or officials and his love for the GAA shone out through thick and thin. In my time in Offaly his beloved Raheen won the Offaly Intermediate Championship, which brought joy to Dinny also.

I am naming Dinny Kelly among this list of famous GAA people not just on his own merits, worthy and all as they undoubtedly are, but because for me he represents the hundreds, probably thousands of people throughout the GAA who are like him. They are the REAL heroes in the GAA just as much as the Matt Connors, Colm Coopers or Bernard Brogans because they were there in good and bad times and it was they who first instilled in young boys the love of the game and ignited their desire to some day pay for their county.

I was a lot better off for having met and been friends with Dinny Kelly, and many other such men, and the wonderful words of sanity he often spoke to me when the going was tough in Offaly football.

COLM O'ROURKE AND GERRY McENTEE Without the combined leadership qualities as well of course as their magnificent football skills it is very unlikely that Meath would have come back from 15 years of Leinster failure to emerge as a major force in football highlighted by their ferocious battles with Cork in the late 1980s. Seldom have two players played such vital roles in bringing their county to the top on and off the field as these two men and they were pivotal in the emergence of Sean Boylan as a brilliant manager of Meath in those and subsequent years.

They were already experienced performers having won

Sigerson Cups with UCD where McEntee was the winning captain in 1978 but there were many more years of disappointment before Meath eventually made the breakthrough in 1987 and '88 and went on to beat Dublin four times in five years in Leinster finals.

Apart from his other qualities Colm O'Rourke deserves great credit for putting up with Joe Brolly and Pat Spillane on The Sunday Game for so long and playing the role of straight man to the clowns! I have known Colm since the mid-seventies when he arrived into UCD and on the first day I was supervising trials for the Freshers panel he came across and said to me : 'You must be McGee'. It was typical of his lack of shyness as I had become a little bit famous at the time having being involved in a rake of Sigerson wins and two All-Ireland club championships – and he has never looked back in that area!

As teenager with Meath in 1976, he assumed the task of kicking a penalty against Dublin, then at their peak, in the Leinster final that could have decided the game but his shot went wide and The Dubs went on to win two successive All-Irelands. It was one of many setbacks. Including serious knee injuries, to the man born in Aughavas, Co. Leitrim but whose family moved to Skryne in Meath when he was a child. But setbacks never scared O'Rourke and he went on to have a glorious football career winning two All-Ireland titles and five Leinsters.

Gerry McEntee was one of the last great midfielders of the traditional style of high catchers but it was his overall contribution to the development of that Meath team in the years leading up to those All-Ireland successes that was so important, something that was also true of O'Rourke. That was particularly true of the latter in the final of 1988 after McEntee had been sent off early in that game. Raw courage and controlled abandon was required when that occurred and no better man to provide it personally and inspire others to emulate him than Colm O'Rourke.

Colm has since emerged as one of the most successful colleges managers in the history of the game thorough his leadership of St Patrick's Classical School in Navan where he has been long-time principal and has sent many of his pupils on the road to football greatness with Meath county teams.

Genuine Meath football supporters constantly dream of the day when the dream-team to manage the Meath senior team will emerge – Gerry McEntee and Colm O'Rourke but the success of their respective careers, O'Rourke as school administrator and McEntee as a brilliant medical man, may have held them back. I have always admired the attitudes of these two Meath goliaths and see them as examples of what real Gaelic footballers should be.

PAT DALY has been one of the most important people involved in Gaelic football for many years even though a lot of people would not immediately recognize his role. Pat a former national teacher and a native of Waterford took on the job of initiating, managing, and supervising coaching in football when he joined the staff of Croke Park where he is now Head of Games Development and Research.

In his time in Croke Park Pat has produced a mountain of information and knowledge in all its forms about football coaching which has served the GAA very well. The annual Games Development Conference held in Croke Park has now acquired an international dimension and reputation and attracts nearly 1,000 attendees.

Pat Daly has been responsible for making coaching, at all levels, accessible to the masses in the GAA and that has been its greatest success. Even parents who have little or no knowledge of Gaelic football can acquire all the knowledge they need from Croke Park via Pat Daly's department.

Pat has also undertaken extensive research into all aspects of coaching, an area which has expanded immensely in the past decade particularly. Some GAA people may say nowadays that coaching has gone too far especially at the highest level but without keeping up to date on world trends in coaching the GAA would be lagging behind other international sports. With Pat Daly's enthusiasm and expertise that is not likely to happen.

Coaching has done more to level the playing-field in Gaelic football in the weaker counties and clubs than any other GAA development and we may thank Pat Daly for being the catalyst for all of that.

JOE KERNAN was always a hero of mine from the time I first watched him playing for Armagh. He was a swashbuckling, flamboyant personality, the sort of player that the fans always looked to for a bit of excitement, drama and in Armagh's case a goal or two when most needed. Crossmaglen his native parish was not the successful club in Joe's time as it later emerged to be and indeed it was Joe as manager of Crossmaglen after his playing days who laid the foundations for the club's historic achievements in the Ulster and All-Ireland series.

I particularly remember Joe Kernan's performance in the 1977 All-Ireland final against Dublin which the latter won by 12 points but his defiance stood out that day when he banged in two goals in the space of five minutes against that very tough Dublin backline. Armagh and Joe were heartbroken that day but 25 years later everything changed in Armagh GAA on September 22, 2002 when inspired by their manager Joe Kernan Armagh beat Kerry in the All-Ireland final by 1-12 to 0-14.

This was one of the greatest occasions for a final that I have seen in Croke Park and while some may argue that Armagh should have won more All-Irelands that matters little in the context of Armagh football. Having lost to Kerry in 1953 and Dublin in 1977 Armagh had crossed the great divide between All-Ireland winners and non-winners and Joe Kernan, with his ability as a manager and his outgoing personality that pleased so many neutrals, has ensured that Joe Kernan would be on anybody's list of outstanding GAA people.

TOM WOULFE was born in Ballybunion, Co Kerry in 1915 but unlike many of his fellow countymen he did not become famous in the GAA as a great Kerry footballer laden with All-Ireland medals. But he still performed one of the most important functions in the past century by originating the campaign to abolish Rule 27 of the organisation as far back as the sixties. That rule more commonly referred to as The Ban had been there from the early years of the last century and it decreed that no GAA member could play, organise or attend what were described by the GAA as 'foreign games' soccer, rugby, hockey and cricket under penalty of heavy suspension.

Tom Woulfe like many other GAA members always saw the Ban as a sign of an inferiority complex in the GAA, afraid to compete on equal terms with all other Irish sporting bodies. His campaign to end the rule largely consisted of swaying public opinion through newspaper articles, letters to Editors and debates etc.

Rule 27 could only be voted upon every three years which was in itself restrictive of debate but Woulfe, who was a lifelong member of the Civil Service GAA club in Dublin, kept plugging away though often faced with bitter and extremely hostile attacks from leaders of the GAA all those years.

Eventually after a national plebiscite among all GAA clubs took place in 1970 The Ban was wiped out almost unanimously and Tom Woulfe has always been regarded as the man without whose persistence The Ban could have remained for many more years.

Tom was not a volatile character nor did he make vehement attacks on GAA officials, something which was not reciprocated in those times. I knew him well and he never lost his fervour for change in the GAA if he thought it was for the good of the organisation. History will record Tom Woulfe's contribution to the GAA in the same light as any of the great players who have adorned his native county in the last century.

MICHAEL CARTY People in the GAA media world are often assailed with questions from the public about who was the best this, that or the other in Gaelic football and the answer is sure to evoke a strong discussion. A question I have often been asked is: 'Who was the hardest player you have come across in your time in football?' It is important to specify what exactly the word 'hardest' means or more precisely what it does not mean by MY definition- others will have their own idea with which I rarely agree.

Hardest in my book means a tough, hard player who can give and take abuse when required as part of the cut and thrust of a close, competitive game but with the proviso that everything is within the rules apart from an accidental foul. On that basis I have no hesitation in giving the distinction to Michael Carty from Castletown in County Wexford who played for Wexford for many years and also had a distinguished career with UCD being one of the few players in history to win five Sigerson Cup medals from 1973 to 1978, as well as two Dublin SFC medals and captained UCD to All-Ireland club victory over Nemo Rangers in 1975. Mick got a special thrill from that because the trophy for the competition was the Andy Merrigan Cup named after the great Castletown and Wexford footballer who had been tragically killed in a farming accident a few years earlier.

Mick encountered many of the great players of the time with Wexford and UCD such as Tony Hanahoe, Brian Mullins etc. in UCD-Vincent's games. He once played in a Sigerson Cup final in Belfast with a broken wrist but played on regardless. He had the ability to hit hard but fair, something which was very common in those days but no so much so today. Nobody looked forward to being marked by Carty who usually played either at centre half-back or midfield and he realised at an early stage that defending and tackling was his greatest asset while attempting scores was something best left to one of his colleagues. A player like Michael Carty has always been invaluable, even to this day, to any team because they instil confidence and belief particularly whey your team is struggling. Being hard but fair is very different to being a hatchetman or a sneaky off-the-ball fouler but unfortunately such players are often confused in the public mind with being 'hard men'. Cowardly is a more relevant description in my book. Michael Carty was proof that you can be hard AND fair at the same time.

MICK O'DWYER There are so many aspects of Mick O'Dwyer's life in the GAA that sometimes the more obvious traits of his personality can easily be forgotten. We all know he was a brilliant footballer, an outstanding team manager and the rest. But for me the most important aspect of his career was his own personality. Since managers arrived on the GAA scene in the nineteen seventies to replace people who were called 'Trainers' O'Dwyer has become the longest serving manager the GAA has ever, and I dare say will ever see – from 1974 to 2013. What I associate most with the man is his own personality. He was a lovely man, a term rarely attached to a GAA manager I admit, but the test is that hardly anybody disliked the Waterville maestro. That is not to say that every GAA person believes he was the nicest person in GAA history at all but rather to get it across that Dwyer, as Kerry people invariably referred to him, never seriously annoyed people in the GAA including the other managers that he encountered.

He was, of course, a trickster, a manipulator of public opinion, a cute Kerry hoor and a lot of other things all of which were acceptable in Gaelic football and its periphery. You simply loved having a chat with Mick O'Dwyer because he loved Gaelic football as a passion and that always overcame any disappointments or sorrows he endured through football in his long career. And no manager in football has suffered such a severe disappointment as O'Dwyer on September 19, 1982 when his wonderful and seemingly invincible Kerry team was deprived of their own and particularly Micko's life-long ambition to win five successive All-Irelands. But as always and despite his devastation he was first man along with then Kerry chairman Frank King into the Offaly dressing room to offer congratulations and in his case we all knew both meant it.

That was the most difficult time of Micko's life as he admitted in his biography and there were many dark days and months of loneliness and frustration back in his native Waterville. But then hardship and deprivation was nothing new to this man from his youth and gradually the lure of football brought him back to life. Even another shattering last-minute goal conceded to Cork in the Munster final of 1983 did not lead to despair but instead he led Kerry to three more All-Irelands in a row including two victories over arch-rivals Dublin and one over Tyrone.

Eventually pulling out of the Kerry football system proved awkward and tough for Mick O'Dwyer but to the utter amazement of the GAA world at large, and particularly Kerry people, he landed in Kildare to manage their county team and after some hiccups in 1998 he eventually brought Kildare to their first Leinster title since 1956 and went on to narrowly lose the All-Ireland final to Galway after a thrilling game of high quality. Later he moved to take over Laois, by then perennial losers, and brought them to a Leinster final victory in 2003, their first title since 1946. But even more dramatically when he finished with Laois Micko headed for Wicklow who were lodged in Division 4 and in the space of a few months the county went mad about football because of the charisma of the man and his own attachment to Wicklow. He had several notable achievements in the Garden County including many Qualifier victories and winning the Tommy Murphy Cup in Croke Park. Having left Wicklow he finished his career with an appointment with the Clare football team.

Everywhere he went in all those counties Mick O'Dwyer was respected and liked to an extraordinary extent bearing in mind his age and long time at the game. It all proved the man's amazing personality that allowed him to become immune to the sort of rows we often get in the GAA or the disappointments that inevitably come with being a county manager. And above all there were no excuses by O'Dwyer when games were lost. Maybe a wry smile that spoke louder than words, but never an excuse or a whinge.

So many managers at the present time could learn a lot from Mick O'Dwyer's behaviour and demeanour and the manner in which he conducted himself whether winning or losing. He never imposed a media ban either. Like everybody else in the GAA I was very fond of Mick O'Dwyer and I was always glad to meet him at a match or a function. A lifelong teetotaler he was a most sociable person and would talk forever.

He was a wonderful adornment for the GAA and is definitely entitled to be acclaimed as the Best Manager in GAA history because of the diverse range of his contributions across several counties. If class is a measurement of success then Micko was the best.

JIM McGUINNESS did amazing things with Donegal county football teams in recent years by changing the whole attitude to the inter-county scene in a short space of time. It is no exaggeration to state that Donegal had a rather fractious relationship with county football for a lifetime. They managed to make the All-Ireland breakthrough in 1992 but another 20 years went by before another All-Ireland was won. For a county with as huge a population and geographical area as Donegal this was a very poor return.

Donegal developed a reputation, rightly or wrongly, of their footballers being rather free and easy as regards team discipline, training and overall approach to playing for Donegal. We constantly heard reports of mini-rows, absenteeism from training and generally the notion that if every player good enough applied himself to the Donegal county team all the time they could be a major force in the game long-term.

Those of us involved in third-level GAA games going back the years would have agreed with that as many of the best players who lined out for colleges like UCD and UCG in particular came from Donegal and were outstanding performers at that level. Then along came Jim McGuinness a man who himself was well immersed in third-level football having played and been successful with Tralee, Sligo and Jordanstown, making him possibly the best educated county footballer in Ireland at the time.

Jim then turned his attention to the inherent problems of the Donegal county team. He set up new structures for selecting, training and managing the team and was handed unlimited power by the Donegal County Board.

But McGuinness did not merely organise new structures, he also formulated a new system of playing Gaelic football that to most GAA people was revolutionary. In the process he completed the already commenced project by other counties of dismantling the century long traditional lineout system for playing the game. Gone was the old system of team formation that was: 1, 3, 3, 2, 3, 3.

Instead to the casual observer, apart from the goalkeeper the other 14 players could play anywhere they wished or more precisely anywhere McGuinness wished. The policy was to play as many as 12 players in the backline when Donegal were defending and if and when they regained possession to then have several players to dash forward into attack to receive the ball from outfield players. There were many variations of this style but that was the gist of it for the common GAA man.

Initially it led to terribly defensive games such as the semi-final meeting between Dublin and Donegal which finished Dublin 0-8 Donegal 0-6 in a game that was described among other things as a travesty, an abomination, the destruction of Gaelic football and a reneging on everything Gaelic football stood for. But McGuinness, by now Public Enemy No 1 as far as GAA people were concerned, ignored the criticism and instead commenced to refine his basic defensive theory to facilitate the team getting more scores and he won the All-Ireland the following year, 2012.

As usual in this situation nearly every manager of a club team decided to copy Donegal and we had an orgy of club championship games with combined scores less than 20 than points.

McGuinness imposed draconian powers on the Donegal players particularly in relation to discipline and training. He could justify all that by winning the All-Ireland but the wider GAA public wanted nothing to do with his style.

The man has to be admired for breaching the boundaries of tradition as teams like Down (1960) and Kerry and Dublin (in the seventies also did). Personally I totally disliked the Donegal approach because it confined the game to a handful of undemanding skills they perfected to the exclusion of many more. The handpass was crucial to the Donegal style and stopping opponents when they had possession was also a key part of their game. Time will tell if Jim McGuinness will be able or willing to further develop the Donegal style to make for a more expansive game that the followers of the game definitely desire. But Jim McGuinness deserves great credit for his bravery in breaking the shackle of conservatism in football. Only time will tell what his, and Gaelic football's legacy, will be in 10 years' time.

LIAM MULVIHILL 'What can you say about Liam Mulvihill only fair play to him. Oversaw the introduction of sponsorship of teams and the actual championships, expanded live television to provincial finals and St Patrick's Day games, regular live TV, football and hurling Qualifiers, redevelopment of Croke Park, abolition of Rule 21, opening up of Croker to the soccer and rugby shower. Would like to have seen the issue of discipline addressed more directly but that's only a small criticism when you look at his other massive achievements, and he still managed to stay sane all those years.'

This is an anonymous message posted on a website after Liam Mulvihiill retired from the positions of Director General of the GAA in 2008. Presuming it was written by an ordinary GAA member it is not a bad assessment of Liam's 29-year 'reign' as the boss of the GAA. He served under 11 different presidents, in itself a wonderful example of diplomacy as those distinguished men varied greatly in their views of the GAA and in many other ways. But it was Liam Mulvihill who had to strike a balance between a person like the late, gentle Paddy McFlynn from Down (1979) and the much more abrasive ones like Peter Quinn (1991) and Sean Kelly (2003).

There is a common mistaken belief among GAA people that the Director General is like a Chief Executive of a company and runs the show completely. Not so in the GAA at all. Liam Mulvihill certainly, like the present holder Páraic Duffy, has some power over administration matters but not over things like fixtures, championship structures, objections or even financial matters. The DG has a say in those things but not the final say – in fact it is often hard to pinpoint who exactly has that say on GAA matters – but it usually ends up with some committee or other to make decisions and even then the 300-plus Annual Congress may have the final say.

Complicated? You better believe it!

Despite all that Liam Mulvihill is regarded as the man who supervised, and far more than that, inspired the biggest changes in the profile and image of the GAA in its history. The massive developments mentioned at the start are proof of that and of course there were many more such that he played a key role in. But the development of the new stadium is surely the real monument to Liam Mulvihill because the concept originated with him and without him, despite all the experts who were on hand, it would not have been carried out so expeditiously. During the project he had to deal with a small army of GAA officers from presidents down and a large number of high-profile politicians who insisted on interfering and tried to direct the GAA in a certain way to suite THEIR own ends. Remember when Bertie Ahern as Taoiseach offered the GAA over £90 million on the Friday night of a Congress to change direction regarding Croke Park and get involved with Abbotstown?

Hopefully Liam will sit down and write a book about his time as boss of the GAA as it would make fascinating reading in those latter areas in particular.

Patience of course is the first essential for any person employed full-time in Croke Park because every member of the GAA seems to think that the people who work there need to be told how to do their job the way the public require it to be done. This applies more than anyone else to a Director General and Liam Mulvihill proved many times over the years that patience is a virtue he had in spades. I have seen and heard several leading GAA officials up to provincial chairmen lambaste Liam Mulvihill on some topic or other, usually in an attempt to cover their own backsides over a problem that was initially of their known making. I have always said that the only reason a lot of people went for election in the GAA was because they did not have the liathroidi to contest real election before the electorate at large.

Liam's Annual Reports were masterclasses in the sort of State of the Nation addresses than any proper organisation should have but often does not. Unfortunately the attention paid by ordinary GAA people to those reports was scant and often totally ignored. It is the same with Páraic Duffy although modern technology does at least broadcast his reports to a much wider audience nowadays.

When he was appointed in Croke Park in 1979 the GAA was a very different organisation to today. The Ban had only been abolished in 1971 and a lot of the festering sores in Irish sporting life brought about by that Ban had still not healed. If one had stated in 1979 that the top people in the FAI and the IRFU would he holding meetings regularly with the GAA their sanity would be seriously doubted. Eventually they not alone talked together but worked on projects such as the opening of Croke Park in almost total harmony. Liam Mulvihill was central to that happening and the GAA has been the better of it.

Getting rid of discriminatory laws like Rule 21 and the ban on GAA grounds being available for other sports changed the face Irish sport like never before. The lingering doubts that many Irish people had to the perceived insular attitude of the GAA were soon dispelled and the wider Irish public developed a very positive attitude to the role of the GAA in Irish society. Gradually those horrible words, 'THE GAH', began to vanish from the vocabulary of Irish sport

Without the calm, methodical approach of Liam Mulvihill these things would never have taken place to the extent that they did. The continuity of his position in Croke Park, for 29 years was vital in maintaining steady progress in all those area rather than a stop-start approach, which might have been the case if each president of three years was making his own decisions. There were also some decisions over the years that were foisted on Liam Mulvihill by a president against his better judgment but he kept his peace! Equally there were decisions, particularly on some controversies that Liam would have wished to progress in a way that he believed was the correct way but he was overruled by a president. What did I say earlier about patience? Liam also learned early on that silence is golden.

As a Longford person, I am proud to say I have known Liam for many years and indeed my brother Fr Phil was instrumental in encouraging Liam to get involved with county board administration in Longford where he soon became the youngest county chairman in Ireland at age 24, after a few turbulent years in GAA politics in Longford, before being appointed to greater things. He was very much the outsider of the candidates for Director General in 1979 but it turned out to be one of the most fruitful decisions ever made in the history of the GAA.

PÁRAIC DUFFY By comparison with his predecessor Liam Mulvihill as Director General, Duffy's tenure has been relatively calm. In Mulvihill's time there were many controversial times such as the opening of Croke Park, building the new stadium and doing away with Rule 21. But the GAA is never short of important work to do and Páraic Duffy has maintained the steady hand on the GAA tiller of his predecessor. Possibly the most important development in the long-term will be the ratifying of the Gaelic Players Association (GPA) as an integral part of the GAA structure after several years of uncertainty as to the rationale for the players' body and their place in the organisation. After a lot of debate and very divided opinions among ordinary members, who initially assumed that the GPA's main aim was to bring professionalism into football, at county level this notion was safely put to bed by assurances by the GPA and the GAA that this was never on the cards.

Eventually a proper structure and a working relationship between the two bodies emerged and nobody can argue now but that the GPA is playing a very important role in player welfare – which is now its main activity.

What was a major achievement by Páraic Duffy also was his direction over the finances of the GAA during the disasterous economic period of the past five years. The GAA largely maintained its income, attendances held up remarkably well and for the first time the GAA took promotion, advertising, etc of the games seriously with wonderful packages to suit supporters at most big games. In Duffy's time the Croke Park development was fully paid off ahead of schedule and commercial revenue continued to improve despite the recession.

Like President Liam O'Neill, Páraic Duffy has been particularly interested in promoting the cause of the Irish diaspora around the world through the GAA. As a result we have GAA units on the five continents and in places that most of us had to look at the world map to see where they were. The Department of Foreign Affairs has acknowledged that the role of the GAA in giving an identity to Irish people abroad and connecting them to the fatherland has been hugely successful.

On the more practical side of football the decision to set up the Football Review Committee (FRC) and the consequent changes that brought about was very close to Páraic's heart as a very knowledgeable football person from Monaghan. He was particularly happy that the FRC motion to eliminate the modern third-man tackle, a very dangerous ploy, was passed and is now fully operative.

Duffy's current term of office ends in 2015 but there is little doubt that he will be re-appointed for a further seven year period, if that is his wish.

S EAN KELLY was the first Kerryman to be elected GAA President and therefore a lot was expected of him. His period in office will always be associated with the opening of Croke Park to soccer and rugby. This was to be one of the last great debates in the GAA, couched in ordinary terms as a relatively simple motion, but possibly the last legacy of the GAA's ultra-nationalism of the previous century and the deep-seated and genuine opposition of nationalists of a certain hue about the watering down of any of what they perceived as a core value of the GAA. The debate was brought about, not by the GAA directly, but by the fact that international rugby and soccer games would not be available in the former Lansdowne Road because the stadium was to be knocked down and rebuilt.

It soon became clear that both sports would have to play their big games outside Ireland and this evoked enormous passion among all sports people and indeed the general public. Immediately the focus came on Croke Park's magnificent new stadium with its 82,000 capacity. But old-time GAA people never liked to be brow-beaten into any change and this was no exception. Opinions hardened on all sides and 'the national interest' became the focal point of the debate thereby putting the pressure almost alone on the GAA.

Kelly played a masterly diplomatic role in this project placating the GAA traditionalists on the one hand and the latent anti-GAA rugby and soccer people who never had much time for the GAA anyway and were somewhat reluctant to concede that the GAA was going to bail them out. As always, personalities emerged from all sides with very vocal opinions such as Michael Greenan from Cavan who was particularly virulent against Sean Kelly even though he was a member of the Executive of the GAA. Many former presidents such as Jack Boothman and Con Murphy also opposed the idea but Kelly stood his ground and stood by his beliefs. It was a very impressive performance, which managed to keep the GAA intact and avoid a possible split.

So on April 16, 2005 in Croke Park the vote was taken to change the relevant rule, Rule 42, and Seán Kelly calmly announced the result: For 227, Against 97, motion passed.

Possibly the most famous vote ever held in the GAA and certainly a result that changed the face of Irish sport forever. And as always GAA people closed ranks and got on about their GAA business. When Ireland faced England in Croke Park in 2007 there has rarely been a more tension-filled occasion and people wondered how the playing of 'God Save the Queen' would transpire. In the event it went perfectly well and the full house gave a marvellous round of applause for the English anthem. But it paled into insignificance compared with the volume created for Amhran na bhFiann and to cap it all Ireland beat England 43-13.

Seán Kelly had many other achievements in his presidency but inevitably his name will be linked with opening Croke Park forever.

TONY O'KEEFFE from the Austin Stacks club in Tralee was at the heart of Kerry football for many years since he first became acting county secretary in 1981 after the death of the incumbent Andy Molyneaux. A secondary teacher in the town and a brother of All-Ireland winner Ger and also a first cousin of great Kerry star John O'Keeffe, it could be said that the right Kerry breeding was in him.

Administration was his forte when he ceased playing for Stacks and he spent 11 years as Kerry secretary during which the county won four All-Irelands. It was part of his task to cope with the trauma that hit Kerry football when they not alone lost the Five-in-a-Row in 1982 but also lost by a last minute goal to Cork in the 1983 Munster final. It really did look like the end of the world for Kerry fans just then but history tells us that Kerry always rise again. And what a comeback it was again under Mick O'Dwyer with a three-in-a-row that included two All-Ireland final defeats over Dublin in 1984/'85.

Tony proved to be an outstanding legislator in the GAA and was recognised by several GAA Presidents for that. He was chairman of the old GAC and presently he is chairman of its successor the CCCC, the body that makes all the important decisions in the day-to-day running of the GAA. Tony was also a member of the FDC in the late nineties which proposed radical ideas for changing the All-Ireland football league and championship but which were found to be too radical by counties and beaten at Congress.

After that a small committee, of which Tony and myself were members, came up with a proposal for the All-Ireland Qualifiers and the rest is history. Tony O'Keeffe still has a lot to contribute to the GAA as an administrator and no doubt future Presidents will still value his logical approach to coping with the gigantic bureaucracy that is the GAA.

MATT CONNOR Such is the high reputation that Matt holds in the pantheon of great Gaelic footballers it is hard to realise two things, firstly that his inter-county career only lasted six years and ended at the age of 24 when most players are only reaching their peak and secondly that so many members of the GAA public still talk about his exploits even though it is now 30 years since his career was cut short by a car accident on Christmas Day 1984. It was my great privilege to have been involved with Matt throughout his senior career and of all people I have always recognised the genius that he was and for once that description is not sporting hyperbole but cold common sense.

Only a handful of footballers have had the talent that he had, people like Purcell, Heffernan, Higgins and O'Connell for instance. There has never been any doubt about his football talent but what made Matt's name so prominent in the GAA world and beyond since the late seventies was not just talent but also his demeanor, the way he carried himself in the heat of battle and the modesty that dominated his career and his life to this day as he moves about in a wheelchair.

In modern day sport, genius can often be tainted by arrogance, false bravura or exhibitionism. That was never the case with Matt. Instead it was his humility, consideration for beaten opponents and a total lack of arrogance even when he achieved some of his most remarkable scores in front of large crowds.

People still talk of Matt scoring 2-9 against the great Kerry team at its peak in the 1980 All Ireland semi-final just a few weeks after he scored the decisive goal against Dublin in the Leinster final without which Offaly would have faded away after what would have been three successive championship defeats in Leinster. That was THE most important goal of Matt's career because it paved the way for All-Ireland success in 1982. And in that famous final, at a time when Offaly were hanging on for dear life with time running out, it was solely Matt's decision to convert two frees into points rather than play the dramatic role by going for goals. And how justified he was for doing that.

Matt was quiet-spoken, rarely involving himself in tactical talks etc. and why should he when he had such talent that could thrive in almost any style of football required on a particular day. On only one occasion did I chastise him in front of the Offaly panel. In 1984, when Monaghan beat Offaly in the Centenary Cup semi-finals, we played an important tournament game the following Sunday evening in Clonbullogue on the Laois-Offaly border with a very large crowd looking on. Maybe I was in bad humour but I thought the lads had been less than enthusiastic about proceedings in the first half. At the break I picked out Matt Connor and gave him hell for his apparent carefree attitude. As usual he did not comment but he ended up scoring 3-5 in that game with one of the goals being a classic shot from 25 yards out on the right wing that nearly beheaded the goalkeeper.

While I was astonished at many of the great scores Matt scored in grounds all over Ireland I also watched him do incredible things with a football in club games, particularly when his team, Walsh Island, played their great rivals of the time Ferbane. Some of his most brilliant scores came when playing for 'The Island'. However my abiding memories of Matt Connor come not from Croke Park or other big stadiums but from the many training sessions I was in charge of in those years with Offaly.

Matt was always serious about training as were all the lads and the training games were often barbaric in intensity. Every player wanted to outdo Matt if he got the chance but rarely did that happen. I particularly recall the duels between Matt and the great goalkeeper Martin Furlong. This was serious stuff. Furlong was a fierce competitor and hated having to pick the ball out of the net. Matt seemed to take an extra delight from beating Furlong with his genius. It is goals, and saves, from those sessions that stick longest in my memory.

Following his serious accident Matt adapted quickly to his new situation and was fortunate to be able to retain his position as a Garda based in Tullamore. When we organised a fund-raiser six months after the accident nearly 15,000 tickets were sold and as a special concession it was agreed that for the first and only time in Ireland the Allstars teams in football and hurling would play as a team against Offaly in O'Connor Park. It was a unique honour for a very unique footballer. Matt was fortunate to marry a wonderful wife in Siobhan and his interest in Offaly football and sport in general has never wavered.

There is no need for me to elaborate at length on the greatness of this man – the fact that 30 years after his short career he is still a household name throughout the GAA world is ample proof of his stature as one of the greatest footballers of all time.

BENNY GAUGHRAN arrived on the scene about a decade too late to link up with the Louth team that won the 1957 All-Ireland final against Cork. Maybe it was that which made him so determined to be successful in his own playing career. His greatest successes came with UCD and he had the honour of captaining the college team to Sigerson Cup success in January 1968 after a long absence. That was an unusual Sigerson competition because the format that had survived for about 60 years of two semi-finals and a final played on the last weekend in November had to be changed.

Preparing for that Sigerson was the first time that I organised morning training, 7am to be precise, to emphasise the dire situation that UCD had not won the competition for five years. So creating a sacrifice scenario was the remedy used to get players to concentrate on the target since the competition was due to be played in Dublin that year. The ideal captain to lead UCD into this manic training regime was Gaughran, one of the most dedicated players I have ever encountered. Right from his first playing Gaelic football it was clear he would be a special competitor and he certainly led by example in those training sessions in frosty November. Everything was going fine until the Wednesday before the competition was due to start when after coming in from another session the news came on RTE that the Sigerson was postponed because of the recent Foot And Mouth outbreak in Ireland.

The competition was then fixed for late January 1968 and UCD went on to beat UCG in the final in Croke Park. From that year onwards the Sigerson Cup was changed to being played in February and so it has remained.

That win had an unexpected bonus because shortly afterward

an invitation came from John Kerry O'Donnell in New York, a close friend of Kerry star Donie O'Sullivan who was on that UCD team, to play in the prestigious New York Mayor Lindsay Games in June in Gaelic Park, New York, a trip of a lifetime then. Benny Gaughran captained that UCD team when they played a soccer game against prisoners serving life sentences in Hartford State Prison, Connecticut that UCD won on a pitch surrounded by armed guards. But things like that never worried Gaughran and he went on to play many serious matches against St Vincent's in the Dublin senior championships in which he really proved his worth.

Benny also featured in an historic decision when UCD became the first team to be thrown out of a Sigerson Cup final. He had received his primary law degree but applied for a new qualification called Diploma in European Law. UCD beat a star-studded UCC side, led by Moss Keane, in the semi-final and were preparing for the final against Queens. But the Higher Education GAA Authority raised an objection to Benny and about an hour before the final was due announced that UCD were thrown out and UCC told to play. The Cork lads had of course been out celebrating as only students can on Saturday night and not surprisingly lost that final but there were very strong emotions around Galway at the final and the after-match function later on.

After he left UCD, Benny played on in Dublin club football into his forties such was his enthusiasm for the game and his loyalty to Louth football never wavered despite difficult times on the playing field. In many ways he was a model player who made the most of his abilities and he was a man I always admired through thick and thin.

L IAM O'NEILL from Laois was unique in modern times in that he was unopposed for the position of GAA President in 2011 and this was clearly a mark of the man's ability in GAA administration that such a thing happened. His background as principal of a two-teacher school in rural Ireland and coming from a family of twelve was typical of many presidents in the long history of the GAA, he was a product of the GAA grassroots and set out to achieve a series of significant targets but not necessarily earth-shattering ones like the opening of Croke Park.

I did not know Liam very well when he asked me out of the blue to become chairman of the Football Review Committee to look at some aspects of football that could be improved so that the game would be more attractive to players and spectators. Unusually for presidents he did not appoint the members of the FRC but instead asked me to form a small committee of my own choosing. He also placed a time limit of about a year to come up with proposals and that too was unusual because generally committees appointed by GAA presidents serve for three years.

It is well known now that the FRC came up with a series of changes to football playing rules that while not individually dramatic, as a package aim to make football more positive and interesting with the Black Card overshadowing several other proposals such as officially recognising the advantage rule

The success or otherwise of Croke Park committees largely depends on the backing they get from the current president and in that regard Liam O'Neill was excellent. The odds were heavily against any of these proposals getting the two-thirds majority needed at a GAA congress but following a lot of discussion, debate and consultation in the 32 counties and beyond most things were passed.

O'Neill was involved in many other initiatives such as bringing the various GAA bodies, Handball, Camogie and Ladies Football, closer together for the benefit of all bodies. Discipline, fixture planning and the promotion of hurling are just a couple of the many projects Liam O'Neill was involved in and his ability to take on some of the more virulent criticism that is directed at the GAA has impressed many ordinary GAA people who sometimes believe they are getting a raw deal from GAA critics.

Liam will be remembered as a positive, down-to-earth president of the GAA working closely with Director General Páraic Duffy for the advancement of the organisation. Within the many restrictions that operate in the administration of the GAA he has done very well and as a relatively young man he surely has more to offer to the organisation at various levels.

GERRY DINEEN was often described as 'McGee's right-hand man' when he was a hard-working member of the UCD football club at team management and club committee level. He was a certainly an all-round man in every sense of the word during the 1970s which probably explains why he did not actually play football in the college. Gerry was one of many student-teachers from StPatrick's Training College in Drumcondra who when they completed their two-year course went on to spend one further year in UCD which qualified them to sit for a BA degree. Several footballers availed of that facility including players like John O'Keeffe and Jackie Walsh of Kerry and Eamon O'Donoghue from Kildare.

Gerry Dineen was from Cork and needless to say we were never allowed to forget that and he often found himself in delicate situations when UCD played UCC in the Sigerson Cup but his loyalties always remained true to UCD. Gerry had another attribute – he could sing. And in UCD in those times there was plenty of scope for singing occasions with the senior team winning major titles almost every year in the seventies. He was a 'wing man' for Jackie Walsh from Ballylongford, son of the legendary Johnny of Kerry fame and it was rare not to see them together in a GAA connection.

As a staunch Corkman he also had the verbal tenacity to put opposing players or supporters into line with a few cutting remarks that tended to make them wither away in haste. Because players from third-level colleges are transient by nature and only attend the college for a few years, with odd exceptions of course like Jim McGuinness, when Gerry remained on as a mentor after he graduated he was a great asset to have as such people in UCD were quite scarce. He was a central figure in establishing the success of the UCD All-Ireland 7-aside competition and other organisational chores in the college.

Gerry has long since left Dublin to return to Leeside and is presently involved with Cork Development Squads. But his name will ring a bell with many, many former UCD GAA people because Gerry was the sort of guy it was hard to forget! I was always grateful for his humour in fraught situations– and of course his singing, 'The Boys of Fair Hill', the unabridged version I might add, still rings through my head on occasions.

S EAN O'NEILL is one of those rare individuals who always exuded class in his life. As a footballer he was probably THE outstanding ambassador to represent the new dimension in Ulster and Ireland football when he first came to prominence as far back as the Sigerson Cup final of 1958 when he played on the Queen's University team that won the Sigerson Cup for the first time. That result coupled with Ulster's first Railway Cup success in 1942 has always been regarded in Ulster as a landmark event in the history of the province. Queen's beat UCD in a replayed final in Fermanagh before a massive crowd. The following year Down won their first Ulster title and in the next year Down won their first and historic All-Ireland final. Sean O'Neill was a seminal figure in all these games and he won another Sigerson in 1964 and a third All-Ireland in 1968 as well as a record number of Railway Cup medals.

Sean O'Neill stood for the new breed of Gaelic footballer of that time, a genius on the field based on skill and a subtle football intellect and confident and flamboyant in his verbal capacity at times. Everybody who met Seam O'Neill in those times knew that a new football force had arrive on the scene with Down and he was critical to that happening.

As a player he was brilliant, there is no other word for it, and who can forget the goal he scored early on in the 1968 All-Ireland final against Kerry when he reacted quickest to a ball that had struck the upright high up. Sean served as Legal Advisor to the Ulster Council for many years and has retained his keen interest in football all his life. Those of us who watched Sean O'Neill as a player and the influential part he played in the emergence of Down and Ulster as major forces will never forget the imprint on Gaelic football he left behind him.

G ERALD McKENNA Because the GAA in Kerry has been for so long dominated in the public mind by the success of their footballers with their 36 All-Irelands it is inevitable that some other important aspects of the GAA can get overlooked, at least outside the county. GAA officers in Kerry have often fallen into that category with the notable exception of Sean Kelly who became the first Kerryman to become GAA President in 2003. Many people had believed long before that that Gerald McKenna would have achieved that distinction before Kelly but the Ballyduff man decided that the presidency was not for him, otherwise he would certainly have been a strong contender on more than one occasion.

We expect Kerry people to have a generous sense of humour, in fact most people believe it is in their DNA, even though I have met some cranky Kerrymen in my time as well!.

But Gerald is not one of those and his ability to produce repartee and humour at even the most contentious debates at a GAA Congress is legendary and has often been useful in defusing heated arguments on the floor of Congress – even when Cork delegates were involved. It would be foolish however to regard this Kerryman as some sort of court jester in GAA terms because he is anything but. He has spent a lifetime involved in officialdom in Kerry GAA.

It is accepted that but for the persuasive powers of Gerald McKenna, who was chairman of the Kerry County Board for most of the 1970s, Mick O'Dwyer's period in charge of Kerry would have been much shorter than it was. When Kerry were beaten for the second year in a row by Dublin in the famous 1977 All-Ireland semi-final the knives were out in some parts of the county for Mick O'Dwyer. Coupled with the anger of being beaten in a final and semi-final in successive years by Dublin was the debate about the style of football being utilised by O'Dwyer and the players with their liberal use of the handpass which to some Kerry traditionalists was football heresy.

The approach of the 'dissidents' in Kerry was to try to unseat the chairman Gerald McKenna as that was seen as ensuring that O'Dwyer would also lose out without the strong backing of McKenna. Eventually Gerald McKenna beat his opponent Fr Linnane, former trainer of St Brendan's Killarney college teams at the county convention. That ended the controversy and Mick O'Dwyer went on to guide Kerry to four successive Sam Maguires and three more after a two year gap in 1982/'83. So Gerald McKenna's role in those victories should never be dismissed.

Later on Gerald spent around 25 years as a member of the Central Council and he has been ever present on important committees in Croke Park to this day. He is a wonderful ambassador for Kerry GAA and a man who was liked by GAA people from all parts of Ireland with whom he came in contact. I am glad to have known the man and had many an interesting chat with him, always with the caveat that one needs to take some of his utterings with just a tiny grain of salt!

S EÁN McCAGUE became GAA President at a particularly difficult time in 2000 as the controversy over yet another GAA exclusion rule, this time Rule 21 which debarred RUC or British forces from being members of the GAA was on the agenda for some time. Eventually when the motion did reach the Congress table in 2003 under McCague's presidency five of the Six County counties voted against the motion, Derry, Antrim, Down, Armagh and Tyrone but Monaghan voted for and Rule

21 was removed from the GAA rule book. It had been a difficult period in GAA politics as already moves were afoot to propose the opening of Croke Park for rugby and soccer but he showed great bravery and political dexterity to ensure the motion was passed

The Monaghan man was first of all an outstanding team manager of the Monaghan team and guided them to their best-ever period winning Ulster titles in 1979, 1985 and 1988. On one famous occasion Monaghan drew with Kerry in an All-Ireland semi-final only to lose the replay. Along with then Monaghan county secretary Páraic Duffy, now Director General, Seán helped make club football in Monaghan more amenable to producing quality county players and with good results.

He took over as President when the motion proposing the Football Development Committee's (FDC) radical change for restructuring the entire inter-county format had been defeated. But he realised that about a dozen leading counties had actually voted in favour of these changes and because of that he believed there was a need for some sort of change. He formed a small committee from members of the FDC, myself included, chaired by the same Páraic Duffy and they produced the All-Ireland Qualifiers in 2001 which was the first time the straight knockout championship had been altered in the GAA.

Seán, believe it or not, was assistant manager to myself for the International Rules series in Ireland in 1987 and Australia in 1990. During his period in office there was much toing and froing regarding the attempts by Taoiseach Bertie Ahern to build a National Stadium and relations were often fraught between the government and the GAA as regards funding as the Croke Park development was already in train. But the GAA stood it's ground that Croke Park was to remain an independent headquarters for the GAA and obviously under Sean McCague's guidance that battle was won. So in an unspectacular way McCague's presidency was a most fruitful one for the GAA in difficult times.

Chapter 43

Paying Players – I Predict It Will Come Within A Decade

ACCORDING to the rules of the GAA the Association is strictly amateur as laid out in Official Guide (2012) as follows:

GAA Official Guide 2012
9. 1.10 Amateur Status

The Association is an Amateur Association. A player, team, official or member shall not accept payment in cash or in kind in conjunction with the playing of Gaelic Games.

A player, team, official or member shall not contract himself/itself to any agent other than those officially approved by Central Council. Expenses paid to all officials, players, and members shall not exceed the standard rates laid down by the Central Council. Members of the Association may not participate in full-time training. This Rule shall not prohibit the payment of salaries or wages to employees of the Association.

Penalty: Twenty-four weeks Suspension or Expulsion.

•   •   •

It is interesting to note the equivalent rule as it was written in the 1992 version of the Official Guide. Included then, after 'in cash or in kind' was the phrase 'or other material reward' but that has now disappeared. Also included was this: 'No member shall be associated with any commercial enterprise in connection with membership of the Association' which is no longer there either.

The removal of those words from the current Official Guide tells us how the strictly amateur status has been dissipated in the intervening years. The new wording has facilitated an influx of money into the GAA that was never allowed prior to then. And we can take it as read that the watering down of the former strict amateur code will continue mainly because the GAA itself is unable to prevent that happening.

For example it is a certain fact for many years that county and club team managers are being paid all over the country with millions of euro changing hands annually.

County managers can receive anything between €25,000 to €50,000 per year, with club managers rarely getting less than €100 per training session and the GAA despite gallant efforts has been unable to prevent what is a blatant breach of the amateur rules and it is normally done with the full co-operation of leading county board officers such as the chairman, treasurer or secretary. Hundreds if not thousands of people are being paid to take charge of club, college, third-level and underage teams in open violation of the GAA's own rules. Amateur how are you!

Now, I am not attaching any blame to any of the people who are receiving money for any of these operations, I am simply pointing out that millions of euro are currently going into the pockets of people involved in training and playing teams who can no longer be described as 'amateurs' as defined by the GAA's own rulebook.

Many county players are also being paid 'in cash or in kind' as the Official Guide quaintly describes it. Leading players can collect anything between €1,000 and €10,000 for taking part in commercial promotions including media related ones such as television. Even a cursory look at the newspapers will confirm this and some superstar players are nearly in the 'celebrity' or 'socialite' class, God help us! The GAA has sanctioned these sorts of payments in recent years. So GAA players are no longer amateurs in the correct sense of that word.

At another level there is no doubt that some players have transferred to clubs other than their native one in exchange for money or 'benefit in kind' – particularly in Dublin.

Breaches of the amateur rules are now seemingly being accepted by the GAA so the question that follows as we look towards the next 10-20 years is where will these developments that have occurred over the last 20 years take the GAA. What will the equivalent rule in the Official Guide read like in 2034? Will there be a rule there at all?

Or will it lead the GAA towards the word that dare not speak its name: PROFESSIONALISM? I believe it will, of a kind. The current dispersal of money to a large number of well-known players in many counties will continue unabated as commercial interests at last begin to appreciate the marketing potential of top GAA players. Now when GAA people mention that word they immediately conjure up a situation where there will be a transfer system as in other professional sports, which would of course destroy the inter-county system overnight.

We will not get full pay-for-play in the GAA for quite a while but even a cursory glance at past experiences in many other previously amateur sports indicates that Gaelic footballers will be receiving regular payments in some guise within the next 10 years.

There could be limited forms of pay-for-play rather than direct professional comparison with other sports. There could be payment for players without any possibility of transfers so that the present system would remain as it is.

For a start the GAA already has strict rules as to the eligibility of players to move from their native county to another one. That would eliminate the transfer threat overnight and I am sure that rule could be made even more severe than it is now. The correct terminology then would be pay-for-play whereby each county could give money within their means to their county players in a tightly controlled manner.

Richer counties like Dublin, Kerry or Tyrone could pay their players a lot more than Longford or Leitrim and that would undoubtedly magnify the current inbuilt inequality between counties. But bearing in mind the current concern in the GAA about the gap in financial resources available to many smaller counties, a pay-for-play system in the future could solve that problem by allocating additional finance to those counties to help balance the opportunities between large and small counties.

Right now every section of the GAA, including the GPA, is adamant that nobody wants pay-for-play but as I have outlined already such promises regarding amateur status have been meaningless in the past and there is no reason things will be any different in the future. So think forward 20, maybe even 10 years from now and ask yourself will there be any serious amateur status left regarding inter-county players?

Personally I doubt if there will because the GAA is already a massive commercial operation outside the usual GAA financing such as gate receipts and that is sure to continue regardless of how the Irish economy is operating. The GAA is a very well-run organisation and its commercial wing is constantly expanding so there will be a lot of money available in 20 years' time, Garth Brooks or no Garth Brooks.

And remember this – thousands of dedicated GAA people actually favour, even now, some form of compensation being given to the present players because of the tremendous dedication and time they give on behalf of the sport they love. In the type of society we have been living in for many years now in Ireland the notion of people applying themselves assiduously to a cause that requires a lot of time, hard graft, and serious interruption to family life, not to mention a lot of personal abuse at times, and not getting any financial reward seems almost anathema to a lot of Irish people.

This is very relevant in summertime when hundreds of thousands throng GAA stadia to watch their counties play big games and get great enjoyment from that. Many of these people genuinely believe that some form of compensation should be made available to county players and most would regard it simply as a gesture of appreciation for all the enjoyment they receive from watching Gaelic football. My guess is that there will be a slow but steady demand from GAA people to give something tangible back in return to those young men who brighten up so many people's lives.

Every other sport that was previously amateur, most notably athletics, rugby union and cricket have traversed the road to professionalism and often it was a confrontational road that caused a lot of disputes and aggravation. Were the GAA to agree to bring in some form of pay-for-play in the future it need not be so contentious. Common sense and strictly enforced rules, as opposed to the failed current rules on amateurism in the GAA at the moment, could leave all sides winning sometime in the future.

•　　•　　•

One of the fundamental objectives of the GAA is getting maximum participation among young people for the playing of football and hurling. At present there are more young people playing GAA games than ever in the history of the Association. Elaborate coaching structures backboned by extensive investment in many parts of Ireland have ensured that we have never had as many youngsters playing football.

But at the same time as that is proceeding there are huge dropout rates among young men in their teenage years and this is a major worry for GAA legislators. There are many reasons for this dropout such as keener competition from rugby and soccer, burnout because of young people being over-used in their mid-teens, and the changing social habits of young people, which leaves a very wide range of non-sport activities available to them today. That competition in sport was always there but the increased popularity of rugby on television and the presence of top rugby players living in many parts of rural Ireland has certainly been a factor. In the 1960s and 70s rugby union was largely confined to large urban areas and televised games were few and far between. But the game had been democratised far more now and thousands of GAA followers regularly attend rugby matches particularly to watch what was recently the Heineken Cup.

An ever-increasing number of young boys are playing rugby with the extra incentive that Gaelic football lacks of aspiring to someday play rugby professionally. This aspiration has always been available for young soccer players but somehow the attraction of rugby seems to be more popular with many young boys nowadays.

The changing patterns of attendance at the major sports events is also a threat to expansion in the GAA on the future. Traditionally the three major sports in Ireland – GAA, soccer and rugby – had largely segregated followings with each set of supporters being confined to their own sport. So the GAA usually had their own almost exclusive audience for their games. But over the past decade, mainly through the influence of television, the three main sports have now had cosmopolitan followings and large numbers now attend two or more different sports. This applies particularly to rugby and GAA attendances so it would not be unreasonable that some previous GAA followers would spend more of their time watching rugby. There is no reason why the reverse would not also be true but there is not much evidence of that so far.

One of the reasons that soccer and rugby evoke more interest at certain times of the year is because from late September until May the live television coverage of GAA games is scant compared to summertime. Only TG4 consistently cover winter football games for instance and Setanta usually cover about a dozen national league games – something that is very much appreciated by GAA people while other television channels, most notably RTE, saturate the market with rugby and soccer.

This is a serious deficit in media coverage in the GAA and one that the organisation will have to address as a matter of urgency rather than giving a free hand to their keenest rivals.

Another reason for teenage dropouts from football is the crazy fixtures programme that applies in many counties in which boys aged 17-20 are usually the biggest losers and end up disillusioned with football. Talented boys in that age-group are often flogged to death by a myriad of football team managers making unreasonable demands on them at a time when their studies are the most important thing in their, and their parents, lives. The pressure often leads to these talented players walking away from football and who can blame them particularly of they are from less successful counties where they see little future for winning things.

●　　●　　●

The greatest practical problem facing the GAA at the moment in relation to the core value of organising the games is fixture-making. Quite simply there are far too many competitions at present, a lot of them need to be abolished and only then can a proper national fixtures plan be provided.

At club level where more than 98 per cent of all football is played, there is huge anger and in some cases despair by club players in many counties about the lack of proper fixture making.

One of the main reasons for this, but not the only one, is the role of the county teams and their managers. In most cases these managers are operating in conflict with club fixtures to a greater or lesser extent, which is obvious from May to September. This is borne out by a dangerous development in recent years whereby senior club championship games are called off for as long as the county team is still in the championship. Dublin and Donegal are just two prominent counties where this has been applied.

Now there is a basic principle in the GAA that the club is at the heart and soul of the organisation. This has always been clearly understood and with around 2,500 GAA clubs it is not hard to see their importance. But young men of today are leaving Ireland in droves every May or June to work abroad because they have no surety of getting a club championship game for months on end.

This problem is getting worse, not better, despite the valiant efforts of the GAA to provide regular games for players. As a national body the GAA cannot instruct individual county boards how to run their own competitions which means that Croke Park has little or no say in fixture-making in any county.

If, as is the situation at the moment, there are not enough dates to play all the games now being listed, at a suitable time of year, the obvious solution is to get rid of some competitions. If the National League started in January we could get rid of all those subsidiary competitions such as O'Byrne Cup, FBD, McKenna etc. If counties want to use these for preparations then play them under lights in December. Bringing the league forward three or four weeks would release that extra time for starting off the county championships.

But serious rationalisation is also needed such as amalgamating Under-21 and Minor grades into U-19, eliminating the All-Ireland Junior championship and scrapping second chance games for the losers of the four minor provincial finals. If the GAA is serious about getting counties to play a proper programme of games in summertime then it is time to scrap the Qualifiers also. The 16 teams that lose their first game in the Sam Maguire Cup could then play a subsidiary All-Ireland that would serve several useful purposes.

Of course one of the best ways of creating more time in early summertime for club games is to start the All-Ireland championship from a position of having eight teams in each province as was put forward by the FRC recently. With four eights per province the first two rounds of the All-Ireland championship could be completed in three weeks. Imagine the excitement, publicity and revenue that system would engender during the first two or three weeks of June! Those fixtures would leave us with the four provincial finals to be played off in July with the rest of the All-Ireland series remaining as it is.

If the GAA wants to bring some freshness to the closing stages of the championship then why not play a round robin between the four provincial champions, something that would financially compensate for the absence of Qualifiers and provide more top games for television – six as opposed to the present two.

All or some of the changes I mention would clear the way for more county championship games to be played in summer months, in May to August. It is important to stress that many counties are working hard to improve their club fixture-making in summertime but an extra push from Annual Congress delegates would help things greatly. My suggestions are my personal views, I am sure other people could have even better ideas to achieve the same objective, to give club players a chance to play championship football at the best time of year.

●　　●　　●

In future years, the GAA simply cannot ignore floodlit football. It is very popular with all the great football codes, Rugby, soccer, American football and Australian Rules for instance. Floodlit games played regularly develop a life of their own and draw huge television audiences. It is not realistic that over the next decade or so floodlight Gaelic football games will not become part of the fabric of the GAA. The problem as of now is a financial one. Players, as represented by the GPA claim that amateur players cannot afford to take time off in order to prepare for and play in night-time games. The GAA claim that players cannot be compensated in this manner as it is a breach of amateur status – that phrase again! These two conflicting views seem incompatible but money, even in the GAA, has a habit of solving many hitherto insolvable problems and this is surely one of these.

I have no doubt that within five years or so we will see regular floodlit football in all parts of Ireland and the GAA will be big beneficiaries. Television companies will have more opportunities to bid for rights and above all the GAA public will be able to watch big games on television regularly from November to April, weather permitting! Handing large amounts of GAA coverage for six months of the year over to other competing sports simply does not make sense now that the leading football codes are competing head-to-head nowadays in every way, but particularly in television.

●　●　●

Alcohol abuse is one of the greatest social evils in this country for centuries and is particularly rampant in modern times particularly among young people. The GAA is the largest organisation in the country and therefore has the ability to influence young people in various ways through its 2,500-odd clubs. I believe the GAA should take a stand against alcohol abuse by not accepting sponsorship from any alcohol-related commercial bodies. That includes the banning of local pubs putting their name on GAA jerseys as well as the large corporate drinks sponsorship.

Despite the blandishments of alcohol companies that sponsorship does not increase the abuse of alcohol, any person familiar with the pub or club scene knows that is not the case. I am a consumer of alcohol myself in moderation as are the vast majority of GAA members. But by flaunting alcohol in any form of promotion in the GAA context the organisation is, in even a small way, condoning the abuse of alcohol.

The GAA can afford to avoid alcohol sponsorship and would gain enormous credit throughout the country if they took this sort of stand. After all alcohol abuse is one of the greatest causes of physical and mental damage to young people at the present time, including young GAA members.

Epilogue

Larry McGann Has The Last Word – As Always

IWAS worried for a couple of months before finishing this book. My great friend of long standing and confidant on GAA things that matter, Larry McGann, hadn't phoned me for ages and I wanted to let him know about the book. But then out of the blue the phone rang at eleven o'clock one night and Larry was off and running, as ebullient as ever. 'Larry' I said, I was about to start ringing up people fearing the worst because I didn't hear from you for months'.

'Don't worry a mhic,' retorted Larry with his booming voice as strong as ever, 'lads who played with me for Knocknavanna Gaels back in 1969 when we won the Junior championship, now we were real men and we knew we would be around for a long time. There is no mystery to my absence though, I was away in Australia visiting my eldest daughter about 20 miles outside Melbourne, the first time I managed to fly that far. Now it's a great country but I didn't realise that it was the middle of winter out there and every time I rang back to Knocknavanna I was told it was the best summer in 20 years. But sure you can't win them all.

'Anyway when I got back the other day I got wind that you were writing a book. Holy God, I said to myself, was it not bad enough having to read him every Monday in the Independent without him writing a book as well. So I had to find out what was in this book and that's why I'm talking to you now,' added Larry.

I told him that the book was top secret until it appeared in the bookshops but knowing Larry as a veteran GAA politician I knew well that this answer would not suffice. In the GAA, there are no secrets as Larry well knows, having served as captain of Knocknavanna Gaels, gone on to train the team for years and taking over as chairman when the much loved Canon Maguire finally departed this life. Larry even served on the county board and was a selector of the county junior team too – a genuine GAA allrounder and an expert at extracting news without the recipient realising it.

'Well I know you will be writing about that 1982 All-Ireland anyway, sure your name will be attached to that as long as you are alive. I was there that day in the rain long before ever I met you and you know, I was all for Kerry to win. They were such a great team and O'Dwyer was a genius of a trainer I thought they deserved an honour that no team had ever won, the five-in-a-row. Anyway you were lucky enough with that auld goal from Darby, that kick could have gone anywhere in the rain. But Offaly probably deserved it in the end.

'Ah, but that was REAL football that day from both sides, Jack O'Shea, Eoin Liston, Sheehy and O'Keeffe, sure we will never see lads like that again and the Connors and O'Connors and Sean Lowry. Anyway I read a lot about the Black Cards that yourself and a bunch of your friends brought in this year. I was surprised to see you being appointed to chair that Football Review Committee in 2013 because I always thought you were seen as an 'anti-establishment man' but I have to admit you and the other members did a grand job.

'My old football colleagues in Knocknavanna seem very happy with how it worked out and are anxious to see more of those cards being used. It has opened up the play, let good footballers play good football and sure there are far less frees. Maybe you crowd in the FRC knew a bit about football after all. But you should have done something about the handpass, it's crazy the way it has taken over from kicking. When I was playing for Knocknavanna Gaels, it was all kicking; we used to move the ball on, the only ones that were handpassing were students or lads with a yellow streak in them who were anxious to get away from an oncoming tackle and we had REAL tackles in those days.

'But you may get on to somebody up there in Croke Park or that McEnaney man from Monaghan about the referees because many of them seem to be afraid to use Black Cards when they should and I see a lot of them opting for yellow ones instead.'

I nipped in with a rare interruption to say to Larry that the FRC had indeed studied the use of the handpass over the previous 20 years and contrary to public opinion, and Larry McGann, handpassing went in cycles and there were years when very little of it was used.

No joy there – Larry is adamant: 'That handpassing is the ruination of football, get that crowd in Croke Park to do something about it before fellows like me stop going to matches altogether'. Yes Larry.

'Now,' said Larry, sounding more serious, 'I hope you are not running down Knocknavanna Gaels in this book of yours. I remember the very first time you wrote about me and the club, back in 1982, and you were saying we used to write the team out on the back of a cigarette packet and I would have to sweep out the dressing rooms before the players arrived as the litter was still there from the last game. And you were complaining about the grass being too long, only having a bag of sawdust to mark the pitch and cut up fertilizer bags to use as flags.

'I have to admit all that was true but it was the same with most clubs and nobody even mentioned running water or showers that time. Sure we didn't have showers in our own houses let alone the football club. You should let people who don't know a lot about the GAA the advances we have made in this regard. GAA dressing-rooms nowadays, including Knocknavanna Gaels, are like hotels, an absolute delight with all modern facilities. Would you be shocked to realise that in our dressing-rooms there is even a small mirror on the wall before every player's position. That was passed at a recent AGM by a couple of young bucks attending UCD in Dublin. Weren't you involved with that crowd long ago, maybe that's where they got these bad habits?' said Larry with a huge loud laugh, because of course the man has a great sense of humour. How else could he survive as a GAA official for over 40 years without a break?

'I am sure you will be writing in this book about the time we got rid of the Ban away back in 1971. I was a delegate that day in the Queens University in Belfast to see that happen and I was delighted. Now don't get me wrong, I am as strong a nationalist as the next man in this country but that bloody Ban was a horrible nuisance. Some of our young fellas started watching a lot of soccer when television came in during the sixties and the next thing they started drifting to some local town to play soccer. Only for The Ban being lifted Knocknavanna Gaels could have been wiped out if the lads playing soccer were caught and suspended. That was one of the best moves the GAA ever made.

'I was delighted too when that Kerry lad Seán Kelly was President and pushed through the motion to let anybody that wanted play in Croke Park – with the exception of Garth Brooks of course – but that's another story. The GAA spent the soccer and rugby money very well and our own county got great new training facilities for the county teams from that.

'Now in my time the best thing that ever happened the GAA was building the new Croke Park. As a small farmer myself, I was aware of running your business well and I have to say I was all for the development from the start and I had full faith in the GAA bosses to get it right. There were no flies on that Mulvihill man from your own county of Longford. He didn't say a whole lot but he made sure the whole project was kept going steadily and finished before time. He should have been a government minister, you know, and maybe things would have got done a lot quicker.

'But come here a minute, my daughter has the internet in

Australia and I was able to keep in contact with things back home and I could even watch the wife, Christina, on the computer and have a chat – by the way you know she stopped washing the Knocknavanna Gaels jerseys when I was voted out as club secretary. She had been doing the job for free for 25 years or more and she swears she will never change her mind. She is a woman of principle as I learned long ago.

'I haven't a clue how that internet yoke works but it does a great job. I was following the GAA for the past couple of months and it struck me that all these team managers talk too much nowadays and most of it is balderdash. I hope you were not like that in your day but of course there was no internet then. Why do these lads have to rant and rave all the time and then they won't even let their own players talk to the newspapers even before the big matches when the fans love to read what players are saying.

'Years ago I had many a strong argument at the creamery most mornings during summer months over something a famous player had said in the paper. It was mighty craic and added greatly to the excitement of the big game coming up. Now the managers want to impose a vow of silence – are they afraid the players of today are not capable of talking for themselves?'

Larry McGann's mother was from County Tyrone and he always had a special interest in that county's GAA fortunes and indeed all the Six Counties. During the troubles he often visited his mother's home place so he was always well briefed on The Troubles and particularly the hard time GAA members had then. So when Derry came along in 1993 to win the Sam Maguire Cup, he was delighted and then Down the following year too. But when Armagh and Tyrone began to dominate Ulster from 2000 onwards Larry never missed a big game in Clones or Croke Park.

'They were two great teams that time,' said Larry. 'The commitment, the intensity and the fierce rivalry would often make the hair on the back of your neck stand up – sure it was like my own playing days. It was great to see history being made when they both won first All-Irelands. I know a lot of people in my part of the country, while they were glad to see Tyrone and Armagh win, were critical of some of the football that was played by both counties.

'But that is a matter for the team managers and the players. Tyrone or Armagh did not play the traditional game, they went in for a lot of packed defences and crowding out players with the ball but no supporter of either county complained. And like Kerry and Dublin before them, the two counties began to vary their play somewhat which eased the criticism slightly but there was a still a lot of disappointment around the country all the same at the way football was going,' said Larry.

I knew this was a delicate subject for Larry but I ventured to ask him about the political situation in Knocknavanna Gaels club because I knew he had been shafted from his position of secretary at the previous AGM leaving him with no officer job for the first time in over 40 years.

'Ah, that was a sore blow to me personally, no doubt about that,' he admitted. 'The worst thing was that I had no inkling it was going to happen but at the AGM in the local school, I got a bit suspicious when I saw young lads sneaking into the back rows at the meeting – lads I never saw at a meeting before. I only discovered afterwards that these lads had hatched a plan the week before in The Eagle Bar after a training session. They persuaded one of their mates to go forward for secretary and they had their homework done because I lost the vote 24-19. It was a desperate shock to me because I was only into my second year as secretary.

'But look, I have always been a realist in GAA matters; take the knocks and get on with it, and after a few days I had got over the shock although the way some of my own age group sympathised with me afterwards you would think I was dead.

'I rang the daughter in Australia and told her I was heading off if she wanted me because I was free for the summer and away I went. I had a great few months over there and anyway didn't

Knocknavanna Gaels get beaten in the first round of the championship so I didn't miss much. And I gave myself a little smile when the result came through. These bucks might realise that they don't know everything about football just yet.

'Because I was staying near Melbourne, I headed to watch some Australian Rules games and the locals are mad about their football. I enjoyed the games but it's not a patch on our own Gaelic football in my opinion. They run around a lot and catch plenty of high balls but they don't have as much skill as good Gaelic teams. They get huge crowds there and of course there are big games every week unlike in our game where you could go four weeks without a match. But I would still prefer a local derby between Knocknavanna and our next-door neighbours any day.'

It was past midnight by this stage but Larry was showing no sign of slowing down before I gently veered him away from the phone by telling him I still had to write a bit about himself and Knocknavanna Gaels for this book and time was running out.

'Well, fair enough, I will let you go but remember it's people like me that are the backbone of the GAA and you should be writing about us in that book, not the big shots in the padded seats in Croke Park or the boyos on the television telling the rest of us how to run football and hurling. It's the Knocknavanna Gaels of this country that have made the GAA what it is today, remember that because I know I am right about it.'

Yes indeed Larry, I know all that and from past experience. Don't I know Larry McGann is always right when it comes to GAA. Start plotting for the next Knocknavanna AGM Larry, it will keep you busy over the winter!

Acknowledgements

I COULD not have compiled this book without assistance from a wide range of people around Ireland for whom I am deeply grateful. These include the following, in no particular order, and if I inadvertently omit anybody my apologies in advance.

My publishers, Ballpoint Press & P.J. Cunningham, Gerry Dineen, Cork, Tony O'Keeffe, Kerry, Pauric McShea, Donegal, John O'Leary, Derry, Peter Brady, Cavan, Meg Higgins, Cavan, John Green Jnr, Longford, Jim O'Sullivan, Cork, Brendan Cummins, Meath, Paddy Kerr, Monaghan, John Donoghue, Meath Chronicle, Jim Carney, Tuam Herald, Martin Carney, Mayo, Eamon O'Donoghue, Kildare, Larry Tompkins, Cork/Kildare, Stephen Darby, Offaly, Richie Connor, Offaly, Sean Lowry, Offaly, Vincent and Florrie Cryan, Portarlington, Tommy Moran, Leitrim, Michael Casey, Longford, Jackie Devine, Longford, Mike Kenny, Longford, Liam Mulvihill, Longford, Peter Reilly, Longford, Tom Woulfe, Dublin/Kerry, Pat Daly, Croke Park, Kevin Griffin, Mayo, Páraic Duffy, GAA Director General, Seamus Foley, Dunshaughlin, Patsy McLoughlin, Dunshaughlin, Staff of National Library and Pearse Street Library, photographers at Sportsfile and Fionbarr Callanan, Austin Kelly and Dave McEvoy of the Ripley Court Hotel in Dublin, and last, but not least, Larry McGann, Knocknavanna Gaels!

Index